Without Bounds

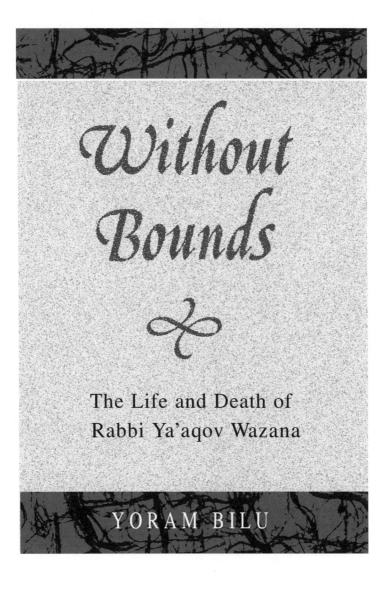

Without Bounds

The Life and Death of
Rabbi Ya'aqov Wazana

YORAM BILU

Wayne State University Press   Detroit

Library of Congress Cataloging-in-Publication Data

[Le-lo metsarim. English]

Without bounds : the life and death of Rabbi Ya'aqov Wazana / Yoram Bilu.

    p. cm.—(Raphael Patai series in Jewish folklore and anthropology)

    Includes bibliographical references.

    ISBN 0-8143-2902-0 (alk. paper)—ISBN 0-8143-2903-9 (pbk. : alk. paper)

    1. Wazana, Yâácov. 2. Rabbis—Morocco—Biography. 3. Medicine, Magic, mystic, and spagiric—Morocco. 4. Medicine, Popular. I. Title. II. Series.

BM755.W343 B5513 2000

296'.092—dc21

[B]   99-054753

Raphael Patai Series in Jewish Folklore and Anthropology

A complete listing of the books in this series can be found at the back of this volume.

GENERAL EDITOR:
Dan Ben-Amos
University of Pennsylvania

ADVISORY EDITORS:
Jane S. Gerber
City University of New York

Barbara Kirshenblatt-Gimblett
New York University

Aliza Shenhar
University of Haifa

Amnon Shiloah
Hebrew University

Harvey E. Goldberg
Hebrew University

Samuel G. Armistead
University of California, Davis

Guy H. Haskell
Emory University

For Tami

Contents

Contents

Preface

Looking back, I think my fascination with Wazana was born in the graveyard in Kinus, where I first heard some of the legends about him. When it emerged that I had stumbled across a mass of highly unusual and unique cultural material, I became intent on organizing the stories and committing them to writing. The task was hardly a straightforward one. Portraying such a remarkable figure as Rabbi Ya'aqov Wazana requires an integration of the inherent drama, color, and excitement of oral transmission, with a critical interpretation consistent with the principles of academic reporting. Having said that, it is the integration of these factors that endows this book with its present form. It is my belief that the investigation and analysis of Wazana's life story can provide a source of interest, not only to scholars and researchers engaged in anthropology, psychology, folklore, North African and Judaic studies, but to the lay reader as well.

Before proceeding, I think it would be useful to offer a general outline of the following chapters and to point to the differences between them. Chapters 1 and 2 make up the introduction, which discusses the challenges of portraying a figure from the past, whose sole reality rests on a collection of stories and personal recollections. These chapters also describe the technique used for assembling the data. Chapter 2 ("They Remember Wazana") is the most "literary" in the book: here, my goal was to capture the ambiance and impressions of the interviews I held with Wazana's former acquaintances. The middle thirteen chapters, which make up the body of the book, recall significant events in the healer's life in chronological sequence. Although the presentation is mostly descriptive, it uses what Clifford Geertz (1973) terms "thick description"; namely, it constructs a meaningful narrative configuration from composite primary interview material, while locating the related events in their cultural context. Although, by definition, "thick description" incorporates an amount of exegesis, the significant body of interpretation has deliberately been confined to the three summarizing chapters. This final section embarks on an analysis of Wazana's character from various theoretical perspectives anchored in psychology and anthropology. But here, too, I have made every effort to minimize the use of professional terminology. My book on Wazana appeared first in Hebrew in 1993. I added to the English version an epilogue that depicts Wazana's amazing "resurrection" following the publication of my book in Hebrew, and the role I inadvertently played in his afterlife.

If not for the candor of Wazana's former acquaintances and their willingness to share their memories with me, this book would never have been written. It is therefore with sincere gratitude and appreciation that I now thank David Edri, Zion Eliyahu, Eliyahu and Tamar Elmaliakh, Moshe Elmaliakh, Mima Almakias, Simi Almakias, Rabbi Ya'aqov Buskila, Masoud and Beha Ben-David, Ya'aqov Biton, Yosef Dadon, Yaish and Aisha Dadon, Rabbi Masoud Dadon, Eliyahu Wazana, Hayim Wazana, Ya'aqov Wazana, Shaul Wazana, Avraham Vaknin, Rachel Vaknin, Avraham Suissa, Shlomo and Ito Suissa, Eliyahu Peretz, Yehoshua Peretz, Rabbi Yitzhak Peretz, and Shlomo Revivo. I would also like to express my great appreciation to my friends David Azoulai and Rabbi Azar Elmaliakh, to whom I am indebted for much of the knowledge I gained regarding the Moroccan Jewish community in general, and Rabbi Ya'aqov Wazana in particular.

As is customary with anthropological reporting, the identities of all interviewees have been disguised—with the exception of a number of members of the Wazana family. I hope that those who would have preferred to see their real identities in print will appreciate my reasons for not divulging them. My approach has been to select from the material gathered in order to create a particular narrative and interpretative framework. While this has always been carried out with complete fidelity to my informants' reminiscences, I chose not to expose their identities in association with this framework, since it is usually far removed from their accounts. As far as the localities are concerned, the names of the small, cooperative villages (moshavim) have been changed, but not those of the towns and settlements where population size makes identification of individuals improbable.

I would also like to thank Moshe Idel, Eyal Ben-Ari, Harvey Goldberg, Zali Gurevitch, André Levy, Amia Lieblich, and Emanuel Marx for reading early drafts of the book, and for sharing their constructive comments with me. Final responsibility for the end product is entirely mine.

Finally, I thank the Eshkol Institute at the Faculty of Social Sciences of the Hebrew University of Jerusalem, as well as Edgar Siskin and the

Preface

Jerusalem Center for Anthropological Study, which he directs, for their contribution to the completion of this study and its being brought to print. I owe special thanks to the Lucius Littauer Foundation for supporting the English translation of the book and to the translator, Ruth Freedman, for her commitment and enthusiasm.

1

In the Footsteps of Wazana

This is a book about memories; to be specific, memories shrouded by a haze of yearning and puzzlement. The object of these memories is the shadowy, enigmatic figure of Rabbi Ya'aqov Wazana, a Jewish healer who lived, practiced, and died in the Western High Atlas Mountains of southern Morocco in the early years of this century. Although Wazana forms part of a briskly vanishing past, his image lingers on with the utmost clarity in the minds of those who once knew him, people now residing in Israel's cities, development towns, and *moshavim*. "There was nobody like Wazana in all Morocco," summarized one informant, his voice mellow with fondness and admiration, as he thought back on the marvelous acts, the healing in particular, Wazana performed for Jewish and Muslim patients alike. "When we had no doctors, he was our only physician," was the conclusion of another.

There is no doubt that Wazana's life is obscured in mystery. The puzzle of his lifestyle, his contradiction-ridden personality, the miracles, and above all, the story of his death, still haunt his former associates and friends. Impervious to time, this enigma lives on, powerful as it ever was. At family and social gatherings, Wazana is a perennial topic of conversation; past patients continue to pray for his assistance in times of hardship or sickness. Forty-five years have lapsed since his death, and many still reach out to him in their dreams.

It is for all these people, my informants, that I wish to provide a voice, hoping that along the way I will not only capture their memories and longings, but also the mystery and tension conjured by the name of Wazana. Making use of the tales recounted to me in Hebrew and Moroccan Arabic, I have endeavored to outline a portrait of Wazana that I believe sheds light on his elusive image. In unraveling the riddles of his life and death, we embark on a journey through time and space, back to the reality once experienced by the traditional Jewish communities of South Morocco in the 1930s and 1940s. But before setting out on this dark and winding road, it is important to note that the figure awaiting us at the end is indeed a slippery and elusive one. Even those acquainted with Wazana, whose roots sprang from the same cultural soil as his, have failed to understand him fully. How then can a researcher from another time and culture comprehend this remarkable individual? Similarly, even if that researcher possesses extensive knowledge of the society that gave birth to Wazana, and a deep appreciation of its cultural codes, there is every likelihood that the effort to cross the ocean of informants' stories and reappear with the "real" Wazana exposed, will probably prove futile. For we must bear in mind that a personality is more than just an abstract of cultural symbols (cf. D'Andrade and Strauss 1992; Spiro 1993; Strauss and Quinn 1997). This is especially pertinent when the personality in the spotlight is as rare and unusual as Wazana's. Second, if stories telling of the past are the only means at our disposal of shedding light on a bygone figure, then the chances are that the illumination will prove very faint indeed. Experienced clinicians are often thwarted in their efforts to delve into the human psyche—even when the object of their examination stands before them unmediated and exposed to their scrutiny. The task becomes significantly more intimidating when the figure under investigation has no independent life other than that existing in the memories of others.

By far the greatest obstacle in the quest for Wazana is the circuitous layers of mediation interposed between subject and researcher (Bertaux 1981). Regardless of the depth of the inquiry, we cannot expect to arrive at a reliable biography based on any verifiable historical reality from the stories gleaned from the healer's acquaintances. In a sense, the Wazana narratives are created the moment they are spoken: they are replete with personal evaluations and interpretations no less than with actual facts (cf. Bruner 1991; Crites 1986; Gergen and Gergen 1983; Good 1994: ch. 6; and Schafer 1981). Furthermore, the informants' memories have been, and continue to be, affected by their experiences in the present. Thus, even if the stories describe actual events that did occur, we must consider that they are inevitably influenced by the flaws of human memory. Distortions creep in, and over time, become increasingly important as the informants' present lives become more deeply entrenched in their Israeli experience, and the distance between the past in the Atlas Mountains and the present in Israel continues to expand. Some informants offered personal impressions of encounters with Wazana apparently rich in detail and seeming to carry the stamp of reliability and realism. However, we should not infer historical truth from such stories simply because they seem to proffer nuggets of everyday reality in the Atlas Mountains. The problem of historical veracity is exacerbated if we consider that most stories were exclusive (i.e., belonged to only one specific informant), and could not be validated by additional sources.

In contrast to the category of unique, personal stories, there were other stories, which, apart from minor modifications, appeared to be common to several informants. Note however that due to their obviously legendary qualities, the "shared" accounts must be taken as particularly problematic to obtaining a reliable portrait of Wazana. In this category are legendary accounts full of supernatural elements—saints (*tsaddiqim*), demons, and acts of magic, such as traveling great distances in no time, producing barrenness by sorcery, or locating lost objects or money by magic. Since the majority of readers would not accept beings such as demons, or activities such as magic as givens in their social universe, their presence in Wazana's story may be hard to digest. Still, before dismissing such phenomena as figments of the imagination, we must bear in mind that the events we are about to encounter were an inherent part of an authentic cultural experience particular to traditional Moroccan life, and that for Jews and Muslims alike, saints, demons and sorcery formed part of normal, day to day reality (see Crapanzano 1973, 1980).

This book is not concerned with challenging the reliability of the personal or the more "realistic" type of story, nor does it intend to speculate about the veracity of the seemingly legendary narratives. I propose instead that the entire corpus of Wazana stories, including those with the troublesome combination of spectacular feats and everyday minutiae, expresses an intrinsic truth peculiar to the informants' narrative perspective and thus endows the figure of Wazana with meaning (Bruner 1990, 1991; Spence 1982). However, the fact that our perception of Wazana is filtered through the informants' eyes does not mean we have to buy their portrait of him wholesale. The fact, for example, that many of the people believe in demons does not mean we have to, and in no way does it rule out a discussion of demons as metaphorical rather than ontological characters, or the use of analytic tools foreign to the cultural system that produces demons.

The attempt to expose Wazana's long-vanished figure demands great delicacy given the difficulties that beset quests such as this into the past. We clearly cannot expect to garner the "real" Wazana from the wealth of stories about him; at best, we can present a coherent reading, perhaps one of many possible chronicles of his life. This book will concentrate on the perceptions of Wazana held by people who have been molding his image for decades, and on the ways they have chosen to represent him to this researcher. The complexity generated by the extensive layers of mediation asks for an interpretation of Wazana from a number of perspectives on distinct analytic levels. Particularly, a two-tiered approach is needed, one involving an exploration of Wazana's unique personality, combined with an analysis of the cultural context and lexicon of symbols relevant to the healer and his acquaintances (cf. Bourguignon 1979; Ingham 1996; Kilborne and Langness 1987; and Obeyesekere 1981). My examination of the healer's life thus involves the integrated exploration of the individual and his society from both the psychological and anthropological points of view. The analysis will track Wazana's life narrative as it was reported by the informants.[1]

I came across Wazana first in early 1975, and the passing years have in no way reduced my fascination with this character. Just like his acquaintances, I have been enthralled by the wake of mystery and nostalgia he left behind. This preoccupation has taken me on a journey countless miles long, up and down the country—from the northern Lebanese border, to the southern development towns in the Negev. With an address book that swelled steadily with names of people who shared their secrets and memories, I set out to collect every crumb of information related to this remarkable character, trying to construct a coherent portrait out of the rich, often bizarre mosaic pieces supplied by his family and acquaintances. The result is here before you. The picture of Wazana arising from these pages has no pretense of being exhaustive or entirely coherent, since the riddle of Wazana's life may never be fully solved. Nonetheless, I have no doubt that his story is well worth the telling.

2

They Remember Wazana

My arrival at the *moshav* is greeted by the usual silence. Summer mornings are generally marked by a stillness that lies heavy over the small, lopsided houses on the stony Judean plain. The men and children are usually working in the green-brown fields, and so the silence over the sun-baked roofs is broken only by the sound of women's voices, the drone of a distant tractor, or some squawking hens. But, on this particular morning the silence remained intact. Even the old men in the synagogue, and the women who normally chatted outside the store had disappeared. "Where is everybody?" I ask old Sa'ada outside the *moshav* clinic. "There," she says, waving her hand in an arc through the hot air in the direction of the west. My gaze follows her movement to the last of the houses beside the reed-covered *wadi*, then up the hillside to a dark knot of figures beside a fence. I see several white dots shimmering in the sunlight. Sa'ada's explanation is wasted on me since she only speaks Moroccan Arabic, and so it is a while before I realize she is talking about a funeral.

Curiosity overcomes my misgivings about the heat and I go marching off across the hot, dusty *wadi* toward the cemetery where the entire male population of the *moshav* sits waiting in the shadows of the fence and the oak trees. They are seated in groups, chatting amongst themselves to pass the time. As I stride up to them, my friend and mentor, Yosef Abutbul, rises to greet me. Old Meir Yifraḥ died in a distant hospital and everyone is waiting for the body to come. Attaching myself to one of the groups, I try to follow the conversation, which is in Hebrew interspersed with Arabic. They gradually turn to reminiscing about life in the old days, back in Morocco: miraculous feats of *tsaddiqim* (saints), and exotically named native settings like Ait Bouli and Ait Abas, Netifa

17

and Demante, Beni-Mellal and Taroudant. The same names over and over: Rabbi David u-Moshe, Rabbi Shlomo Ben Leḥans, Rabbi David Dra HaLevi, Rabbi Amram Ben Diwan. All of a sudden Yosef Knafo stands up and stares beyond the circle, his eyes bright with excitement. He motions the others to be silent: "They may be righteous, holy men, but still, nobody was like Rabbi Ya'aqov Wazana in all Morocco." With this he proceeds to rattle off a string of tales, which flows like a rising stream, evoking the magic of the famed healer who performed exorcisms, removed spells, brought the dying to life, and made lost objects materialize from thin air. Though most of the people seem familiar with the stories, they nevertheless listen spellbound, interjecting his narratives with expressions of wonder and surprise.

My research on Jewish Moroccan ethnopsychiatry led me to *moshav* Kinus in 1974, and there my attention was first drawn to Wazana's existence. Some early misgivings with regard to my visit gradually faded when I returned to the *moshav,* and even stayed a few weeks at a time. I found many of the people I spoke to unusually frank on the subject of their life problems and experiences with healers. Their stories, and those of the rabbi-healers whom I interviewed later, provided me with sufficient material to build a detailed picture of the traditional healing system they had brought with them from Morocco to Israel (see Bilu 1978, 1985a).

While many of my interviewees spoke often of life in Morocco, they rarely touched on Wazana, and I realized slowly that very few had known him personally. Yosef Knafo, from Ouarzazate, who praised Wazana in the cemetery, was one such acquaintance, as was Yosef Abutbul, my agreeable host in Kinus. The Abutbul family had originally lived in Mezguemnat, Wanzurt, and Tezort—a cluster of tiny villages, home of the Berber tribespeople in the Tifnoute region of the Western High Atlas Mountains of southern Morocco. I discovered that Wazana was born near them in the village of Assarag, and that he lived most his life in that remote, alpine region. Yosef Abutbul, who came to Israel as a boy, often mentioned the way Wazana had treated his family, noting particularly the fact that the great healer had saved his mother during the near fatal birth of her first child. Abutbul was the first to mention the circumstances of Rabbi Ya'aqov's death, and I later learned he had written down this and other stories about Wazana, and sent them to the Israel Folktale Archive based at Haifa University.[1]

A few people in Kinus suggested I should visit Atseret, a *moshav* perched atop an isolated hill in the Adulam region. They pointed out that the people in Atseret had retained their traditional healing practices to an unparalleled degree. They were right. The rich data on traditional healers furnished by the interviewees from Atseret allowed me at last to finish the study I had begun in Kinus. While assembling data on traditional healing practices in Atseret, I was struck by the regularity with which

They Remember Wazana

Wazana's name cropped up. People in Atseret who had known Wazana in Morocco all came from the neighboring villages of Agouim and Imini on the mountain road leading from Marrakech south to Ouarzazate. They recounted that, at the height of his fame, Wazana abandoned his home in Tifnoute, and moved eastward to Agouim, where he lived until his death. Because the interviewees from Kinus and Atseret knew Wazana at different periods of his life, I found that by stringing their stories together, I could obtain a more coherent picture of Wazana's life story. Some interviewees regarded themselves as close friends of the healer, and their accounts indicated that their relationship extended beyond his role as a healer. They treasured recollections of social gatherings in which laughter and alcohol played a large part; they referred to trips to other villages on which Wazana had accompanied them. I learned that the Ben-Hamo family had been especially close to Wazana. The five Ben-Hamo brothers, now living in Atseret, informed me that their friend, the healer, often stayed in their father's house in Agouim. Rabbi Shalom Ben-Hamo, a *shohet* (ritual slaughterer) and part-time healer, thinks of himself as Wazana's disciple. His older brother David, claims Wazana is a savior who tended his family whenever need arose. David conscientiously commemorates the anniversary of Wazana's death with a family *se'udah* (festive meal).

At Atseret I came across Rabbi Yitzhak Pehima, the one-time *shohet* and teacher from Imini, now living in the town of Kiryat Gat. Pehima often comes to visit his former neighbors from Morocco. Like Rabbi Shalom Ben-Hamo, he spent many hours in Wazana's company and the latter had acquainted him with the esoteric healing arts. Once we were standing near a pool that overlooked the village, high above the straggling houses and the chicken houses whose sounds and smells permeated the *moshav*. He leaned over to me, whispering gently: "Atseret and Agouim, they're the same." I immediately knew he was not just referring to the makeup of the population, but to the geographical similarity between the two locations. Atseret in Israel and Agouim in Morocco were both hilly and remote and the *moshav* possessed a combination of plant life and smells that reminded him of the life he had left behind. At events I attended in Atseret, I too felt that strange sensation of frozen time. An example of this was the *hillula* (memorial celebration)[2] in Atseret commemorating the death anniversary of the illustrious *tsaddiq* Rabbi David u-Moshe, whose shrine lies near Agouim.[3] I recall that an elderly man began singing a Berber tune in a cracked, worn-out voice, an elderly woman accompanying him in a croaky duet; around us *zagarit* ululations soared through the night air as a chorus of female voices joined the old-timers. At these gatherings, it was inevitable that everyone settled back to listen and tell their colorfully dramatic stories about Wazana.

I too was enchanted with Wazana. If I doubted his existence that day in the cemetery because the quality of the tales was so legendary in

19

texture, subsequent interviews with the residents of Kinus and Atseret clarified that Wazana was indeed real—and had been the healer and close friend of many individuals I had come to know.

The former residents of Agouim and Imini now living in Atseret referred me to their network of friends and family outside the *moshav*. These contacts in turn supplied me with names of others associated with the healer. Over a two-year period, beginning summer of 1986, I managed to trace and interview more than thirty men and women scattered throughout Israel's cities, towns, development towns, and *moshavim*. Sometimes I would be accompanied by my assistant, Matan, who conducted some of the interviews in Moroccan Arabic. We were welcomed with the traditionally warm hospitality that marks this community. Everyone seemed happy to speak to us, and without exception tried to cooperate and supply information.

27 November 1986

Ramle, home to Masoud and Tamu Tubul, whose address was supplied by Rabbi Yitzḥak Peḥima, Tamu's son-in-law from Kiryat Gat. The Tubul family lives in a spruced up multi-entrance apartment block, recently renovated by a neighborhood rehabilitation project. Urban scenery such as this, characterized by shabby complexes, the outgrowth of an accelerated building boom in the 1950s and 1960s, became a familiar backdrop for the interviews. The elderly couple's home was simple and modestly furnished. We were ushered into a guest room with sofas draped in colored sheets to protect them. A plain wooden closet stood against a wall, and there were pictures everywhere: Moroccan *tsaddiqim*, Israel's third president, Zalman Shazar, and of course family snapshots. A carpet, no doubt lovingly transported all the way from Morocco, adorned one wall. As we entered, Masoud Tubul, an old man with glasses and a white beard was lying down with a handkerchief over his face. He had a cap on and wore a robe of heavy, black material. His age was evident from his blurred speech and hazy memory. He constantly digressed, unaware that he was doing so. His wife Tamu, on the other hand, was alert, lucid, and high spirited despite her eighty years. She sometimes silenced her husband in midspeech and assumed the narration herself, excusing this on the grounds that his memory was not what it was. They squabbled incessantly, it was hard to tell whether in anger or jest. Neither was comfortable speaking Hebrew and so they quickly reverted to Arabic.

Tamu had important information concerning Rabbi Ya'aqov's father, Rabbi Avraham, who had died in her first husband's house in the village of Amassine. On marrying Masoud, her second husband, they went to live in his village, Assarag—Wazana's home before he moved. These were the first people we met who had lived near Rabbi Ya'aqov

Masoud Tubul

before he left Assarag to live in Agouim. Masoud recounted that he had gone to search for the healer on his donkey to break the grim news of Wazana's father's death.

After the interview, Masoud walked us to the car, and posed for a photograph outside his newly refurbished home. I have him on film, stiff and erect, back straight, his arms by his sides, wholly unperturbed by the neighborhood children watching the proceedings and finding it all rather amusing.

23 April 1987

We left early for Atlit for a meeting with Makhluf Ben-Hayim. I already knew that it was in Makhluf's home in Agouim that Rabbi Ya'aqov had died. Makhluf lives in a rectangular block near the railway tracks in the southern part of town. We found this short, wizened old man with his bushy beard, shaved head, and black beret eagerly awaiting our arrival. His wife, Aisha, served us snacks of mint tea, cold drinks, buns left over from the Mimuna,[4] and some dried fruit. She seated herself a short distance from us, and, apart from a few comments, made no attempt to interrupt.

Makhluf had been the blacksmith in Agouim. Other informants mentioned that no one could shoe a Muslim horse better than Makhluf. In Israel he worked for a national construction company until retirement. He explained that the relationship between his family and Wazana predates his own birth. He is assured that all his children, three boys (one named after Rabbi Ya'aqov) and four girls, owe their lives to the healer who cured their mother of a demonic sickness which produced recurrent miscarriages. Makhluf provided important details concerning Wazana's death. Like David Ben-Ḥamo, his former neighbor from Agouim, whom I knew from Atseret, he holds a feast each year in Wazana's honor.

I had further proof of this man's staunch loyalty to Rabbi Ya'aqov on another occasion. Annually, on the fifth of Adar, a celebratory *hillula* is held in honor of Rabbi Yosef Abu-Ḥatsera. The late Rabbi Yosef, a

Makhluf and Aisha Ben-Ḥayim

22

descendent of the revered Moroccan Abu-Ḥatsera family,[5] had a large following of former residents of Ouarzazate, Telouet, and Tazenakht in southern Morocco. In Israel, many of these families settled in Atlit, where Rabbi Yosef visited them regularly. Rabbi Yosef himself had taken up residence in France. On his last trip to Israel, during which he died, the much venerated rabbi paid his accustomed visit to Atlit which, incidentally, now boasts a monument in his memory. One year I attended the *hillula* organized by the mayor of Atlit, himself from the village of Imini. In a banquet hall, on a platform which faced three rows of tables, sat a row of VIPs: Knesset (Israeli parliament) members, guest rabbis from other cities, members of the Abu-Ḥatsera family, and Rabbi Yosef's sons— French speakers in conspicuously well-tailored suits. Speeches extolling the *tsaddiq* and his family preceded the meal which was accompanied by songs performed by local artists praising the rabbi and his righteous ancestors. As the evening wore on, the festivities rose to ecstatic heights as dancing celebrants, swaying in time to the rhythmic drums, bore the *tsaddiq*'s sons around the hall on their shoulders. The sons kept showering the crowd with *arak* (alcoholic beverage) and handing out small pictures of their father as they moved around the hall. Meanwhile the jubilant crowd jigged in circles, kissing their hands as they whirled by.

It was against this heady background of elation that Makhluf chose his moment for a skirmish with one of Rabbi Yosef's most ardent admirers—the mayor's father. Makhluf meant to be provocative, and he was: "Maybe you think *ait* Abu-Ḥatsera is such a big deal," he declared archly, "but that's because you didn't know *ait* Wazana . . ."[6] This was Makhluf's way of making it clear that in his opinion, the Wazana family deserved no less respect and adoration than the Abu-Ḥatseras. The fact that he picked a quarrel with the Abu-Ḥatsera dynasty in their stronghold surely reflects considerable acrimony at the irreverence shown the Wazana family. The magnitude of the discrepancy in status of the two families is underscored by the fact that few who had attended the Abu-Ḥatsera *hillula* chose to take part in the modest feast prepared by Makhluf in Wazana's name. This corroborates informants' testimony bearing on the disparity between the two dynasties which in fact operated in the same area of the Atlas Mountains. I shall be referring later to accounts pointing out the hostility and condemnation displayed by Rabbi Yosef Abu-Ḥatsera toward Rabbi Ya'aqov.

Having taken leave of Atlit, we drove to Givat Ada via the hamlet of Binyamina, across some undulating agricultural hill country speckled with vineyards, fields, and orchards. Here, single-story houses surrounded by a natural oak forest form a marked contrast to the urban scenery so far encountered on our travels. Despite the pleasant route, our destination is again a working-class neighborhood on the eastern outskirts of Givat Ada, known locally as Yoseftal. We are looking for Rabbi Azar Gabai, whose address was provided by his sister in Atseret. Rabbi Gabai was waiting in an armchair in the hallway outside his apartment. One of his hands and both his legs were badly crippled by chronic arthritis, but apart from that, his appearance was similar to the now familiar southern Moroccan mountain Jew: thin and dark in appearance, with angular features, a white beard, and wearing the apparently standard black beret. Rabbi Gabai had presence, and an aura of serenity and self-possession radiated from him. Despite his handicap, he looked younger than his seventy years. Azar Gabai comes from Amassine, where Wazana's father died. Although he was trained as a *shohet,* he had prospered in Morocco as a businessman. In Israel, he supported himself with savings at first, but when his funds ran out, he settled for a job in a local canning factory. He has come to terms with his decline in fortune and health, and at this point in his life obtains great pleasure in his ten children and twenty-five grandchildren. He only met Wazana briefly as a young man while studying the laws of ritual slaughter. Nevertheless, Rabbi Gabai was able to provide vital and in fact exclusive information concerning the healer's training.

The day, which began in Atlit, ended in the town of Ḥadera where we went in search of Rabbi Moshe Tubul. Lacking a precise address, we had no alternative but to ask around at different apartment blocks bordering on the Sela and Rasko neighborhoods in the west of the city until we found him. Seventy-eight-year-old Rabbi Moshe was a stout, vital man with a beard and a black hat. He suffers from asthma, and his breath came in a whistle as he spoke. My first glimpse of him found him sitting on his porch, absorbed in copying a Torah Book onto parchment. In Morocco he lived in Tezort, but his travels as a *shohet* and *mohel* (ritual circumciser) brought him to the same localities as Rabbi Ya'aqov. He related that he had spent considerable time in the vicinity of Amassine, Agouim, and Imini. His job had been to slaughter animals for *hillulot* (pl. of *hillula*) held at the tomb of Rabbi David u-Moshe. Since retirement, he has taken up writing Torah scrolls and amulets and serves as *shohet* for the community whenever needed.

This interviewee had tacit reservations regarding Wazana, whom he seems to have known well. While referring to the healer as "the one who used the outsiders" [evil spirits], Tubul nevertheless refrained from disparaging Wazana outright, and carefully avoided saying anything derogatory. He told me that, when his first wife experienced hemorrhaging which prevented her from conceiving, he had no qualms about turning to the healer for help. Despite the fact that the treatment was successful, and his wife gave birth, sadly she and the child died. Rabbi Moshe subsequently remarried a woman twenty years his junior, and fathered eight children. The child of his old age, an adolescent daughter, was born when he was over sixty.

Rabbi Azar Gabai

Without waiting for us to leave, Rabbi Moshe resumed his work. I paused at the threshold to look back, and saw him for the last time, bowed over his parchment, quill in hand, deeply absorbed in his task once more.

4 May 1988

A cool, sharp wind carrying the scent of spring blossoms greeted our entry to *moshav* Makor on the Lebanese border. The northern mountain scenery was breathtaking, and the pastoral setting that met our eyes, the white houses stark against the lush green woods, were a marked contrast to the security fence and army outpost with its Israeli flag billowing in the breeze. The population of Makor is mainly made up of Iranian and Moroccan Jews. It was the most northern of our destinations. Hardly any of the square, red-roofed houses still have their original facade: most have been renovated, or demolished and rebuilt with luxurious extensions that seem frivolous considering the financial straits the *moshav* is in. In a file of modestly restored houses on a short stretch of road tucked away

Chapter 2

Rabbi Moshe Tubul

from the main road lives an extended family from Amassine affectionately known to the rest of the residents as the Gabai "clan." Again we find the familiar-looking Moroccan mountain Jews: the men mostly lean, the usual beret, the women fuller figured, affable, smiling. Matan and I went to different houses, delivering greetings from the Gabais' relatives in Givat Ada, Yavneh, and Atseret. Food appeared on the table wherever we went and naturally we partook—it would have been considered discourteous not to. There was no shortage of Wazana stories, and there were many who seemed well acquainted with him. It was a brief visit since other plans forced us to cut the round of interviews short. It was the Lag Ba'Omer eve, and we had decided to drive to the *hillula* at Rabbi Shimon Bar-Yoḥai's shrine not far away, in Meron.[7] With a few of the Gabais leading us in their cars, we headed toward Meron.

The *hillula* was in full swing when we reached the place. Just before the main gates we met a congested muddle of pilgrims all moving slowly up the hill toward the sages' shrine. There were literally thousands of families forcing their way through a sea of tents, cars, and stands stocked with goods of every description, representing the temporal as well as the spiritual worlds. We merged into the crowd and jostled our way through an improvised amusement park, lottery booths, pony rides, and exhibition tents, past a police recruitment stand on the hood of a jeep, the Lubavitch

Gabai family in Makor

"*mitzva* tank," and a stall with Druse ornaments that also sold extra-thin pita bread and local cheese. Nearer the shrine, the more "frivolous" merchandise began to give way to the spiritual. There were candles, oil, and pictures of *tsaddiqim* heaped on stalls everywhere you looked, with the frowning visage of Israel's national saint for the 1980s, Rabbi Yisrael Abu-Ḥatsera (affectionately known as Baba Sali), another scion of the holy family, glowering down from most stalls. It was pandemonium as fundraisers and representatives of religious organizations shouted competitively for donations from passersby.

We could see the shrine, lit from afar by two massive torches whose guttering flames cast a pink shadow over the white stucco building encasing the shrine. There was an indescribable crush inside as hundreds of people crowded around the tombs of Rabbi Shimon and Rabbi Elazar his son. Everyone was trying to touch the railings surrounding the pair of graves, which were buried under a mountain of candles, head-scarves, and currency thrown by the celebrants. The murmur of prayer, and the incessant sound of weeping permeated the site, and, from the corners of the chamber, women's voices steadily intoned the Maghrebi healing song, "*Ha wa za idawina*" ("Here he comes to heal us"), accompanying their supplication rhythmically on tambourines. Some managed to wade through the crowd with trays of food, offering the other pilgrims a taste of their thanksgiving offerings. On the roof of the shrine, Hasidim dressed

27

Hasidim dancing in the *hillula* of Rabbi Shimon in Meron. Note the three-year-old boys, brought to Meron for their first haircuts, on their fathers' shoulders. Mothers and daughters are peeping through the railing separating the men and the women.

in their black garb, twirled in circles of ecstasy, each man clutching the waist of the person in front, all united in a hopping, jerking, sweating human chain. A rabbi with a long beard, waving a handkerchief, led the rest of the dancers in song, mangling the syllables of a hymn of praise to the *tsaddiq*. The dancers chanted after him in a hypnotic monotone: "Our Master Bar-Yoḥai, Bar-Yoḥai our Master."

The next morning, we ascended to the ruined ancient synagogue of Meron, and stood a while, observing the melee of people, tents, and cars far below. I asked myself how many of the celebrants, many of them Moroccans, knew Wazana. On the way back from the synagogue, Matan and I agreed to split up and search among the tents for people who might have known Wazana. We found each other an hour or so later, with nothing to show for our efforts. It was not only disappointing, but increasingly clear that Wazana was a distinctly localized hero, known only in a small area of southern Morocco. His acquaintances, who nowadays were scattered throughout Israel, represented but a tiny minority among the huge Israeli Moroccan community.

As we slowly homed in on the inner circle of "Wazana's people," we learned that the healer had been celibate throughout his life, and that he died childless, a long way from his native village. All efforts to locate Wazana's close family through the phone book had been in vain, and my attention therefore focused on his former friends and neighbors from the Western High Atlas. We returned to Atseret several times more to interview people from Agouim and Imini who had been unavailable during the first round of interviews. On one such visit we were introduced to David Samuel, the only non-Moroccan resident. David joined the *moshav* upon marrying an Imini woman. Originally from Iraq, David had never met Wazana, but nevertheless was sufficiently well informed to suggest we speak to Rabbi Ya'aqov's blind kinsman, Shaul Wazana, who lived in the Mediterranean resort town of Natanya. I knew Shaul by sight, having spotted him at several Maghrebi *hillulot*. He was a fattish man, invariably dressed in a brown *jellaba* (hooded robe) and black fez, who always sat at the hub of the action, telling jokes and receiving cash donations in exchange for his blessings. Shaul is a prominent figure within the community, and reputedly possesses an extraordinary memory: it is rumored that once he hears a name, he never forgets it. We were fortunate to have met David since before he linked Shaul to the healer, I had not associated him with our quest.

As we stood talking to David, wondering what to do next, his eyes suddenly gaped in amazement. He was staring at a large man in the company of a young girl, who was approaching where we stood, tapping his white cane as he went. It was uncanny to find ourselves in the presence of Shaul Wazana, robed, as usual, in a brown *jellaba* and black

Shaul Wazana

29

fez. Shaul explained that he had come to the *moshav* to buy chickens. We greeted him with enthusiasm, delighted that fate had intervened in this way on our behalf. Shaul confirmed his kinship to Rabbi Ya'aqov Wazana and, after some hesitation, agreed to meet us once he had completed his purchases and visited some friends in the village. We tensely awaited his reappearance, wondering whether he would keep his promise. When he finally arrived, he invited us to enter the home of the girl we had seen with him in the street. Matan conducted the interview in Moroccan Arabic, which I do not understand, so I sat to one side, relishing the blind man's lilting intonation and observing his rich body language. It occurred to me that because of his blindness, Shaul had not pushed himself to integrate into present-day Israeli society. He has maintained the same lifestyle and routine that he pursued in Morocco, traveling among the communities he feels comfortable with, wearing his traditional garb, exchanging blessings for donations, never missing a *hillula* celebration.

Shaul had little to say on the subject of Rabbi Ya'aqov, although he had known the healer well. He did recall however that he had met him at the tomb of Rabbi David u-Moshe, shortly before Rabbi Ya'aqov's death. However, he was happy to discuss other members of the family, whom he described as "glorious *tsaddiqim*." Our fortuitous encounter with Shaul did not allow us to complete Wazana's family tree. Nevertheless, it did assist us in clarifying the impressive lineage and entailed privileges enjoyed by Rabbi Ya'aqov in the past, and Shaul in the present. Shaul succeeded in clarifying another point for us: for him at least, Rabbi Ya'aqov could claim the dubious privilege of being one of the least illustrious members of the family.

Slowly we traced other members of the family. The first of these I met in "Rabbi David u-Moshe's house" in Safed. In 1973, the venerated *tsaddiq* from Morocco, Rabbi David, had appeared to forestry worker Avraham Ben-Ḥayim in a dream, declaring his wish to live in the home of Ben-Ḥayim in the Canaan neighborhood (Ben-Ami 1981; Bilu 1987). The latter obediently allocated the saint a room in his apartment, and informed all his followers in writing that the saint had appeared to him in a dream. He invited everyone to attend a *hillula* whose attendance far exceeded expectations. Henceforth, each year on the new moon of Ḥeshvan, thousands of pilgrims flock to this shabby Safed neighborhood, to pour over gardens and sidewalks and squeeze into the tiny, specially adorned room in Avraham's apartment. Unlike the pilgrimage to Meron, this celebration is exclusively for people of North African extraction.

From information I had received, I knew that Wazana had lived quite close to Rabbi David u-Moshe's tomb, and that he had often visited the *tsaddiq*'s grave. I therefore decided to travel to Ben-Ḥayim's home in Safed in the hope of meeting people who might have known the healer. In Safed, I fell into conversation with a bearded man dressed in black and wearing a

On the way to the house of Rabbi David u-Moshe, Safed

homburg who responded with alacrity to my questions. I discovered that one of his kinsmen had married Rabbi Ya'aqov's only sister, and that as a young boy, his job had been to attend Wazana's father, Rabbi Avraham. Our conversation was brief and ended all too soon. My new acquaintance was in a hurry to return home, and I decided to accompany him, down the hill leading out of the Canaan suburb, and recorded his account of the Wazana family as I went. Before disappearing down a narrow alley, he gave me a list of Wazana's family now living in Be'er Sheva.

I drove south to Be'er Sheva and wandered around for some hours before finding Masouda Buskila, whose home was predictably situated in a sprawl of long multi-entrance concrete slabs: part of the so-called D neighborhood. My target is married to Moshe, son of Esther Ohana, Rabbi Ya'aqov's sister. Masouda's Hebrew was far from fluent, but her manner was spirited and bright, and punctuated with dashes of humor. It was this meeting which finally rewarded my patient survey with the long awaited entry to Wazana's native village and the heart of his family. Her refrain, "I grew up in his house," was her way of emphasizing how close she had been to the healer. Both Masouda and her sister-in-law, Hana Buskila, venerate Wazana as their family *tsaddiq*, and their families look to Wazana for help when bad health or misfortune strike. They light candles to his memory daily and hold commemorative feasts to mark his *hillula*.

31

Flocking at the entrance of the house of Rabbi David u-Moshe

המקום הזה קדוש
לכבוד הרב הגדול
המלוב׳ן כמוהר׳׳ר
וד ומשה זיע׳א

ק פ ה

Interior of the house of Rabbi David u-Moshe; the inscription reads, "This place was consecrated to the great rabbi, the miracle maker, Rabbi David u-Moshe"

    In contrast to the passionate, but rather inarticulate Buskila sisters-in-law, Rabbi Shmuel Suissa, Wazana's distant relative from Be'er Sheva, was polished, ceremonious, and slightly pompous. He is a teacher and author of religious textbooks. Of all the people I had interviewed, Suissa came across as the best educated. He is from Idirghan, a small village in the Sous region, and his first meeting with Wazana took place when the healer came to treat his family. Suissa told us that he had spent many years in Casablanca where he finalized his religious education and went on to teach in a Jewish school.

On arriving at Suissa's apartment, I was led through a living room whose walls were lined with book shelves and portraits of distinguished rabbis before being shown into the bedroom where Rabbi Shmuel, who is crippled in one leg, lay, the lower half of his body covered in a sheet. His face was youthful, his eyes slightly slanted, and his head shaven. He seemed delighted to be given an opportunity to talk about himself: the books he has written, his Jewish and secular knowledge, his eloquent sermons, his talent for enthusing people with religion, the melody of his voice in synagogue. In the midst of recounting Wazana's exploits, he even managed to introduce Spinoza, Heine, Ben Gurion, and Bialik (Israel's national poet) into the conversation. Suddenly the conversation turned to a seance he had performed, in which he had summoned the spirits of Ben Gurion and Bialik. At this point I had the sense of drawing a step closer to his kinsman, the extraordinary healer. Thus, with his eyes tensing in recaptured horror, he leaned over conspiratorially, lowered his voice and whispered to me that after death, these two great historical figures were sentenced to the tortures of hell—for their sins of irreligiousness.

The Itung neighborhood, a miserable spot on the western outskirts of Pardes Ḥana, is home to the eldest living member of the Wazana family, a man sharing the name Ya'aqov with the object of our quest. It is no surprise that the neighborhood is another jungle of multi-entrance apartment complexes with a few dingy shops, a bomb shelter, and a large concrete yard lined with clotheslines weighted down with laundry. Our target, Ya'aqov Wazana, is blind and lives with his widowed daughter and her children. Their apartment somehow manages to combine a mixture of refinement—its walls overlaid with fine wood—and dilapidation—the floor tiles are crooked and wobble when walked upon. Kitschy pastoral scenes and the ubiquitous portraits of *tsaddiqim* abound. Rabbi Ya'aqov waited for us in his living room and struggled to sit up as we entered. He was very old indeed—over ninety—and his white, hooded *jellaba* and snow-white beard carried the air of a far off time and place. Fortunately, Rabbi Ya'aqov was lucid and focused. His brother Avraham, who later joined us, was also blind, just like the third brother, Shaul from Natanya, whom we had already met. The old man's patient delineation of his family tree was frequently interrupted by praise for *ait* Wazana's celebrated *tsaddiqim*. His nephew and namesake, the subject of our inquiry, was conspicuously absent from this litany of praise; in fact our informant seemed to relate to him with a modicum of contempt. It was evident that he did not regard him as a worthy inheritor of the family blessing and privilege.

As old Ya'aqov plumbed his memories, around us the household was making ready for the wedding of one of his grandsons. Toward the end of the interview, we were joined by yet another grandson in jeans and an undershirt, and sporting a heavy gold chain. He asked his grandfather to talk to us about the friction between the Wazana and Abu-Ḥatsera families but the old man was averse to developing this theme. It was clearly a delicate subject. All he said was that a dispute on a point of religion had arisen, a religious dispute, nothing more. After the interview, he motioned to Matan and I to approach, and resting his hands gently upon our heads, he blessed us.

Thus, with the blessing of an old man in a white *jellaba* echoing in our ears, we took our farewell of the Wazana family in Israel.

Old Ya'aqov Wazana (namesake and cousin of Rabbi Ya'aqov)

3

Ait Wazana

These are the generations of the Wazana family as revealed to us by its oldest descendant, Ya'aqov son of Rabbi Yaish, at his home in Pardes Ḥana:

> Rabbi Avraham begot David who begot Avraham and my esteemed father, Yaish. And Rabbi David had many children whom he sent forth to different towns saying: "Go out and live by what you find." To them he bequeathed a bountiful inheritance which they received from the towns of Ait Wauzgit, Agouim, and Sour. Rabbi Avraham Wazana, son of Rabbi David and brother of my father [Rabbi Yaish], went to Ait Wauzgit, where he found a wife and begat Ya'aqov in Assarag, in Tifnoute. I too was named Ya'aqov by my father.

This chronicle describes the generations of the Wazana family. The founder of the dynasty was Rabbi Avraham, known as el-Kebir, ("The Great"), to distinguish him from his grandson Rabbi Avraham, father of Rabbi Ya'aqov. His son, Rabbi David, bestowed on his many descendants a birthright of areas of religious authority.[1] As we shall hear later, the Jews acknowledged the privileges handed down by the early Wazana forebears (*zekhut avot*), and assiduously took care of their descendants' sustenance.

The above description of a four-generation family tree was provided by Ya'aqov son of Yaish who, like the hero of our story, the healer Ya'aqov son of Avraham, is the great-grandson of the dynasty founder, Rabbi Avraham "The Great." The historical accuracy of this interviewee's information is questionable considering his comment that Rabbi Avraham, and another ten sages, were exiled to Morocco from Jerusalem after the destruction of the Second Temple by the Romans (in the first century C.E.). This particular detail is a typical theme in the legendary genre establishing the antecedents of Moroccan *tsaddiqim;* the legends of many of the saints often place their subjects in the Holy Land prior to their appearance in Morocco, depicting this as the consequence of exile (Ben-Ami 1984: 41). This "historical depth" thus establishes the figure of Rabbi Avraham as a recognizable legendary archetype, but it is probably illusory. Search as we might, we were unsuccessful in unearthing any missing links in the family genealogy supporting this version's historicity.[2]

The advent of Rabbi Avraham el-Kebir in southern Morocco is particularly dramatic, and his travels through the Dra Valley on the road to Ouarzazate, where he first comes to light,[3] are replete with miracles, as befits a great *tsaddiq.* According to the legend, Rabbi Avraham was traveling toward "an Arab town full of bandits and murderers," on the banks of the Dra River, when he altered his course to visit an ancient Jewish cemetery, intending to pray at the abandoned graves. Upon reaching the cemetery, he discovered an Arab shepherd grazing his flocks. The *tsaddiq* ordered the shepherd to leave the holy site, but the latter stubbornly refused, threatening to kill Rabbi Avraham. As a punishment, the Arab's gun was turned to stone and his entire flock became headstones. News of the miracle spread to the town, and the local ruler decided to ride out to meet the saint, to apologize for the incident and mollify the holy man. Rabbi Avraham asked the ruler to erect a wall around the cemetery, which he did, and the local Arabs were ordered to carry out this task. The wall was erected in two days, and the sage was finally escorted into the town amidst great ceremony and rejoicing.

The townspeople implored Rabbi Avraham to stay, but he was determined to continue on his way. He set out again, reaching his next destination in a trice, due to the miracle of *qfitsat haderekh* ("contraction of the road"; see Ben-Ami 1984: 66; Willner 1969: 295). On Friday afternoon, Rabbi Avraham, accompanied by a sizable escort consisting of Jews and Arabs, decided to halt beside the spring of Eben Zagart, in the area known as Frenin. It was just before the Sabbath, and the saint, not wishing to profane the holy day by continuing on his way, sent his escort back to their homes. The Muslims thereupon returned to Dra, while Rabbi Avraham dispatched the Jews to Ouarzazate to inform the community to expect his arrival once the Sabbath was over. The messengers' traveling time was miraculously foreshortened. Upon hearing of Rabbi Avraham's decision to spend the night at the spring, the Jews of Ouarzazate were seized by terror since the place was believed to be haunted by bandits and wild beasts. Indeed, the saint was attacked by local Arabs but they became paralyzed whenever they approached him. All the while, the sage went on quietly preparing his Sabbath meal, engrossed in prayer. The Arabs eventually fled, leaving Rabbi Avraham all alone in the wilderness.

With nightfall, the rabbi found himself surrounded by lions, tigers, hyenas, and snakes which did him no harm. They were sent by Elijah the Prophet to protect the *tsaddiq*. Indeed, throughout the night, the mystical figure of Elijah appeared on the hilltop overlooking the spring, maintaining an all-night vigil, drawn rifle at the ready.

Rabbi Avraham spent the Sabbath in prayer and study. After performing the *havdalah* (the ritual to mark the close of the Sabbath), one of the lions turned to him angrily and said: "Rabbi Avraham Wazana, is it permissible to fast on the Sabbath? Do we have to fast while you eat?" The lion begged the saint to depart so that the beasts might eat. However the Rabbi declared: "I will not move until people arrive with transport to escort me away from here." The lion responded, "You have no need of horses, climb on my back, and I will bear you where you wish"; and the Rabbi was thus transported to Ouarzazate on the back of a lion, the other lions racing in convoy around them. Meanwhile, the town's Jews were in deep mourning, convinced that the *tsaddiq* could not have possibly survived a night alone in the wilderness. They even hired Arabs to search for his remains. Their amazement, at the spectacle of Rabbi Avraham entering through the city gates, mounted on a lion, with an escort of lions, knew no bounds. Some tried to attack the lions, but were frozen to the spot whenever they approached the cavalcade, which made its way through narrow streets to the *mellaḥ* (Jewish quarter). Rabbi Avraham then commanded the elders to feed the lions with the remains of the Sabbath meal to reward their work. Finally, he uttered the divine name and the beasts vanished into the air.

Rabbi Avraham's remarkable entry into Ouarzazate established him in the minds of the local Jews as a saint and miracle-worker, preparing the way for the emergence of *ait* Wazana as a holy dynasty. It was no surprise that varying versions of this legend were told by Rabbi Avraham's descendants in Israel, or that the events were augmented with colorful details accentuating the family's ancestral merit (*zekhut avot*). The miracles that Rabbi Avraham performed on his journey through the Dra Valley to Ouarzazate—overpowering Arab assailants, the incident in the desecrated cemetery, and the cemetery's subsequent restoration, traveling great distances in a flash, and supremacy over wild beasts— these are all standard saint legend motifs (Ben-Ami 1984: 56–68). It is very unusual, however, for all of these to appear in one story, and the fact that they do is impressive justification for the family's claim to holy status. The young Rabbi Ya'aqov would no doubt have heard these and related stories, and we may conjecture that the legends bolstered his faith in his own powers resulting in his characteristic confidence and sense of purpose.

The saintly Rabbi Avraham bowed to the appeals of the Jews of Ouarzazate, remained in their city, and subsequently married a local woman. A year later, a son, David, was born and, even as a young man, showed signs of inheriting his father's merit.[4] The legend, which occurred prior to David's marriage at the age of sixteen, offers testimony to his supernatural powers: "There was a young girl from Ouarzazate who owned a beautiful hen with brightly colored feathers. This hen would follow the child wherever she went, and even slept next to her. One day, the girl was playing with the *kaid's* [local ruler] children when the *kaid's* daughter grabbed the hen and took it to her mother who thereupon slaughtered it." When news of the Jewish girl's distress over the loss of her pet reached David's ears, a miracle occurred. As the *kaid's* wife sat plucking the dead hen, the feathers she plucked became fastened to her face. Try as she might the woman could not free herself of the feathers because Rabbi David had declared that, "The one who stole the chicken will be transformed into a chicken, and the one who caused its death will surely die." The first part of the curse came true immediately as the *kaid's* daughter became a chicken and went strutting after the Jewish child. Rabbi David was ordered before the *kaid* and offered the latter a cruel choice: "If I restore your daughter, your wife will die, and if you choose your wife's life, your child will remain a chicken for the rest of her days." The *kaid* asked for his daughter back, and Rabbi David ordered him to shut his eyes. When he looked again, his daughter was standing before him. However, upon returning home, the *kaid* found his wife's lifeless body. Following this incident, word of Rabbi David's powers spread far and wide. Shortly afterwards, his father arranged for him to be married to a girl from the community. According to one version of this legend, Rabbi David married the chicken's owner.

An echo of this story, which starts out innocently enough as a fairy tale, but ends with a ruthless act of vengeance and death, may be heard in the events surrounding Rabbi Ya'aqov's death. As we shall see, although differing in detail, the legends share a structure that is strikingly similar.

A year after Rabbi David's marriage, his father, Rabbi Avraham, died. The legends surrounding his death, which are replete with miracles, are consistent with his eminence as a *tsaddiq* of great merit. In conformity with the customary model, the principal miracle entails prediction of the time of his own death. According to one extant version, on the night he died Rabbi Avraham invited two hundred scholars to join him in a feast. Following the afternoon and evening prayers, Rabbi Avraham requested the assembly to recite the prayer Shema Yisrael three times, and then to read from the Book of Psalms until midnight. At the stroke of midnight the sages were gradually overcome by sleep, and no one was awake to witness the Rabbi's soul depart. Straight after his passing, Rabbi Avraham informed his best pupil in a dream that his body was lying ready and awaiting burial in the cemetery at Ait Budiel. Upon awakening, the company of sages discovered the Rabbi's disappearance and hired an experienced Arab horseman to ride to Ait Budiel to search for the body. Rabbi David intervened and had the Arab transported miraculously to the cemetery where he discovered the saint's body already washed and wrapped in shrouds. A gathering of local Jews and Arabs was already waiting there since the Rabbi had also appeared to a righteous woman in her dream, revealing the whereabouts of his body. When the Arab reported his findings to the Jews of Ouarzazate, many were dismayed to learn that the *tsaddiq* should be buried far from their town. Rabbi David thereupon begged the community to honor his father's wish saying, "Do not move my father's body. I will take his place when the time comes: let him be buried there [in Ait Budiel] and I will be buried in Ouarzazate."

The nuclear motifs appearing in the legend of Rabbi Avraham's death recur in the death stories of other members of the family: foreknowledge of the hour of death which allows the *tsaddiq* to prepare, asking to be buried in a remote cemetery, and the involvement of a Muslim horseman are common elements in the death legends of Rabbi Avraham and the father of our protagonist, Rabbi Ya'aqov.

Within a short time, the tomb at Ait Budiel became known as a holy site, the destination of pilgrims and the source of omens and miracles. There is a story that when the French elected to pave a road through the cemetery, their trespass on the *tsaddiq*'s realm was paid for with the lives of several workers, forcing the project to be abandoned. Close by the tomb runs a stream renowned for its supernatural powers: "The waters rise and fall like a fountain, and any attempt to divert its water is punished with instant death." On a visit to Morocco some years ago, Shaul Wazana and his brother went to see the tomb of Ait Budiel. They found it still intact, on the banks of a newly constructed artificial lake.

Rabbi Avraham's famed entry through the gates of Ouarzazate, and the subsequent miracles, established the Wazana family name solidly among the firmament of southern Moroccan saints. The wonders performed by his son and successor, Rabbi David, further consolidated the family's *zekhut avot*, which was handed down the generations in an unbroken line. The story of Rabbi David's great miracle, which placed him in the position to bequeath his legacy and birthright upon his descendants, is an excellent example of the scope of his powers. Not only did mortal beings, Jews and Arabs alike, as well as subjects of the animal kingdom, answer to his bidding, but as we shall see now, also the inhabitants of the "other world," the demons (Arabic: *jnun*), were subservient to his will.

Once, the legend goes, Rabbi David was invited to visit the Jewish quarter (*mellah*) of Sour, a village situated somewhere between Assarag and Agouim, west of Ouarzazate, to bestow his blessing on fifteen young brides. The day appointed for the weddings was Thursday, and Rabbi David agreed to arrive the day before. Thus, on Wednesday morning he ordered his messenger to harness the horse in readiness for the journey.

Chapter 3

The messenger expressed doubt that they would arrive in Sour on time, reminding the Rabbi that "the journey from here [Ouarzazate] to Sour cannot normally be done in less than three days." The *tsaddiq* ignored this, and whipping up the horse, raced over the villages of Amassine and Agouim, arriving at Sour that very day. Upon arrival they were puzzled that no one came to greet them. However, an old woman they happened across explained that the whole community had gone down to the river with the brides and grooms. "At that time the Jews had no *mikveh* [ritual bath] in which the brides and grooms could immerse themselves and therefore used the river." As the old woman finished speaking, cries were heard coming from the direction of the river. Rabbi David hastened over and learned that the first bride to enter the water had disappeared beneath the surface. The Jews of Sour were terrified and shocked, feelings of anguish and grief quickly replacing their earlier expressions of happiness and joy.

According to the legend, Rabbi David remained composed and quickly ordered the community leaders to erect a large tent and call everyone inside. When all were gathered, he told them to remain silent and motionless until his task was done. He then proceeded to divide the people into two groups, marking the border between them with his silver-handled walking cane which was covered with his cape. Before the eyes of the astonished assembly, the Rabbi pronounced a magic formula, at which flames erupted out from beneath the cane, followed in quick succession by a cloud of mysterious spirits rising from the ground. The spirits sought to approach the *tsaddiq* in order to kiss and embrace him, but Rabbi David rebuked them gravely, saying: "You evildoers, have you no shame? Does it not say in the holy Scriptures, 'Daughter of such a one is destined for the son of such a one even if they are from different lands?'[5] And have you not transgressed the holy commandments . . . by snatching her just before the *sheva brakhot* [the seven blessings for the bride and groom which form part of the wedding ceremony]?" The spirits from under the ground that were, in fact, none other than demons, swore that they had had no hand in the deed but Rabbi David did not relent. He continued summoning them, legion after legion, until only a single blind demon remained in the river. To force the last demon to appear, the *tsaddiq* captured the rest inside the tent, compelling them to stand, hands folded behind their backs in submission, and announced that "none would go free until the missing girl was returned." At this, the blind demon appeared, and indeed it was he who had stolen the young girl for his bride. Trembling before the *tsaddiq,* he told how he had taken the girl because, "she entered the river and didn't call on the name of the Holy One Blessed Be He." According to another version, the girl wounded the demon's eyes as she was bathing and was snatched away in revenge.[6]

After assuring himself that no intimacy had taken place between demon and human, that the girl had eaten nothing in the kingdom of the spirits, and that her clothing had been restored, Rabbi David commanded the demon to return the girl. As the community watched, amazed, the trembling, weeping girl suddenly reappeared. The *tsaddiq* then commanded her captor to remove all the golden jewels he had given her, forcing him to swear to leave her alone forever. "You are forbidden to cross her path ever again. If you approach her, you will surely die." Saying which, the Rabbi struck the ground with his cane, and the demonic legions vanished as though they had never been. The brides finally resumed their immersions in preparation for their nuptials, leaving the bewildered Jews crowding round the *tsaddiq* to receive his blessing. In their gratitude, they vowed to take care of his sustenance for the rest of his days.

Rabbi David's clear-headed response to the pledges borne on this tide of emotion marks the point at which his own, and his father's charisma became institutionalized as a permanent family resource. He admonished the Jews of Sour against empty promises, saying: "He who makes a vow and does not fulfill it—will be punished by death." He offered an alternative whereby "whoever owns one hundred cows will set aside the butter produced in a day. He can enjoy the milk, but the butter must be collected. Anyone who reaps from the wheat or the barley should set aside a tithe. And anyone who returns from a journey [on business] should set aside a tithe [of the profit]. Further, whenever you hear the name Wazana, when someone bearing that name comes to ask something of you, you shall present it to him."

It is to this system of earmarked allocations that the Wazana family refers when speaking of "the inheritance that was bequeathed [by Rabbi Avraham] in Ait Wauzgit."[7] With regard to Ya'aqov Wazana, the healer, interviewees outside the family circle left us in no doubt that the "inheritance" was a real aspect of their lives in Morocco: "none of us [the Jewish population] would touch it [the produce]. It was his father's inheritance, his father's merit," explained Rabbi Yitzḥak Peḥima. Peḥima, a one-time resident of Imini and Agouim, recalled how, "we all used to give him donations. Tithes." Rabbi Moshe Tubul, the *shoḥet*, healer, and scribe from Amassine, noted that "people set up a sort of fund for Rabbi Ya'aqov; he came around every month or two, and took what we set aside for him. He knew the gifts were waiting. We gave it to him because of his father—because of his forebears' privilege." According to Eliyahu Tubul, who came from the same village as Rabbi Ya'aqov, his father, Rabbi Avraham, had been "a great rabbi and at the beginning of each month we used to give him gifts from our crops, or else some sheep or cattle. If he didn't receive something at the beginning of the month, then the cows would stop producing—no calves, no milk . . ." The Wazana family enjoyed this arrangement in Morocco, and at least one of them, namely blind Shaul Wazana, still does in his own way.

Chapter 3

The miracle performed by Rabbi David in Sour is of particular interest in light of the association his descendant, our protagonist, had with the demonic world. These ties apparently spring from an established family tradition wherein the *tsaddiq* held incontrovertible mastery over "those underground," that is, the demons. However, there is a marked difference between Rabbi David's relationship and attitude toward the demons and that of Rabbi Ya'aqov. In contrast to Wazana's tendency to smudge or remove the boundaries between the human and the demonic, the miraculous incident at Sour serves to emphasize the scrupulous segregation between the two worlds. Rabbi David is uncompromisingly meticulous in ensuring that no mark of impurity from the "other" world remains to sully the abducted bride. The girl is restored to her "natural" place (under the wedding canopy, next to her intended husband), and the demon is forced to swear never to approach her again. These segregative precautions represent a far cry from the behavior of Rabbi Ya'aqov, who, in explicit contradiction of his illustrious grandfather's act of restoration, takes a demonic wife—rather than a human bride.

The central role of the blind demon in this story is of great interest in light of the fact that blindness is common to the Wazana family. "In our family when you reach the age of sixty or seventy, you turn blind," commented blind, old Ya'aqov Wazana from Pardes Hana with resignation. And as if to emphasize this fact, we were joined in the interview by his brother Avraham, also blind. The best known of the Wazana brothers in Israel, Shaul, has been blind from childhood, while the eldest brother, Yitzhak, who is no longer alive, lost his sight a short time before he died. According to Ya'aqov Wazana, neither his cousin, the hero of our story, nor his father, Rabbi Avraham, were spared this fate. Indeed, two of the interviewees who had known Rabbi Ya'aqov well in Morocco, claimed that the healer's eyesight had deteriorated in his latter years, even though he never suffered total loss of sight. From Rabbi Ya'aqov's elderly cousin we also learned that the healer experienced temporary loss of sight during the year he spent in Casablanca. The interviewee explicitly linked this occurrence to Rabbi Ya'aqov's marriage to the she-demon (to be dealt with in full later).

What is the cause of the Wazana family's blindness? The older Wazana men, all of them blind, can offer no satisfactory explanation. However, one of Shaul's younger sons did hint at the possible reason for their reluctance to talk about it. He suggested that the blindness was the result of a curse which had been placed on one of the Wazana ancestors following some dispute over the naming of a newborn. It is tempting, in Rabbi Ya'aqov's case, to forge some kind of inverse association between his partial sight loss toward the end of his life, and the trait that so clearly characterized his actions—namely his insistence on *looking* into the forbidden, his tendency to expose things preferably left concealed. We will examine this trait later, in our detailed exploration of Wazana's personality.

The deterioration from the ranks of the powerful and illustrious previously enjoyed by the Wazana family during its Moroccan heyday, to the humble standing characterizing it today, is somewhat problematic, and even painful. It is apparent that while certain historical Wazana *tsaddiqim* continue to be venerated by Moroccan immigrants from Tidili, Tifnoute, Ouarzazate, and Skoura,[8] contemporary members of the family lack the prestige that surrounded their ancestors. The disparity between interviewee Ya'aqov Wazana's past and present standard of living reflects one aspect of this decline. "When we lived in Ouarzazate, we were very rich. We had a dozen houses that people rented from us. Our home also served as the synagogue, and three *minyanim* [prayer groups] would pray there each day and join the family for meals. I used to be a salesman, and traveled all around the villages. Then the French came along and brought their own kind of blessing. I had a cement factory with a hundred and forty workers. We abandoned it all to come to Israel." His arrival in Israel, as an older man, heralded a significant fall in fortune: initially working for the Jewish National Fund, he barely managed to scrape together a living as a farm laborer. Of all the Wazana family, Shaul is the most widely known among immigrants from southern Morocco. As we have noted, he visits their different communities, attending every *hillula* in memory of the *tsaddiqim*, and exchanging blessings for money and good humor. Nonetheless, even Shaul, who corresponds most closely to the old-time Wazana *tsaddiqim*, is merely a pale reminder of his forebears. His large circle of acquaintances might marvel at his astounding ability to remember everyone he meets, and may accept his blessings gladly, but they tend to doubt that he possesses any special powers.

Wazana's family and certain acquaintances hotly contend that *ait* Wazana's erudition and powers equal those of *ait* Abu-Ḥatsera. If this is indeed so, then it is puzzling to find that in Israel at least, one family flourishes and is respected, while the other has difficulty maintaining its standing within a small peripheral group of Moroccan Jews. Old Ya'aqov Wazana told me of a bitter argument that occurred between the leading representatives of the two families—Rabbi Avraham "the Great" and Rabbi Ya'aqov Abu-Ḥatsera—on a point of scholarship. He declined, however, to elaborate on the significance or consequence of the disagreement. I certainly sensed tacit resentment toward the rival family, who, in his opinion, has no superior claim to the *zekhut* than he does, but nevertheless enjoys immense prestige among the former Moroccan community in Israel. An explanation for this disparity in status offered by a younger member of the Wazana family does not flatter the house of Abu-Ḥatsera. According to this source, although the families are essentially equal, Abu-Ḥatsera's preeminence in Israel is largely thanks to the greater humility of the Wazana clan.

Whatever the reason for the decline in fortune in Israel, the life of Rabbi Ya'aqov the healer, as we shall see from the coming chapters, is the dramatic epitome of this "degeneration." This man, the historical link between the early Wazana *tsaddiqim* and their present-day descendants, used his family privileges for his own crooked and tortuous ends. It was a path foreign in every sense to that trodden by his esteemed forefathers, and one that would ultimately lead to his ruin.

4

Born in Assarag—
In the Heart of the Atlas Mountains

Wazana was born at the beginning of the century in the village of Assarag, in the heart of the Western Atlas Mountains. This rural area is traversed by the Tifnoute River and lies at the edge of the highest peaks of the Atlas range. Assarag is isolated and hard to reach, especially in winter when thick snow blankets the ground. Far removed from the large Jewish centers on the coast and in the north of the country, the tiny Jewish communities of Tifnoute made their home among the settlements of the Berber tribes. The marginality of the local Jews had a linguistic manifestation: some of them spoke only the local Berber dialect, as opposed to Arabic, the language normally used by Moroccan Jewry. As far as we know, this linguistic anomaly was unknown elsewhere in Morocco (cf. Goldberg 1983: 63).

As in other parts of southern Morocco, the Jews of Tifnoute made their livelihood working as small traders, itinerant peddlers, and artisans. They were tailors, blacksmiths, and metal workers, pack harness makers, and saddle fitters. They manufactured bellows for charcoal furnaces, and specialized in producing different types of footwear: shoes, sandals, slippers, and snow boots. They used to peddle their merchandise among the nearby villages, plying their specialist trades to Jews and their Muslim residents. Only a handful of the Tifnoute Jews actually worked as farmers, but it was not uncommon for people to share in working the land or raising animals with their Muslim neighbors, and then apportion the yield between them.[1] Although not without some tension, life among the Muslims was generally marked by harmonious relations. While Muslim

45

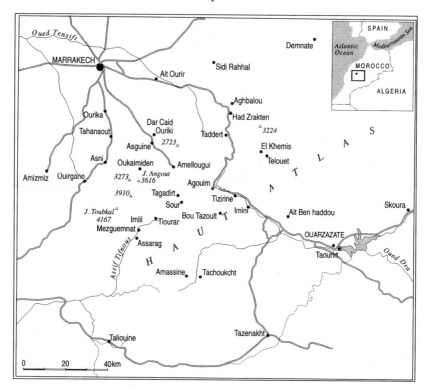

Wazana's Territory
Agouim, where Wazana spent his last years, and where he died, is located in the center of the map on the Marrakech-Ouarzazate Road. Assarag, where he was born, is southwest of Agouim, on the Tifnout River. Ca. 1990

law ascribed the Jews an inferior status,[2] the necessities of day-to-day coexistence tended to mitigate the standing of the Jews. The services they rendered for their Muslim farmer neighbors were material, and thus there developed an intricate network of family and personal relationships which guaranteed the Jews the protection of their neighbors. Prior to the arrival of the French, the region fell outside the sphere of central government control, and in time earned a reputation as the "strife territory" (*Bled-es-siba*), due to the conditions of political instability and lack of personal security that prevailed. Under the circumstances, the patronage enjoyed by the Jews assured at least a tolerable form of existence.[3]

From the safety of the present in contemporary Israel, the former Jews of Assarag look back on life in the village with fond nostalgia. They acknowledge the hardship and extreme poverty, and remember clearly the wretched, humble clay houses they once called home. Neither has the oppressive hand of the autocratic local ruler based in the kasbah of Telouet been forgotten. Surfaced roads, electricity, and running water were unknown until after the last of the Jews left for Israel in the early 1950s. On the other hand, the land was lush and water abundant in both summer and winter. The region was renowned locally for its bountiful produce, the fruit in particular. Compared with the intensity of life in present-day Israel, the agrarian simplicity of Assarag seems an ocean of tranquillity, contentment, and well-being.

In the eyes of the Moroccan immigrants, the heaviest price for leaving Morocco has been the warm, close-knit relationships that typified their life in these small, stable communities. They further yearn for the singular spiritual and religious atmosphere that crowned village life, and the fact that, without exception, the community was devout in its traditions. It is surprising as well as laudable that the inhabitants of these tiny enclaves set such store by their Jewishness. Notwithstanding their isolation, the communities managed to nurture strong ties with rabbinical centers in Marrakech and other cities. Every village or group of villages established its own synagogue and cemetery, and all had the necessary ritual functionaries: a *shoḥet, mohel,* cantor, and teachers of Torah. Occasionally, a few or all of these services were carried out by one person. Until the age of *bar mitzvah* (thirteen years old), boys learned reading, writing, and scripture in the local synagogue (*sla*), and those with ability whose families could afford it were sent to study in a religious academy (*yeshiva*) in Marrakech or Casablanca. Some young men returned home ordained as rabbis or *shoḥatim* (pl.) and contributed to maintaining the essential ritual traditions of Jewish life.

How large was the Jewish population of Assarag? According to the informants, approximately twenty or thirty families; however, this number, which might possibly be a little exaggerated, relates to the beginning of the century (when Wazana was a child). Thereafter, the size of the Jewish community in Assarag gradually dwindled, and, by the time Wazana left following his mother's death in the late 1940s, only a handful of Jews remained. The size of the Jewish population has been offered as the principal reason for Wazana's flight.

As noted before, the healer's family tree boasts both rabbis and sages, some of whom achieved recognition as *tsaddiqim* far beyond the precincts of the Tifnoute region. Hence, Wazana's family history afforded him significant merits of holiness and blessing transmitted through the generations.[4] It is important to understand the significance of this privilege within the traditional Jewish society of southern Morocco, where cults of *tsaddiqim* enjoyed a scope and power unparalleled in any other Jewish group (see Ben-Ami 1984; Bilu 1990; Goldberg 1992; Shokeid 1971; and Stillman 1982). The emphasis placed by mystical as well as other Jewish traditions on the importance of the *tsaddiq* was combined with the traditional Islamic veneration of holy men in Morocco (Eickelman

47

1976; Geertz 1968; Gellner 1969; and Westermarck 1926) to assure the *tsaddiq* a central position in the lives of the Jews. Entire communities made pilgrimages to the *tsaddiq's* grave to mark his *hillula,* individuals visited the tomb in times of trouble, and families lit candles and held thanksgiving feasts at home in his honor. They named their babies after him and prayed to him for help whenever and wherever the need arose. Thus, the bond between the *tsaddiq* and the faithful was close, highly personal, and often lasted a lifetime.

Why did the Wazana family, with its glittering pedigree, settle in the small, peripheral village of Assarag? The legend records a miraculous journey from the Dra Valley to Ouarzazate which established Rabbi Avraham "The Great," the dynasty founder, as a popular *tsaddiq.* As we have noted, his son, Rabbi David, who was no less powerful than his father, established his home in the town of Ouarzazate where he raised a large family. As his sons reached adulthood and were acknowledged as rabbis and sages possessing the family powers, Rabbi David deployed them to different localities to avoid the possibility of competition and conflict. So it was that one of the sons, Rabbi Avraham Wazana, named after his illustrious grandfather, came to the village of Assarag where his own son, Ya'aqov, was born.

5

Wazana and His Parents

Rabbi Avraham and his wife Esther had many children (according to one version, twelve), but apart from Ya'aqov and his sister Ḥana, all of them died in infancy. Thus, Rabbi Ya'aqov was the only surviving son, and this singularity served to intensify the powerful parent-child bond. As I will show, the strong attachment between the healer and his parents was largely responsible for his peculiar lifestyle.

Rabbi Avraham is described as a worthy and steadfast heir to the privileges bequeathed by his ancestors. He was, by all accounts, a pious scholar whose spiritual learning was his sole vocation. In contrast to his son Ya'aqov, he never used *ktiva* (writing) for healing: "His father never wrote [amulets]; he just blessed people and they would all get better." It was the father's custom to visit the different communities of the Tifnoute region, giving his blessing to the Jews he met in return for liberal gifts of their produce. The local Jews regarded Rabbi Avraham as a *tsaddiq*, and the story of his death, which is typical of Jewish Moroccan saint legends, reflects this fact very clearly (see Ben Ami 1984: 63–64). One description of his death is as follows:

> Rabbi Avraham traveled to Talouine [a village in the south of the Tifnoute region] to collect donations. He was given oil and honey. This was his gift. During the evening prayers he told them [the congregants]: "You must read the Shema Yisrael; it is time for me to die," and he asked to be buried in Tazenakht [about 90 km east of Talouine]. He promised that his body would be as light as a feather. They replied: "It can't be [that you're going to die]. You are a

tsaddiq." An Arab passerby overheard all this and said, "If he dies, I will take him to the place where he will be buried—it will take three days." The Arab said this jokingly, in scorn. He wasn't serious. When they finished praying, the Rabbi said "Shema Yisrael" and fell down dead.

When the Arab went to sleep, Rabbi Avraham came to him and began choking him. He said that if he didn't get up he would finish him off. The next day the Arab ran over to the *ḥazan*'s [local rabbi] house, and [asked him] to take Rabbi Avraham. They tied the *tsaddiq* to a mule and his body was so light it took them one day instead of three to reach Tazenakht, which is where they buried him.

Most other versions of Rabbi Avraham's death story correspond to the above version in all the main details except for the locations of his death and burial. Most interviewees, including one woman who said that Rabbi Avraham had stayed in her father's house in Amassine the day before he died, claimed that the *tsaddiq*'s body had been transported miraculously from Amassine to Tamzersht, and not from Talouine to Tazenakht. According to the informants, Rabbi Avraham's burial in Tamzersht as opposed to Assarag, his home, was due to the religious and spiritual merit of the Tamzersht community: "There were more Jews there, and greater holiness, they prayed more and showed more respect. They respected everything. Everyone was sympathetic to everyone else." In this statement, made by someone from Tamzersht, we have an allusion to the deterioration in Jewish life that took place in Assarag, the village where Rabbi Ya'aqov was born and where he spent most his life. Tamu Tubul of Assarag also maintained that Tamzersht had been a place of holiness ("that's where the great *tsaddiqim* are buried"), and referred to the local Arab population as *shurfa* (descendants of the prophet). This direct lineage to Mohammed accorded them an aura of holiness from which the Muslims, but also the Jews of the village, could benefit. It is no surprise that Muslim piety and virtue is offered as a reason for the *tsaddiq*'s burial in Tamzersht. We must bear in mind the closeness of the relationship that existed between the two communities, and in particular, the fact that in the Atlas Mountains, Jewish and Muslim saint cults had many elements in common (see Ben-Ami 1984: 166–84; and Goldberg 1992). This explanation is certainly acceptable in light of the intimate involvement of Rabbi Ya'aqov in Muslim customs and beliefs (to be discussed later). Having said that, there is also the possibility that Tamu's explanation reflects her own warm sentiments toward what she calls "the good Arabs of Morocco." Her version of the story of Rabbi Avraham's death presents the figure of the Arab in a positive light from the outset, and makes no claim of Arab disrespect toward the *tsaddiq*. According to her, the Arab is the first to bring word of the *tsaddiq*'s death, having experienced a vision of Rabbi Avraham, who appeared to him with "an angel hovering above him and rays of light illuminating his face."

An examination of Jewish Moroccan saint legends reveals that it is not uncommon for a *tsaddiq* to request burial somewhere other than his home village or the place of his death.[1] In the majority of cases, the request ascribed to the saint appears in fact to conceal a long history of struggle between two Jewish communities, each desirous for the *tsaddiq*'s resting place within its domain so that the community can continue to benefit from his blessing. Such contests invariably resulted in victory for the larger, more central community, and this pattern of burial relocation therefore mirrors a facet of the social reality of these communities in the early twentieth century. The small, isolated mountain settlements emptied as their inhabitants migrated to the main towns. The burial of these "mobile *tsaddiqim*" therefore reflects the movement toward the new Jewish concentrations on the frequently changing map of southern Morocco. An echo of the fierce inter-community competition emerges in the story of a former resident of Tamzersht who said that, in defiance of the *tsaddiq*'s categorical request, the Jews of Amassine insisted on burying him in their own cemetery. However, when they tried to lift the body, it was as heavy "as all this" (the speaker denoted the neighboring tenements seen through his window), and could not be moved from the spot. Finally, they agreed to carry him to Tamzersht, whereupon his body became as light as a feather.

Most of the interviewees were in agreement regarding the date of Rabbi Avraham's death, a missing detail in the version cited earlier. The death occurred during the festival of Ḥanukka, in the winter month of Tevet, and a thick blanket of snow over the mountains added significantly to the spectacular nature of the burial party's trek from Amassine to Tamzersht. That the journey only took a fraction of the normal time was all the more miraculous, given the challenging weather conditions and the fact that, as one version states, the Jews of Amassine had been ordered by the *tsaddiq* "not to take me by horse, but to carry me yourselves." Whether an animal with an Arab driver made the journey to Tamzersht, or a cortege of Jews struggling through the snow bearing the body of the *tsaddiq* on their shoulders, a considerable distance was covered in next to no time. One interviewee described it as "the same distance as from here [Be'er Sheva] to Haifa on foot [over 200 km]." "The men who carried him said he weighed less than half a kilo, as the saint did not wish to weary them, and rather than taking ten hours it only took two," marveled an informant from Tamzersht.

The motif of the miraculous reduction in travel time also occurs in other legends of *tsaddiqim* in the Wazana family, and signifies the elimination of the constraints of time and space. In much the same way as the presence of thick snow makes the ease and speed of travel seem so miraculous, so the particular day of the week on which the burial takes place is miraculous. Traditionally, the perfect day for a *tsaddiq* to die is a Friday, owing to its proximity to the holy Sabbath day. Furthermore, many legends contain an element of tension over whether the *tsaddiq* can indeed be laid to rest in time for the Sabbath. The suspense ends when time itself stands still and allows the funeral to proceed without desecrating the Sabbath.[2] Rabbi Avraham's death fits into this pattern: his body was carried from Amassine on Friday morning and the burial was completed in Tamzersht that same afternoon. Further miracles occurred; the grave was found already prepared to receive the body, although no human hands had touched it, and having completed their task, the burial party had time to reach home "with the sun still hanging in the sky" (the Sabbath begins one hour before sunset).

If the *tsaddiq* can ensure his burial to be as near as possible to the Sabbath (to benefit from its holiness), this means in fact that he can control the hour of his death. This allows the *tsaddiq* to prepare himself accordingly, and even to orchestrate the surrounding circumstances in order to increase the inherent sanctity and purity of his death. One informant gave details of the ritual purification that Rabbi Avraham discharged in preparation for his death (in addition to the prayers and recital of the Shema in the synagogue). According to this account, he immersed himself in the ritual pool (*mikveh*), trimmed his hair, and fasted until his death. These preparations serve to reinforce the dimensions of sanctity in the death story which, in any case, contains many miraculous elements. Most of these miracles—foreknowledge of the hour of death, imposition of the *tsaddiq*'s will on a rebellious Arab, and the "contraction of the road" (*qfitsat haderekh*)—are frequent motifs in the death legends of Jewish Moroccan saints, and of the saints of the Wazana family in particular.

Most informants agree that young Ya'aqov Wazana (one version states that he was twelve years old) was far away from home at the time of his father's death. It is possible that repeated remarks made to friends years after his father's death—"If I had been there, he would have lived a year longer"—reflect a feeling of a missed opportunity brought about by this absence. Subsequently, the healer reportedly became terrified and threatened by the village in which his father died. Behind his fear apparently raged the conflicting emotions of attraction and aversion: "Part of him wanted to go to Amassine—but he couldn't. He was afraid of dying there like his father. He believed that if he went there he too would die." The impression that a sense of "unfinished business" was responsible for the terror resulting from his father's death is further strengthened by the fact that Wazana was generally a brave man, with a habit of taking risks his acquaintances regarded as an integral aspect of his personality.

While it is generally agreed that young Ya'aqov Wazana was away at the hour of his father's death, a less common version of the story claims that he did arrive in time for the funeral. According to the old couple from Assarag, Masoud and Tamu Tubul, angels came and took Wazana from his home and carried him to Tamzersht in time for the funeral. However, most accounts concur that Wazana was absent from his father's death, and stress his failure to attend the burial. This version is more congruous with the narrative logic of Rabbi Ya'aqov's life story, not merely because it is most common, but because it resonates with the strange acts that subsequently took place and which are remembered to this day by the healer's acquaintances and friends.

As early as 1959, Yosef Abutbul, a native of Tifnoute who heard many stories of Wazana from his parents, sent an account of these events to the Israel Folktale Archive. Here, apart from some minor stylistic adjustments to assist the tale's clarity and flow, is the account written by Abutbul:

> He [Rabbi Avraham] had a son whose name was Ya'aqov. When Ya'aqov was old enough to understand he asked his mother where his father was buried. The name of his village— where he was born—was Assarag. His mother said to him: "Son, your father is buried in the town of Tamzersht." He replied, "I must prostrate myself on his grave, I have to go there." He took some people who loved him and loved his late father. They journeyed until they came to the town [Tamzersht] where they were received with open arms. He asked the townspeople . . . to take him to the cemetery so that he might prostrate himself on his father's grave. They said to him, "we will go tomorrow Master." He said, "I want [to go] now." So they took him, and he took with him the Book of Psalms. They showed him, "This is your father's gravestone." He said, "I want you to stand down there." So they went down and he read Psalms. Suddenly the grave opened, and his father appeared to Ya'aqov just as he was [during his life]. He [Rabbi Avraham] said to his son, "Ya'aqov, Ya'aqov my son. You must go. I bequeath you your vocation for the rest of your life. Just go, Ya'aqov my son, May the Lord bless you and keep you."

The story's opening implies that Ya'aqov was a very young child when his father died. The pain of premature bereavement and sense of agonizing loss, while not stated directly, are clear from the apparent compulsion to mourn at his father's grave ("I must . . . ; I have to . . ."), and the note of accompanying urgency ("I want [to go] now"). Rabbi Avraham's miraculous rise from the grave can be seen as some consolation for his son's absence at the time of his death and burial. The rather ornate written text has Rabbi Avraham pronouncing biblical-style greeting and blessings[3] and bequeathing the profession of healing as compensation for his son's bereavement. Another legend sent by Abutbul to the Israel Folktale Archive confirms that this reference is indeed to healing. In this legend, Abutbul relates that Rabbi Avraham gave his son "his work, and then he [Ya'aqov] wrote [amulets] for everyone . . . and God was with him in all that he did." The healing aspect aside, Rabbi Avraham's blessings to his son also emphasize the transience of the graveside encounter, and the finality of the separation (repetition of "You must go . . . Just go").

Most informants provided a variation of the father and son encounter. They differ over the time lapse between the father's death and his son's appearance in Tamzersht. However, they all emphasize the severe anguish Ya'aqov suffered because of his absence at the crucial moment. For example, a kinsman noted that, "because he was away when the father died and did not see him . . . he went mad." The majority ascribe Rabbi Ya'aqov a highly active role in the encounter with his father:

> Ya'aqov Wazana was in Casablanca when his father died. He went to visit his grave and said, "I have to dig, to see my father's face." They said to him, "You must not do this! It is forbidden. You cannot bring him back." He dug all the same. When the grave was open they found bees on Rabbi Avraham's mouth, and honey pouring from his lips. The body was still intact, and the face was the same as the day he was buried. One of the Jews who accompanied Rabbi Ya'aqov wanted to take and eat some [of the honey]. Rabbi Ya'aqov said to him, "It is forbidden. Do not eat." The man ate a bit and became sick with the falling sickness so that he died, poor wretch!

The sense of non-acceptance of his father's death, giving rise to a powerful and irresistible urge for reunification with him, even for a brief moment, is given explicit and blatant expression here.

Whereas Wazana's connection to his father relates back to childhood (he was very young when his father died), the close bond with his mother, Esther, was experienced over a long period. Apart from a short period when he went to stay in Casablanca, Wazana lived at home with his mother until she died when he was in his forties. From the descriptions, it seems that Wazana was utterly devoted to his mother, a devotion magnified by the lack of other close relationships during most of the time he lived in Assarag. Wazana's friend and disciple, Rabbi Yitzḥak Peḥima, noted in the interview: "He was the only one, just him and his mother, there was nobody else. No father. Nothing. Just him and his mother." A distant relative said: "He lived with his mother in Assarag. He was strongly tied to her and couldn't leave her." Masouda Buskila, a longtime resident of Assarag who is now married to Rabbi Ya'aqov's nephew, gave a firsthand account of Wazana's special behavior toward his mother: "There was no one compared to Rabbi Ya'aqov [in the way he treated her]. He would take her like this [mimed carrying someone], he did anything she asked, he hired a maid to clean for her all her life. He loved her very very much."

Later we will deal with Esther Wazana's attitude toward her son's unmarried state, but for the moment let us examine her death and its effect on Rabbi Ya'aqov's life. Again, there is a consensus among the informants that Wazana was absent from home at the time of his mother's death. There are varying opinions regarding the reason for his absence. Masoud Tubul, Rabbi Ya'aqov's neighbor in Assarag, recalls that Esther Wazana died when her son was away treating a renowned sheikh. He recalls going to look for Wazana, to break the bitter news, on the road to Tamzersht, and that when they met, Rabbi Ya'aqov already knew of his mother's death (although no one had told him), and had even informed the sheikh that it was imperative he return home. According to Masoud, the sheikh's efforts to change Wazana's mind included the offer of a handsome sum of money which was refused: determined to leave, the healer spurred on the mule borrowed from Masoud, and arrived home in time for the funeral. Another explanation for Rabbi Ya'aqov's absence appeared in the stories written by Yosef Abutbul. In contrast to Masoud's version, which stresses Wazana's loving devotion to his mother, Abutbul's account is hardly flattering. It appears below with a number of minor editing adjustments:

> Usually he [Rabbi Ya'aqov] healed Arabs too and they paid him a lot of money. . . . The sheikh of Talouine had no children—just a son who was born when the sheikh was an old man. He [the boy] lay dying after being so sick for many months, his soul wished to depart. . . . He [Rabbi Ya'aqov] lived in the village of Assarag, and his mother was ill.
>
> He [the sheikh] sent for him. They [the messengers] said to him [Wazana], "Peace be unto you, we are here on the orders of the sheikh of Talouine. . . . The sheikh [has commanded] you to come to our village; his son has been seized [by the demons], he is going to die." He [Wazana] said, "How can I go, when my mother is sick?" They said, "You must come. Your mother will not be afraid." He could not say anything; if he refused, they would throw him in jail . . . so he went.
>
> When they arrived there, the sheikh received him warmly. Wazana wrote something for the boy who opened his eyes and began to get well again. Wazana stayed with him for about ten

days until he was better. When Wazana was there the sheikh
brought him a *shoḥet* who prepared doves and all kinds of
delicacies for him to eat. Then Wazana left and the sheikh
gave him a lot of money. When he arrived home, he found
his mother had died. When the seven days of mourning had
ended, he summoned several demons—he was the only person
in the house. He told the demons to bring his mother so that
he could see her. They replied, "There is nothing left to bring
you; only her head is left and part of the body and her hands."
He forced them to bring her so they brought his mother to him
and he saw her.

The details of the drama unfolded in this story serve to dispel the perfect
image of the devoted son. The plot is complex and emotionally charged:
it arises out of a cruel dilemma with which the son fails to cope. Two
non-typical responses—fear (of the sheikh's reprisal for disobedience) and
perhaps greed as well—cause him to desert his mother in her last hours.
Moreover, in contrast to his initial refusal to accompany the sheikh's men,
it seems that he is pleased with the sheikh's hospitality and is in no hurry
to return home. The culinary delicacies he enjoys are indicative of his
virtue: the informant is interested in emphasizing his concern with eating
food that is kosher while at the Arab's house. Nonetheless, the balance
of virtue is heavily weighed against him: as he sits enjoying the lavish
hospitality offered by the sheikh, his mother's life draws to its close. Even
if the reader understands Wazana's initial predicament, his prolonged and
pleasurable stay at Talouine can only be cause for wonder and serve to
cast a heavy shadow on the image of the loving son that emerges from
earlier noted descriptions.

As with the stories of the father's death, here too the story ends
with Wazana's desperate attempt to see his mother. In both cases, the
desire for reunification with his parents stems from the intolerable feeling
of lost opportunity caused by his absence at the critical hour of their
deaths. However, Abutbul's story leads us to surmise that the torment
of missing his mother's death is magnified and mixed with a powerful
sensation of guilt at the bitter knowledge that he could have, but did not,
return home while she was alive. Demons, which did not appear at all in
the story of the meeting with the father, are the ones who assist Wazana's
efforts to see his mother once again. This detail reminds us that he was
no longer a young lad when his mother died, but a famous healer in his
forties, whose primary power source resided in his relationships with the
demonic world. This network had not been established at the time of his
father's death. Wazana's mother, Esther, a good wife and virtuous woman
praised highly by my informants, lacked the degree of piety possessed
by her husband, Rabbi Avraham. This difference is reflected in the fact

that her remains were disintegrated and incomplete, whereas the father's corpse was perfectly intact.

The mother's disinterment appears in other accounts which, unlike the above, do not interfere with the picture of unadulterated love. The account below emphasizes the intolerable pain Wazana experienced when his mother died during his absence:

> There was no limit to his devotion to his mother. When she died, the French had taken him to a place the same distance away as Eilat [Israeli port on the Gulf of Aqaba far from "mainland" Israeli centers], further. Then she died and they [the Jews of Assarag] waited for him. It was hard to contact him. There [in Morocco] they did not leave a dead person for three or four days. They buried them on the same day, you must do that according to the [Jewish] law. . . . He returned home three days later and said, "I must see her." [They replied] "It is forbidden," but he insisted, "I must see her; if I don't I will commit suicide." Why? Because he was so completely tied to his mother—more than a normal son. He was also her only son. . . . After the seven days of mourning he went along with the rabbi and took some men. He removed the earth and saw her, and then put the earth back. That same day he left the village. He was not able to live there by himself. So he moved to a place called Agouim.

As with the father's death, and perhaps even more pronounced, we witness here the sense of panic accompanying the powerful desire to see the deceased parent again in order to take a final leave. This is voiced here as a matter of life and death ("I must see her; if I don't I will commit suicide"). The act of uprooting and relocating to Agouim is explicitly ascribed to his mother's death. A similar rationalization for the move to Agouim was provided by another informant who described Rabbi Ya'aqov's anguish at his mother's death in these emotional terms:

> Why did he leave Assarag for Agouim? There were no Jews there and no mother—his mother had died. He was very, very close to his mother and spent all his time with her. Without his mother around he had no reason to stay. He said, "Everything in this town is black in my eyes." We were told that when his mother died he went completely mad. He went to the cemetery, and slept there all night. . . . [Although] no one could be there, he spoke to *them* [the speaker pointed to the ground to indicate demons]. . . . Who knows, who knows what he said to them, or what he did there. Maybe he spoke to them, maybe he tried to get her, perhaps. Who knows?

Chapter 5

Wazana's extreme reaction to his mother's death, and the powerful emotional tones, testify to his tremendous pain and inability to accept her loss. It is clear that he went through a profound depression at the time. A sample of the quotations presented earlier indicates the sensitivity of the informants to Wazana's unshakable, close relationship with his mother: "He was the only one, just him and his mother, there was nobody else. No father. Nothing. Just him and his mother"; "He lived with his mother in Assarag. He was strongly tied to her and couldn't leave her . . ."; "He had no one else, no father, no nothing, just him and his mother . . ."; "He was utterly devoted to her, couldn't leave her . . ."; "He did whatever she wanted, he really, really loved her." Wazana's stay in the cemetery represents a desperate effort to maintain contact both through physical proximity to her burial place, and by summoning his demon familiars, who lurk around cemeteries, so that he could see her again and bid farewell. After the encounter, nothing was left to keep him in Assarag.

6

A Robe, a *Bordo,* and Other Objects

An interval of many years separated the deaths of Wazana's parents.
Even though his father died when he was still young, and his
mother when he was middle-aged, the death legends nevertheless contain
similar messages. In both cases, Rabbi Ya'aqov's pain and sense of loss
were exacerbated by his untimely absence from home. It seems that he
found the torment of these abrupt bereavements both intolerable and
unacceptable—his non-acceptance being reflected in the bizarre disintern-
ment stories. In both cases the longing, despondency, and melancholy
transcended the serious Jewish legal injunctions against interference with
the dead. Given the emotional attachment to his parents the question
arises to what degree he remained bound to them when they died. Even if
the move from Assarag to Agouim was driven by the pain of separation
from his mother, in hindsight it appears to represent a desire to disengage
from her home and her grave and their associations. In the case of his
father, Wazana was already at a physical distance due to the fact that
Rabbi Avraham was buried not in Assarag, but in Tamzersht, and he
had a terror of visiting Amassine, where the death occurred. However,
it is unlikely that this distancing could dull the memory of the figures
to whom he was so inextricably tied. We have no way of knowing how
much his thoughts turned to them after their deaths, though from the
scant information available it seems he invested considerable effort in
preserving their memory.

The persistent bond that Wazana maintained with his late father was
a natural outcome of the latter's bequest of a career as a healer. Although
Rabbi Ya'aqov's healing style was worlds apart from the traditional family
approach used by his father, it seems he often turned to his father for help

in difficult situations. According to Rabbi Shalom, another healer from Agouim who deems himself Rabbi Ya'aqov's disciple, Rabbi Ya'aqov once declared that "he was not afraid of anyone: he just called on his father, the great kabbalist, and everything would work out." Nonetheless, the continued connection with his father after death failed to assuage his need for a benevolent father figure. Makhluf Ben-Ḥayim, with whom Wazana lived in Agouim, recalled that upon arriving at his house, Rabbi Ya'aqov addressed him thus: "I would like you to think of me as your son, I just need a corner for myself." We should remember that, when he left Assarag and took up residence in Agouim, Wazana was in his prime, a renowned healer and much older than Makhluf.

Did Wazana own any keepsake to remind him of his father? According to a number of informants he did—and they all took care to emphasize the tremendous importance of this object. "He carried his father's *bordo* [walking stick] everywhere, he never let it go, never put it down," recalled one of his friends. An acquaintance from the village of Timjdut rejoined: "He had a *bordo* that never left his sight." Given this attachment, we can imagine Wazana's distress when one day the cane was stolen by Arabs in Timjdut. "He was truly wretched and couldn't stop searching for it, he just kept looking and looking." When friends offered him two new canes to replace the one he had lost, he naturally refused. The story ends on a bright note however. As Wazana and his friends made their way to the home of an acquaintance in the village of Timjdut, an amazing sight met their eyes: the *bordo* came gliding toward them through the air, "like a plane over the roof tops," went straight to Wazana, and landed in his hand. On regaining his composure, Wazana gave his usual broad grin, completely recovered from his previous air of dejection and quipped: "I must have forgotten it here." His stunned companions laughed at this casual explanation. "You probably forgot it in heaven," one joked back. Obviously Wazana's friends believed they were witnessing another of those special trademark miracles that lay at the foundation of his fame, and ascribed the incident to his alliance with the demons.

Wazana's inability to part with his father's cane, the plain symbol of masculinity, paternal potency, and authority, is indication of a profound emotional bond which even death could not sever. It is interesting that Wazana, who on the whole was disinterested in material effects, showed similar fanatical possessiveness toward other objects, including a large, bulky copper ring he allegedly used for controlling the demons; a magic mirror for locating missing persons; and a set of amber beads he twisted between his fingers in the Muslim fashion. He also had a red hat (*tarboosh*), lined with amulets, which he guarded closely, never allowing others so much as to touch it. None of these items belonged to Rabbi Avraham. Though, in one way or another, all of them were associated with the profession of healing that Wazana had inherited through his father's blessing, these articles in fact represent Muslim healing traditions far removed from the path of Rabbi Avraham.

Was there anything to remind Wazana of his mother? According to Rabbi Yitzhak Pehima from Agouim, toward the end of his life Wazana spoke of her often. Pehima related that, after the healer's death his neighbors raided the room where he died, and removed all of his belongings. Only one item was restored to his family, a robe hidden beneath his bed, which one of the female looters presented to Wazana's nephew in Agouim. There is a story that Rabbi Ya'aqov appeared in this woman's dream, threatening to harm her if she failed to deliver the robe back to the family. According to Rabbi Yitzhak, the dress belonged to Wazana's mother and routinely accompanied him on his travels. Rabbi Ya'aqov had a daily ritual by which he remembered his beloved mother: "Each morning, when he was alone, he would unfold the robe, stare at it, and cry for a long time. Then he would dry his eyes with it, fold it up and put it back [under the bed where he kept it]." There can be no more touching statement of longing and sorrow than this solitary and poignant ritual performed by a heartbroken son.

7

Amidst Sages and Demons:
The Apprenticeship of Wazana

What turns a young man from a peripheral village in the High Atlas Mountains into a famous healer? Before we explore the course of Rabbi Ya'aqov's training, let us first reiterate that his impressive family credentials provided an excellent starting point for his career. In Jewish-Moroccan tradition, ancestral privilege (*zekhut avot*) signified a palpable expression of divine blessing and grace granted to deserving individuals, and as such, represented a crucial asset to any healer in the making. As a child, Wazana would have listened to legends of his ancestors' deeds in the Dra Valley and Ouarzazate, and experienced firsthand the deferential behavior of the Jews of the Western Atlas whenever his father visited their villages. This knowledge would have enhanced his feeling of strength and power in two ways. First, he had the backing and support of a line of saintly ancestors, and second, his family had admiration and respect of the Jews of Tifnoute. Wazana's boldness and self-confidence, as we shall discuss later, duly reflect this sense of empowerment.

Members of these Jewish communities believed that the "privileges" bequeathed by saintly forebears endowed their descendants with the power to treat the needy and suffering, heal the sick in mind or body, assist unmarried women in finding a spouse, render childless couples fertile, or return a man's lost property or his stolen beloved. It should be recalled that, for a broad segment of traditional Jewish society, including the communities of southern Morocco, healing was, to an extent, regarded as a skill related to religion, harnessing sanctity and its derivatives (e.g., holy names) to combat the powers of impurity threatening humankind.

This proximity to holiness was more easily attainable in families with many venerated rabbis and sages. In such families, holy healing books were more easily accessible, and it was possible to meet experienced healers familiar with books containing the kind of "writing" used to bring relief from sickness and suffering. We have no way of knowing whether Wazana actually met any healers in Assarag. All we know is that his father, although not involved in "writing" himself, did own kabbalistic books containing holy names and healing formulae. One of Wazana's friends from the village of Timjdut described Wazana's fascination with these books:

> His father had a book so big and heavy he could not lift it. It contained holy names. I don't know what it said. One day, when Ya'aqov was young, his father went out and the boy decided to open the book. He turned to the first page and read what was there. When his father, may he rest in peace, returned to find him reading, he asked: "What are you doing?" Ya'aqov replied, "I am reading this." His father said, "Have you turned the page?" The boy replied, "No," and his father answered, "You are fortunate." He was afraid something might happen to Ya'aqov. From that first page he learned everything he knew. If he had turned the page, you never know what might have happened.

Later it will become clear that the claim that all Wazana's knowledge was contained in that first page of the Jewish book of names is at variance with most renditions of the story of his apprenticeship. The story above however makes two important points: first, that the boy's curiosity in the accessible book of names inspired his early interest in healing; second, we observe that the father responds to this interest in a tone of both concern and disapproval. This is underscored in another account of the incident: "Rabbi Avraham Wazana owned a book containing holy names which he would not allow his son to touch. Ya'aqov used to steal the book and look at it. When his father saw him reading, he tied his hands together and made him swear never to go near the book again. When he [Rabbi Avraham] saw [how far things had gone] he buried the book in the cemetery." Rabbi Avraham's stern stance is portrayed here as the natural consequence of a loving father's fear that his son's budding preoccupation with holy names might lead to serious harm. It was believed that laxity in matters of physical and behavioral purity and carelessness in copying and using holy names entailed tragic consequences. Furthermore, the soul that delved into the mysteries of the kabbala at too early an age was likely to be endangered.[1] No less danger lay in store from such impure forces as demons if a writer of names sought to attack and defeat them. The parents of other rabbi-healers from Morocco reportedly reacted to their sons' interest in healing in a similarly negative fashion (Bilu 1978: 458). Probably such attitudes dissuaded many a rabbi or sage from pursuing a healing career. Indeed, in both the case of Wazana and of present-day healers I interviewed, it is rare to find the model of an uninterrupted, entrusted transfer of the vocation from father to son. There is a distinct cultural emphasis on healing as part of an age-old family tradition; however, as in Wazana's case, there is greater weight placed on ancestral piety and scholarship rather than on writing-based healing arts.

We now know that Wazana ignored his father's outburst. Although henceforth he stayed away from the family book of names, he nevertheless relentlessly pursued his goal of becoming a healer. This is the first sign of those qualities of bravery and persistence that were to transform Ya'aqov Wazana into the idol of the Western Atlas Jews. Yet, without wishing to detract from his qualities, the likelihood is that the loss of his father at a young age effectively removed any potentially serious threat to his chosen career. With neither the guidance nor the strictures of an authority figure, Wazana was free to follow his leanings and curiosity, and give rein to everything that was bold and defiant in his nature. Interestingly, the fathers of most Moroccan healers I met in Israel died before their sons turned to healing. This finding supports the premise that lack of an inhibiting or controlling hand was an important factor on the path to becoming a healer. Beside this practical explanation, it is possible that a specific personality type, whose development was affected by the loss of a father figure during the formative years, is in fact attracted to healing in the first place. We may conjecture that an occupation offering the practitioner powers of this degree may well compensate for early feelings of frustration and helplessness brought on by the pangs of loss and bereavement. In the case of Wazana, this helps us to reconcile the apparent contradiction between the father's inhibiting influence during his lifetime, and the bestowal of the vocation of healing to his son after death.

After his father's death, Ya'aqov Wazana lost all interest in the books of Jewish healing. Without brothers, or guidance of any kind, and with only a tiny number of Jews in his village to restrain him, he felt free to enter the world of Muslim magic and healing. While it was not unusual in southern Morocco for a Jewish healer to acquire some skills from Muslim sources, Wazana took a giant leap by basing his techniques almost entirely on Muslim traditions of Arabic writing. In his quest for these tools, Wazana searched out the Arab magicians of Sous, an area in southwest Morocco known for its sorcerers and wonder workers. These magicians used to travel about the region, stopping every so often to display their arts in marketplaces along the way. They enthralled their audiences with such tricks as turning ropes into snakes, making food and drink appear by magic in an empty box, or by discovering the whereabouts of hidden treasure by writing on a pastry which then transported itself to the treasure's location.[2] Skeptics would describe these feats and others like them as deceit or sleight of hand, whereas the body of believers saw them as sorcery (*skhur*) or the work of demons (*jnun*).

A few healers now living in Israel recounted that they had personally made contact with Muslim magi in the Sous region, and had even invited them into their homes in order to learn their secrets. Such encounters served to augment the existing pool of healing resources with non-Jewish elements, including those based on sacred Muslim texts. Wazana's determination to gain a thorough mastery of Muslim lore led him to meet with sheikhs renowned for their skill in controlling demons. He also succeeded in obtaining certain of their books, although it is not clear how this was accomplished. In order to familiarize himself with these texts, he learned to read and write Arabic, and was one of the few Jews in the region to acquire these skills. Local Arabs, incensed that a Jewish healer had gained possession of Muslim works, tried to take them from him by stealth as well as force. Rabbi Ya'aqov, for his part, took great pains to guard his books, keeping the most precious of these close to his person under his *jellaba*.

Several informants related that "Rabbi Ya'aqov acquired his knowledge from an Arab sheikh he used to meet in a Muslim cemetery; they sat there all day and all night, studying." Rabbi Azar Gabai provided details of the way Wazana "became involved in such things." According to Gabai, when Rabbi Ya'aqov heard of a magician (*talb*) from Sous who could control demons, he went to his village and offered the magician a prized sack of sugar in exchange for his knowledge. The Arab ordered his wife to prepare tea for the young Jew who had come so far, and then asked her to bring in a jar of oil. Saying that Jews are careful about the cleanliness of their food, he asked Wazana to examine the jar to see if ants had crept inside. Wazana complied, but all he could see was his reflection in the oil. As he peered into the jar, the room vanished, "and he was under the ground, among the demons. He thought he was there for four years and that he had married and raised children." He returned to find himself still in the sorcerer's house. The sorcerer, who pretended not to know him, asked, "What are you doing here Jew?" Wazana, who had no recollection of the earlier events in the Arab's house, described his quest for the famous *talb,* and recounted the story of the time he spent under ground. The sorcerer finally disclosed himself and explained: "The pot of tea you left still stands on the stove, see, it has not yet been poured. This is the jar of oil that my wife brought to me, it is still here. I just wished for you to learn that the sugar you gave me was not wasted."[3]

With this impressive demonstration, Wazana chose to remain with the sorcerer for a further six months, studying his secret arts. As his apprenticeship drew to a close, his mentor made him swear to fulfill three sacrosanct conditions: "To keep himself clean, to say the Arab [Muslim] prayers each morning, and to marry one of 'them,' i.e., to choose a woman from under the ground." Here we learn the price for the long-coveted magical powers. The conditions of keeping clean appear straightforward enough; however, the two remaining stipulations offer a serious threat to Wazana's Jewish identity. How could this member of a family of *tsaddiqim,* himself the bearer of the title "Rabbi," possibly recite Muslim morning prayers as a routine? And what does it mean to "marry a woman from under the ground"—a she-demon? These questions will be addressed later, but for now it is evident that they point to the two worlds—Muslim and demonic—into which Wazana was swept in his undeterred pursuit of the magic of the Arab sages. The third of these conditions, and the story of Wazana's sojourn in the depths of the earth, indicate that his ultimate goal was to control the demons. Before we explore how this was achieved, it is important to examine the nature of the demon (*jinn,* pl. *jnun*) and the place of this phenomenon in traditional Moroccan society.[4]

Demons are "spiritual" creatures with supernatural powers that allow them to travel great distances effortlessly and at great speed, to cause injury at the slightest touch, and to disclose anything hidden. Although invisible by nature, they may assume disguises, appearing as animals or even humans, at will. As with humans, they eat, drink, reproduce, fall sick, and die. In addition, demons are divided into the same divisions as humans, and their world mirrors traditional Moroccan society. Thus, their society contains both male and female, young and old, Jews, Muslims, and Christians, tribes, sovereigns, subjects, evildoers, the just, and even the saintly.

The parallel planes that the human and demonic worlds inhabit is reflected in the belief that each person "above the ground" has a demonic counterpart—a "twin" or "shadow" companion for life. The correspondence between these worlds is antithetical in terms of place and time. The demons inhabit the zone below ground (although they can appear above it—existing in water, fire, or air), and the night is their natural realm. Calling demons by name is extremely dangerous, and most believers therefore use euphemisms instead of referring to them directly: for example, "the invisible ones," "the ones underground," "the neighbors," "the others," "the outsiders," or they point silently to the ground, to indicate where they reside. Demons can appear in the human sphere, and their presence can be experienced in different ways. Direct encounters between humans and demons usually occur once and briefly. However, on rare occasions they can establish long-term close relationships. There are stories of sexual relations and marriage between men and female demons, and of humans who either forcibly or by choice join the demonic realm for varying lengths of time. From Wazana's training to the time of his death, there are clear intimations of his close affiliation with the demonic world.

Demons are irascible, ruthless, and tyrannical, and their behavior is capricious and arbitrary. They are therefore extremely dangerous. Although they are not always evil or harmful, and only attack humans in response to an assault on themselves or their children, they make no allowances for the fact that their invisibility makes them vulnerable to accidental injury by humans. The most common type of demonic attack involves the sudden onset of disturbances to physical or mental health. Their assault can take one of two forms: either an external blow, or else the penetration and taking possession of the victim's body. Illnesses caused by the external assault are known in Moroccan Arabic as *tsira* (Bilu 1979), while those involving seizure and control of the victim's body, that is, possession,[5] are known as *aslai* (Bilu 1980).

A demonic attack is especially virulent at circumscribed times and places, near certain objects, when negative emotions are expressed, or during life-cycle transitions. Demons are attracted to heat, water, blood, meat, and certain kinds of dirt. As noted earlier, one is more likely to run into them at nighttime, and on certain days. They tend to lurk in cemeteries, marketplaces, water pools, caves, rock clefts, sewage systems, and slaughterhouses. Some live under the floor of the house, preferring the area near the threshold. Apart from these danger zones, which may be defined in terms of time and space, certain emotional conditions, especially gradations of fear and anger, are believed to aggravate the demons. Similarly, life-cycle transitions and changes can provoke demonic onslaught. For example, pregnant women are vulnerable, the risk of attack rising at the time of birth and immediately afterward. Newborn babies are also vulnerable, particularly boys prior to circumcision. A bride and groom are also at risk, and the interval between death and burial is extremely dangerous for the family of the deceased.

In traditional Morocco there developed an intricate system of prohibitions, customs, and rituals for staving off demonic mischief. Muslims and Jews alike tried to control their anger near meat, blood, dirt, and other matter attractive to demons; they were careful not to pour hot water outside the house for fear of harming demons; they were careful about setting foot outside the house unnecessarily at night, and tried to steer clear of areas purportedly haunted by demons. To appease demons, they placed food that demons relish in the corners of their rooms, particularly next to the threshold, and tried not to leave their own food and drink lying around in open vessels for fear that demons might partake and defile the remaining food.

There were rituals and traditions revolving around birth, marriage, and burial aimed at thwarting demons, and keeping them away by fair means or foul. Specific substances and objects were utilized to these ends. Thus, for example, salt, iron, silver, and tar were used to keep demons at bay, while henna, sugar, oil, and other edibles were presented as peace offerings. Particularly effective in the war against the demons were names, sentences, and formulations believed to possess religious sanctity. In the Jewish context, most writing used against demons was based on kabbalistic "holy names" copied from ancient books similar to that owned by Rabbi Avraham. The Muslims too had their own formulae and invocations drawn from their own religious texts, and it was into these that Rabbi Ya'aqov delved. Although demons were considered dangerous and harmful, the means deployed against them offered a counterbalance to their threat and provided relief for the suffering they caused. Moreover, through a range of not entirely risk-free techniques, demons could be harnessed to human service and set to work healing, amassing wealth, reclaiming lost objects and stolen goods, or defending folk against sorcerers. It was his powerful desire to achieve such control that sent Wazana in search of the Arab magician from Sous. In sum, within traditional Moroccan society, demons were central to people's lives. For anyone born into that cultural climate they were real, a basic given in daily life.

Rabbi Ya'aqov Wazana was by no means exceptional in seeking to harness the demons to his will. Many Jewish and Muslim healers pursued an association with the demonic world, seeking to control its inhabitants in order to alleviate the misery and suffering they caused, and also to exploit their constructive powers for healing and divination. The techniques used to gain control of demons have been described by Moroccan healers living in Israel (Bilu 1978: 469–76), and we gather that these are not much different from those Wazana learned from his Arab instructor.

A relatively simple operation was to light an oil lamp after the Sabbath, cover it with a *tasksut* (a utensil with seven holes used to prepare couscous). If accompanied by the appropriate invocations, a giant demon with seven heads (*afrit*) would appear, each of its heads growing through a hole in the vessel, and would submit itself to the will of the practitioner. The success of this technique was wholly dependent on the practitioner displaying complete self-control and iron-clad courage.

Other, more complex techniques called for a combination of methods carried out over a period of time, for example, burning incense (which the demons like very much) and immersing the body in the smoke (*bkhur*), writing "impure names" on a piece of parchment or paper, allowing the writing to dissolve in water, drinking the solution and then pronouncing invocations for summoning the demons. These ceremonies were performed at night (the demons' daytime), over three successive months. A detailed account of the immersion in impurity technique used to achieve control of demons (inhabitants of the ungodly world), was described by a healer who, like Wazana, learned the secret arts from a Sous magi. The initiate was required to live in filth for seven days, bathe in urine, slay a cat and use its blood to write profane names on human bones, bathe in incense smoke and pronounce the invocations referred to above. To complete the task, the initiate stays in a known demon haunt such as a slaughterhouse or cemetery for a period of time. All techniques for gaining control of demons emphasize fearlessness. Those able to conquer their fear sufficiently will control the demons much as, in one informant's words, "a police officer captures a criminal in handcuffs."

Although we cannot know the method actually used by Rabbi Ya'aqov, his determination and courage obviously surpassed that of any of the Jewish Moroccan healers I met. The techniques they described were extremely perilous, and none of the healers, apart from one, had successfully completed the steps. Some provided highly dramatic descriptions of their attempts, but admitted that, at the moment of truth, they were gripped with such overwhelming terror at the prospect of seeing "the beings from the netherworld" that they retreated, abandoning the project. The only healer claiming to have completed all the tasks and being rewarded with a demon-slave confessed to losing it after a short while. Only Rabbi Ya'aqov endured all of the stipulations unflinchingly. His willingness to marry a she-woman is typical of his courage and the lengths to which he would go to achieve power.

8

A Question of Identity:
Pray as a Muslim and Marry a Demon

"To keep clean, to say Arab [Muslim] prayers each morning, and to marry one of 'them'; that is, to choose a woman from under the ground." As noted earlier, control of the demons was conditional upon meeting these demands, and Rabbi Ya'aqov's firmness of mind to achieve control at any cost led him to abide by these obligations. It was this disposition that made him the singular and remarkable figure he was.

Invariably, Wazana's acquaintances and friends raised the subject of his fastidious attention to dress. His garments were always white, though occasionally covered with a black cloak: his hat was a red, Muslim-style *tarboosh*. His clothes were of especially fine quality, and spotlessly clean—notwithstanding the many dusty miles he traveled from his mother's home in Assarag. This meticulous attention to appearance was a sign neither of narcissism nor foppery, but, as discussed before, was the outward manifestation of his unfaltering dedication to the goal of demonic control through cleanliness. This, however, was trifling compared with the other two conditions he was required to meet.

It did not go unnoticed among Wazana's acquaintances that he prayed "Arab and Jewish prayers," though according to some, "he did not do this openly," but "in secret." The fact that this behavior was tolerated is astonishing, since it constituted an act of heresy that directly interfered with Wazana's Jewish identity. Let us not forget that this rebel was himself a rabbi, the descendant of a respected line of sages and saints, and that his extraordinary behavior was neither short-lived nor haphazard, but deliberate, consistent, and routine ("he never began a day without reciting Arab prayers").

How can we explain this community's willingness to tolerate what clearly constituted distasteful misconduct? Beyond reflecting a certain tolerance and openness, we may infer from informants' attitudes that Wazana was perceived as unique and exceptional, and therefore beyond judgment by conventional standards: "There was no one like Wazana in all Morocco," was a frequently heard refrain. Ultimately, this relentless drive to assume the role of omnipotent healer led him on a strange and tortuous journey, which in the end benefited Jews and Muslims. "He had no choice," declared one informant resignedly, "if you wanted those things [healing powers] you needed to be both a Jew and an Arab."

Why did Wazana, of all people, choose this dangerous road? Because "he was born and raised among Arabs," explained his friend and student Rabbi Yitzhak Pehima. His intimacy with Arab life paved the way to his interest in Islamic customs: "He went to their mosques, learned from their scholars. He only used Arabic writing [for healing], he prayed according to the Arab custom. His occupation wasn't Jewish." Yet another of Wazana's students, Rabbi Shalom, claimed that Rabbi Ya'aqov "knew the Koran by heart—it gushed from him like a stream." He defensively excused his one-time teacher's perverse behavior by rationalizing that prayer cannot be evil—not even Muslim prayer—especially when it was harnessed to the purpose of healing. The same few people who denied the gravity of his actions took pains to justify this Muslim conduct. For example, Makhluf Ben-Hayim, Rabbi Ya'aqov's friend and benefactor from Agouim, recalled that Wazana categorically informed him that his seeming tendency to engage in Muslim practices was just his response to the fact that so many Arabs needed his services: "Why should I use our names when I write for them? Why should I let our holy names be defiled? It is for that reason I use their language."

Whatever his reasons might have been, one consequence of crossing the religious and cultural divide was that Wazana knew impeccable Arabic. He was one of only a handful in Agouim who read the language, and thus "whenever they [the Jews] had contracts in Arabic he was asked to come and explain it to them."

In fact, only a small number of informants actually saw Wazana praying like a Muslim. One individual from Timjdut, with whom Rabbi Ya'aqov had stayed, recalled his astonishment when one morning he went to his guest's room and found it empty, with Rabbi Ya'aqov nowhere to be found. Searching high and low, he finally spotted the healer, crouched in a field, bowing low over the furrows, in a posture of Muslim prayer. Usually, however, Wazana prayed early in the morning, locked in his room, and then went back to sleep. As we see later, these morning devotions followed in the wake of a night of activity, and so the exhausted healer never rose before nine or ten in the morning. On rising, he would slowly get ready for solitary prayer in the synagogue which, by that late hour, had been emptied of worshippers.

Apparently, the routine of "Arab prayer" followed by "Jewish prayer" had no ill effect on Wazana's spirituality. His friends were amazed to see how long he spent in the synagogue each day, wrapped in his *talit* (prayer shawl) and *tefillin* (phylacteries), deep in concentration, "praying word by word by word," clearly and emphatically. So celebrated was his devotion that people complimented one another by saying they prayed "just like Wazana." The healer's close friend, Rabbi Yitzhak Pehima, stated that latterly, after the healer moved to Agouim, he discarded his Muslim practices, and only prayed in the Jewish fashion. Since no one else mentioned a change of this nature, this version most likely reflects Pehima's personal desire to see Wazana's image conform to that of his ancestors.

Wazana's reputation for prayer devotion, and his care, when among Muslims, to refuse food that was not kosher, are details introduced by the informants to reduce the significance of his pursuit of Muslim customs. As noted, Wazana's friends regarded this aberration as an outgrowth of his occupation, which the consensus perceived not as "a Jewish occupation, but the occupation of famous sheikhs." Thus, Muslim prayer was regarded as neither defiance nor heresy, but as one more element within a complex set of behaviors they understood to be emblematic of the healer's desire to control the demons. In his friends' eyes therefore, Wazana's intimate relationship with the demonic world was the driving force that shaped his Muslim identity and gave it meaning.

Wazana's acceptance of the third condition stipulated by his Muslim mentor, namely to marry "a woman from under the ground," is by far the strongest evidence of the lengths to which he was prepared to go to gain control of the demons. In fact, such a marriage existed as a given option within traditional Moroccan cultural reality (Crapanzano 1980), although it was exceedingly rare for such a step to be taken voluntarily due to its dire implications. According to tradition, marriage to a she-demon condemned the human spouse to remaining single "above the ground," with the threat of mortal vengeance hanging over any husband who dared to be unfaithful. It is hardly surprising therefore that human spouses were viewed as pitiable victims who had fallen prey to the wiles of lascivious she-demons. The latter supposedly used their cunning to trap men by appearing as the daughters of Eve and seducing them. Consummation with a she-demon sealed the relationship with a binding covenant of enforced loyalty—from which there was no way out.

Those skeptics who reject the reality of the demonic world will try to find a psychological explanation to account for the relationship between she-demons and reluctant spouses, and will hold some kind of emotional disturbance responsible for this strange form of commitment.

A Question of Identity

The question arises: what kind of emotional constellation could possibly transform a relationship with a woman into a prospect so intimidating that an individual is compelled to seek refuge in the option of a "demonic" marriage? While such a path is both extreme and deviant, it does serve as a cultural option which, to some extent, allows individuals to avoid dealing with emotional inhibitions and their causes, and to escape the grave social penalty for failing to comply with the sanctified value of raising a family. Later on, we shall examine one possible psychological construction of Wazana's demonic marriage, but for now, let us concentrate not on the healer's psyche, but on the way he appeared to those around him. These were not the kind of people who deal in psychological currency.

Most of Wazana's friends ascribe his remarkable healing accomplishments to his union with the she-demon. In their eyes, it was this relationship that granted the great healer the power to transcend the limits of possibility and perform feats undreamed of by normal humans. It is clear that the informants believed that, contrary to the usual pattern of a human male falling victim to a carnal she-demon, Wazana freely entered the demonic union as a means to achieving his ends. Rabbi Avraham Gabai explained this important distinction. First he described the more common instances, in which "one of their women grabs you and says: 'You must marry me.'" Under these circumstances, the victim can only grovel before the she-demon and try and gain his release: "You must say to her: 'I am not of your kind and you are not of mine; it is no good for us to marry. I beg you, please! I cannot do this thing.'" The submissive tone used is meant to demonstrate the sheer terror of a man faced with the prospect of a demonic marriage for, as we know, "he cannot marry above the ground unless she sets him free." If the man severs the union to take a human spouse "they slay him where he stands." In the second category, the active party is the man who exploits such a union to gain control over the demons. Rabbi Ya'aqov obviously belongs in this group: "He went looking for them, he found them, and he took control of them." Even though informants showed no interest in analyzing Wazana's behavior, they nevertheless expressed a sense that his "free choice" was in fact not so "free." They tended to focus on external explanations rather than internal, psychological factors, and substituted the psychological drive with a permanent contractual commitment. "It is a covenant, he cannot cheat on her," reasoned one informant, his friend clarifying, "He had no choice in the matter, it was signed and sealed, like with a judge, he had to accept it." Their conclusion implies that Wazana, who chose a demonic spouse of his own volition and for his own reasons, was ultimately forced to stay with the she-demon, and could not free himself. One informant described this process clearly. It began, she believed, as a seduction, and ended with Wazana's total capitulation and subjugation. "He was forced to marry, he was trapped by a woman [the she-demon]. She said to him:

Chapter 8

'If you want to enjoy life—then marry me.' Wazana agreed. You never come back because you have to return things [favors received from the she-demon]. Because he could not return her favors she had him [he could not escape]." The tension between free choice and forcible subjugation, between initiated union and passive entrapment, is noted in Rabbi Aaron Gabai's succinct description, which captures the two types of demonic marriages: "He ruled them, and they also ruled him. They worked for him until they took him. All his power came from them."

An unusual account of Wazana's marriage with the she-demon was provided by Rabbi Ya'aqov's blind cousin and namesake. He situates the story in Casablanca, during the time in Wazana's life when he was renowned as a healer, and not at the time of his training.

> Why didn't he get married? He performed a *tkaf* [lit. "binding," designates sorcery designed to prevent or put a halt to something] on a woman from Dar el Beida [Casablanca]. He made it so she could never get married. There was some criminal type there who asked Rabbi Ya'aqov to write for him so that the woman would never marry the man she loved. Rabbi Ya'aqov slept alone, and when he got up in the morning he couldn't see. He hired a boy and told him to go to his mother's village [Assarag] and fetch one of his books. About a month later the boy returned with the book. He [Wazana] took different colored candles and said to the child: "I will read and you will light the candles. When I tell you to light the red candle, light the yellow one; when I tell you to light the green, light the red, etc." And so it went, until two in the morning. Suddenly, out of the depths of the sea sprang an *afrita* [giant she-demon]. She said to him: "You will never marry until both that woman and I are married." He began to beg her: "I will come to you for ever and raise you out of the sea, etc, only give me back my sight." She cured him and when his sight returned he fled from Dar el Beida.

How do the events in this somewhat cryptic story lead to Wazana's demonic marriage? Even though the answer is not explicit in the story, we detect an inner logic to the plot based on the "restitution" principle rooted within the traditional conception of disruption and restoration of cosmic balance. This principle governs the interactions between humans and demons. This particular informant, who continually made negative insinuations regarding his cousin from Assarag, accused Wazana (he often called him "Ya'aqov," omitting the respectful "Rabbi") of using sorcery to prevent a Casablanca woman from marrying her beloved. His criticism is further evidenced by his use of a Hebrew slang word for "criminal" to describe the Casablanca man who commissioned Wazana to perform the *tkaf*. For his involvement in black magic (which most healers deny practicing), Wazana was struck blind. To cure himself, he summoned the she-demon responsible for his blindness from the depths of the sea using an esoteric procedure that required lighting different colored candles in a certain sequence, and changing the names of the colors according to a certain code. On appearing, the she-demon announced that, besides losing his sight, the healer was condemned to remain unmarried until both demon and human *tkaf* victim were married.

It is not clear why the "restitution" principle involves the she-demon, unless the latter represents the demonic double of the human victim. As mentioned before, according to tradition, every human has a demonic "twin" whose life is identical in every detail. We may conjecture that by preventing the human woman from marrying, Wazana had also harmed her demonic double. Wazana's words of appeasement, and his promise of an intimate and lasting liaison—"I will come to you for ever and raise you out of the sea"—may be interpreted as a proposal of marriage. He redresses the injustice suffered by the she-demon by marrying her. Although this act of restitution restores his eyesight, it nevertheless binds him to a demonic mate for life.

If the above reasoning is correct, the conclusion of this obscure story contains elements of poetic justice and even irony. To atone for the spell which indirectly prevented the she-demon from marrying, Wazana must surrender himself to her as a spouse. The price is high as he, just like the human victim of his own sorcery, is doomed never to marry on earth.

Wazana's demonic union lasted a long time, during which he fathered two children (according to some, three, four, or even five children). Although only one informant claimed the privilege of actually seeing the demonic family, no one doubted its existence. There were even stories of Rabbi Ya'aqov introducing his beloved mother (who often bemoaned her only son's unmarried state) to his demonic wife and offspring. One version of this story follows:

> One day his mother said to him: "You must get married: you are all that I have, and I would like you to marry and have children that I may see before I die." He answered, "If you swear to me that you will not tell anyone about me, I will show you my children." She then made food without salt,[1] and prepared everything and cleaned his room. He then said to her: "When she arrives, don't force her to eat; let her eat whatever she likes." Then he brought her in, a woman with two children. Her [his mother's] throat was going like this, up and down [from fear and excitement]. She came in with her children and ate and drank and kissed her [his mother].

Ḥana Buskila (married to Rabbi Ya'aqov's nephew), heard the story of the meeting directly from Wazana's mother. According to Ḥana these meetings occurred routinely: "I asked her [Wazana's mother]: grandmother, why isn't Rabbi Ya'aqov married? She replied, 'Listen my dear, but don't breathe a word to anyone. It is forbidden! He already has children, and when I wish to see them, he brings them to me in the middle of the night. I see the children, and his wife. He can't get married [to a normal woman]. He already has children, and he brings them out like kings. I see them, and then, in a flash, he whisks them away.' "

A special relationship grew up between Rachel Ben-Ḥamo from Agouim and Rabbi Ya'aqov, who treated her for an assortment of prob-lems and injuries—among them infertility that lasted for seven years. He also cured her of "evil spirit disease" (aslai). Her husband noted that his wife and the healer "were like two fingers on the same hand; as if he was her father or something. He used to say to people: 'Leave that woman alone, she's mine.' " Rachel added: "I helped him and did his laundry. He loved me like a daughter." No wonder then that of all the informants, only Rachel had been privileged to meet Wazana's demonic children. "He asked me: 'Do you want to see my children?' I was scared, but [all the same] I said 'Yes.' He went like this [she waved her hand]. He said, 'What do you want to drink, tea, coffee?' I said, 'Nothing, I am afraid.' He told me to cover my eyes, and then he said, 'Here is a boy, here is a girl.' I saw big children playing, three . . . two girls and a boy." Even though only Rachel and Wazana's mother ever met his demonic family, everyone accepted it as fact: first, because no one could explain Wazana's supernatural abilities without them, and second, because they took his lifestyle, his daily routine, and particularly his nights, to be a token of demonic presence. Many stressed that wherever Wazana stayed, he was given a separate room so that he and his family could be reunited at night. Former hosts recall him speaking to his demonic kin all night long. "He stayed awake all night," marveled one friend, "he put out the light and, if you slept with him, he would sit up until after two o'clock, and when the cock crowed three times he slept."

Wazana's daily schedule reflected his dual existence. He spent his day sleeping, praying in the synagogue, sitting with friends and healing. As night fell however, his pattern changed as he stepped into the demonic world. A different facet of his identity dominated another part of the day: a Jew in daylight, at twilight, the border between day and night, a Muslim (since Muslim prayer summoned the demons), and with nightfall, the companion of demons.

In contrast to the surprisingly tolerant attitude of the ordinary Jews toward Wazana's multilayered identity, the stance of the clergy was one of suspicion and intermittent hostility. This is particularly evident from encounters reported between Wazana and the esteemed Rabbi Yosef Abu-

Hatsera, both of whom worked in the region. Two informants, Rabbi
Yitzhak Pehima and Rabbi Shalom Ben-Hamo, former ritual slaughterers
and healers from Agouim, knew both men well. Pehima, Wazana's pupil
and friend, had been Rabbi Yosef's attendant, accompanying him on his
travels through the region. The following incident, recounted by Pehima,
occurred at a time close to Rabbi Ya'aqov's death.

> I was Rabbi Yosef Abu-Hatsera's attendant and went
> with him collecting donations in Agouim. We were walking
> down a road lined with trees when he said to me, "I want
> to sleep, you stand guard." I replied, "Go to sleep," and I
> massaged his feet to help him sleep. Wazana appeared and
> offered the Rabbi ten riyals saying, "Bless me." Rabbi Yosef
> blessed him and took his donation. When he woke up, the
> money was still in his hand, and he said to me, "Give this to
> someone who needs it, I will not take it from him." I asked
> him why, to which he replied, "It's none of your business—
> give it to a poor person, I won't have it in my pocket." I took
> the money and went back to the road and gave it to one of his
> [Wazana's] kinsmen.

The spurning of the donation speaks volumes about the extent of the great
Abu-Hatsera's loathing for Wazana. Once, at a *hillula* in memory of Rabbi
David u-Moshe, Rabbi Yosef vented his distaste before Rabbi Shalom and
the other celebrants, calling the healer "impure," and ordering him to be
seated far from his own table. Wazana took revenge with a typical display
of magic, causing the meal to disappear, so that he had to be begged to
restore it. The approving way this incident was reported indicates that
Rabbi Abu-Hatsera's negative stance was not shared by all Jews in Agouim
and the surrounding villages. The descriptions of Rabbi Yosef present him
as patronizing and arrogant, revered and feared alike. As we see later,
Wazana was a pleasant and cheerful character who warmly welcomed
the villagers as his companions and friends. That Wazana was renowned
as an omnipotent healer tempered the communities' squeamishness at
his Muslim practices. At the same time, however, the reservations of the
clerics, headed by Rabbi Abu-Hatsera, imply that Wazana would have
had difficulty finding a place among those communities closer to the
Jewish learning centers of Morocco. In other words, his behavior was
tolerated precisely because of his whereabouts—among the small, sparsely
populated, and scattered communities of the Moroccan Jewish periphery.

9

"There Was Nobody like Rabbi Ya'aqov in the Whole World"

Wazana's notably commanding appearance provided the perfect accompaniment to his amazing exploits. Informants describe him as tall, distinguished, powerful, and handsome, with dark, glossy, well-groomed hair, large piercing eyes, and skin aglow with life and vitality. With his powerful body and handsome appearance, he appeared so youthful that many thought him untouched by time: "Wazana kept his looks until his death: his figure and appearance didn't change—he died in his prime, tall and strong. If you had seen him, you would think he was only twenty."

His distinctive white clothes added further to his aura of grandeur. Wazana, as we know, wore white without fail, and his clothes were always pristine. His red *tarboosh,* which none of the other Jews wore, contrasted sharply with the white of his garments. It is not surprising that some compared Wazana's appearance to that of a king. Ḥana Buskila, his relative, was very firm on this score: "Remember Mohammed el-Ḥamis [Mohammed V, father of King Ḥassan II]? Well, Wazana dressed just like that." Wazana became a model for the local Jews due to his devotion to prayer and his appearance. To compliment someone's appearance, they said: "You look like Wazana."

Judging by the hyperbole, memories of Wazana have not been dimmed by time; the contrary appears true, time has only helped to inflate his already larger-than-life proportions. "You have never seen anything like Rabbi Ya'aqov," declared one woman, "it was seeing the divine presence (*shekhina*), it was looking upon glory, it was a delight to look at him. His face was like Joseph in the Bible story, you couldn't look at him straight."[1] Someone else echoed this theme of a glory too beautiful to contemplate: "He was so virtuous, so dazzling, you couldn't look into his face owing to his *shekhina*. You had to go like this," and she mimed hiding her eyes.

Accompanying Wazana's statuesque build, good looks, and magnificent clothing were outstanding personal qualities. He is portrayed as friendly, sociable, even-tempered, and good-humored: "he was easy to get on with, you could joke around with him." Rabbi Shalom Ben-Ḥamo compared Wazana to his arch rival Rabbi Abu-Ḥatsera: "They were the same height, same breadth, they wore the same style of beard." The similarity ends there. In contrast to the condescending and haughty Rabbi Yosef, "Wazana was always *mabsut* [happy and content], always smiling. He was relaxed and not arrogant, always ready with a laugh, with women, children, Arabs, everybody!" Thus Wazana is presented as down-to-earth, sociable, a good companion, kindhearted, open, and devoid of all pride or haughtiness. The informants were particularly struck by his willingness to befriend everyone he met, without compromising his dignity in the least. "You could get close to him," concluded Rabbi Aaron Gabai, "he had a lot of love for people." One expression of this love was the great kindness he showed; whatever came his way, whether *zekhut avot* donations, or fees for healing and divination, he used to divide unselfishly among his friends.

Rabbi Ya'aqov enjoyed life, and regarded the companionship of friends, a bottle of *arak,* appetizing food, and a quantity of branded cigarettes as a priority. "At night, he sat with cigarettes, tobacco and *arak,* easy, easy, easy. No worries, sharing everything he had. He didn't like money, just a good time: to drink and be happy. Everybody loved him—small children and Arabs as well. On his travels, women would stare through their windows, calling to one another: 'Wazana's walking by.'" He put no effort into money or property, although this was clearly an available option. As someone said, "Money came easily, [but] he didn't want lots of money, he wasn't after money, he wasn't interested in a living." All the same, he never went without, his friends gladly providing all his worldly needs: "He had no property or business, but he always lived respectably. . . . Everywhere he went, they gave him what he needed." The informants sensed that Wazana's lifestyle was guided more by social impulses than by utilitarian considerations: "He loved laughter, friends, having a good time, these were his delight. If he wished for money he could have been richer than anyone; but what did he care?"

Rabbi Aaron Gabai listed Rabbi Ya'aqov's most conspicuous qualities: "He didn't fear anything, he didn't care about anything, and he didn't need anything." The first stresses Wazana's unusual degree of courage, a primary personality trait about which near unanimous agreement existed among the informants. The second concerns his almost total independence from social obligations and conventions—the lack of a family to worry about or property to protect. The third alludes to Wazana's good life, his enjoyments, the way he exploited the pleasures of the moment, undisturbed by such mundane issues as income or family. Rabbi Gabai also referred to Rabbi Ya'aqov's common touch and egalitarian manner: "There was nobody like Rabbi Ya'aqov anywhere. He had the appearance of a great rabbi, not a simple man; but he didn't puff himself up or go around saying, 'I've done this . . . I'm going to do that.' If you asked him, he would say, 'I am a simple man, I'm like you, just kidding with people, I'm a harmless guy.'" Rabbi Ya'aqov's highly regarded family, and his reputation as an omnipotent healer highlighted his lack of pretension and simple ways even more.

The miracles and spectacles Wazana produced for his friends also contributed to his popularity. Wazana was an epicurean who never compromised over quality tobacco, *arak,* food, or drink— even if supplies were rationed. If none were available, he would make them appear. This ability, which skeptics would dismiss as conjuring or sleight of hand, was, in the eyes of his friends, perfect proof of Wazana's supremacy over the demons: "The ones from below—his wife and children—brought him things." Such miracles, which many eye-witnesses reported, were inherently very different from the healing acts which appear later in this book, although the latter too involved demonic collaboration. In healing, Wazana demonstrated tremendous courage, determination, and persistence. His activities were often described in the dramatic language of matters of life and death. In contrast, Wazana used his powers socially in a lighthearted, frivolous way, to produce the kind of wonders that satisfy the taste buds.

Wazana's love of liquor ("*Arak* was his life, but he never got drunk, Heaven forbid!"), and its important role in his social life, explains why most of his feats involve *arak.* It is said that whenever he ran out of drink, he would take an empty bottle, fill it with money and cover it with a cloth. Then, with a flourish, he uncovered the bottle to reveal it brimming with *arak.* Likewise, he would replenish his friends' cigarettes, tea, mint sprigs, food, and drink. He had the habit of plucking cigarettes—"*Casa Sport,* the best in Morocco"—from the folds of his friends' clothes, who would then swear they had no cigarettes on them. If he felt like tea he would rap the wall and a steaming teapot, with enough cups for everyone, would appear. If he felt like mint for his tea, "he would read something," and a sprig of mint would sail down from the ceiling or pop up in a corner of the room. By rubbing his hands together, snuff or amber would appear from nowhere.

Informants recall Wazana's developed sense of fair play: how he never took anyone's cigarettes or drink without compensating them.

There Was Nobody like Rabbi Ya'aqov

When a "victim" discovered the loss of some article, the correct money would always be there in compensation. On the other hand, he had no qualms about punishing anyone who refused his demands. Stories abound of how he made *arak* disappear from the larder of tightfisted friends or neighbors who claimed their *arak* jars were empty. When someone protested their loss, Wazana would give his usual hearty laugh and shrug innocently, "But I thought you didn't have any." On a particular occasion Wazana taught one informant's wife a harsh lesson for refusing to give him the last of the *arak* in her house:

> He went to my wife, she was weaving a carpet at home. He said, "I want some *arak,* look for some." She answered, "There isn't any." He saw that she didn't want to give him the *arak* so he went like this to her eyes [passed his hand over her eyes], then he left her. She couldn't see any more after that. Her eyes became so swollen and red and running with tears that she couldn't move or work. My mother went to her. "What happened to you?" she asked. "I can't see anything," my wife answered. My mother knows Wazana. My mother went to him, "Rabbi Ya'aqov, aren't you ashamed to do [that] to my daughter-in-law?" He replied laughing, "I didn't do anything." He didn't care about anything. Then he went to my wife and said, "Now have you got any *arak?* Just bring out what there is." She brought out what she had—half a glass. He did this with his hands again and her eyes were all right again. When I saw him, he told me what had happened. I said to him, "Is that what you did to her?" and he laughed and laughed. He loved to laugh.

This story demonstrates Wazana's low tolerance for defiance. It also demonstrates that despite his quick temper, he was easily appeased. The informant's memory of Wazana's amusement reflects this too. By all appearances he gained more satisfaction from playing tricks than he did from safeguarding his dignity. In this story, as in many such incidents reported, Wazana maximized his entertainment by playing the wide-eyed innocent, denying any part in the disappearance of food, drink, or whatever, and publicly exposing the lie behind the refusal to deliver some coveted item. Wazana's style, which added to the merriment and frivolity of social gatherings at which he was the star, only served to increase his popularity.

The clowning and fun aspect of Wazana's wonders did not detract one bit from the awe and respect informants felt toward him. Unlike the suspicious among us, Wazana's acquaintances never believed that these acts involved sleight of hand or amateur magic. It was unanimously held

Chapter 9

that demons lay behind his unlimited powers, regardless of the fact that
these powers were revealed through seemingly trivial entertainment rather
than serious matters. There are manifestations of the demons' presence
in other stories. For example, the story of how Wazana once sent his
demonic servants to discipline some friends who refused to bring him
arak from a neighboring village in the middle of the night. The men were
severely battered all night, and were forced the next morning to complete
their assignment. On another occasion, he assigned demons disguised as
horses, goats, and dogs to disturb some sleeping friends, simply to enjoy
their consternation.

The unmediated and hearty, somewhat childish nature of his tricks
is illustrated in the following story: When staying in the village of Tidili,
Wazana sent Rabbi Aaron Gabai, then a young boy, to go and buy *arak*
from one of the Jews. The hour being late, he provided the lad with a
large lamp to help him on his way. As he reached the vendor's house,
two horses went careening past him. Startled, the youth shrank against
the wall, but the larger of the horses hit him. The lamp was smashed by
the impact and Gabai stood, shaking like a leaf, still clutching the handle
in his grasp. The *arak* vendor had no trouble recognizing the source of
the mishap. "Who sent you? Wazana? So then Wazana did this to you!"
Wazana himself hooted with laughter when he heard the tale, and totally
disarmed the boy. "How he laughed. He said to me, 'Look how late you
are, and I'm still here waiting for my *arak*.' I replied, 'You nearly killed
me.' Then he laughed and laughed and laughed: 'What did I do to you?'
I told him, 'You sent the big horse against me, why didn't you send the
smaller horse—it would have hurt me less!' Then he laughed, 'Nothing
happened to you, so what do you care? It broke the lamp? I will pay for
it.' Then we took the *arak,* and drank and laughed. He never did anything
to really hurt anyone, ever! He just liked you to know he was a specialist
at that sort of thing."

If people who did not know him treated him with disdain, Wazana
knew how to put them in their place briskly and effectively. One time
he was buying tea in the marketplace when a Jewish peddler chastised
the healer rudely for rolling the tea leaves between his fingers to test their
quality. In a single motion, Wazana transformed the sacks of tea into bran.
The wretched peddler wept over his loss, imploring Wazana to restore
the tea. As usual, the kindhearted healer was appeased, but not before
rebuking the peddler as follows: "Never talk like that again to people you
don't know. You cannot know who is good and who isn't—only the Holy
One Blessed Be He does, that is his to reckon."

The next story exemplifies the strength of the informants' belief
in Wazana. It also shows that when Wazana's powers were questioned,
retaliation could be excessive as well as dangerous—a fact belied by the

jocular, almost innocent tone of the narrative style. A sense of menace and apprehension at Wazana's power emerges between the lines.

> Avraham Hazan was from Assarag. He said to Wazana: "If you know how to do things show me." Wazana replied, "I warn you Avraham, if I do anything to you, you'll regret it for the rest of your life." Hazan replied, "What can you do? Will I fall down? Will I die?" Wazana said to him, "You have been warned! Now, go into that room, but first tell me, what are you, a man or a woman?" Hazan answered, "What d'you mean man or woman? I've got children, I've got it all." Wazana told him to go and look at himself. He went, took a look, saw he was a woman [physically]. The man came out different. He dropped to his knees, "Ya'aqov, I'm begging you, I'm pleading with you, I beg your pardon, forgive me." Wazana said, "Did I say anything to you? Did I hit you? Did I touch you? Did I give you a potion to drink? Did I throw something on you?" He said to him, "I beg your forgiveness, I was just kidding . . . pardon me." Wazana said, "Go back in your room." He went into the room again and came out a man.

The story above lends emphasis to Wazana's magical powers and unique style. Whoever wields powers capable of manipulating a division as inherently antagonistic as male and female is unstoppable. Wazana's disingenuous and sarcastic response to Avraham's sex change contains a list of typical methods used by healers and conjurers. In doing this he stresses his own superiority over the others—their laborious methods are redundant. He can perform miracles with a mere wave of the hand.

10

Casablanca

Wazana was a local hero whose life was spent tucked out of sight in the remote periphery of Morocco, far away from the cities of the north and the coast. His home in the region of Tifnoute, where the tiny Jewish communities nestled within the Berber tribe villages, was one of the most extremely isolated, inaccessible parts of the country. Only once, during his youth, was this bucolic existence interrupted, when the lure of progress, and the promise of economic betterment under French occupation, drew Wazana to Casablanca (Dar el Beida).

His adventures in the big city with its industry, permissiveness, secularity, and "Frenchness," form a marked contrast to his existence in Assarag, the tiny, traditional mountain village. Accounts of his stay in Casablanca make little reference to any healing activity. In Casablanca Wazana found himself among broad boulevards, sprawling street cafes, wealthy Jewish traders, beautiful women, and European-style palaces where the French officers quartered. In this liberal metropolis, with its cosmopolitan ambiance, Wazana's expertise was most needed to deal with romantic cases: helping brokenhearted lovers win back their mistresses, reuniting lovers, restoring women who had eloped or been kidnapped to their families.

Eliyahu Tubul joined Wazana in Casablanca and was the only informant to observe him in action there. There was one incident which impressed Tubul (a young man at the time) in particular. Alternative secondhand accounts of the case were provided by other informants as well. The case concerned the wife of a senior French officer who abandoned her husband and fled home to her parents in Paris. Owing to her father's position as a general, the incident caused considerable embarrassment in government circles and placed the husband in an extremely awkward position. The officer unburdened himself to the son of a prosperous Jewish merchant and was advised to seek out Wazana. At the meeting, the officer was initially suspicious and even contemptuous of the village Jew in his white *jellaba* and red *tarboosh*. His tune changed when the mediator, in Wazana's name, promised unequivocally that "if he doesn't bring your wife back, you can have him beheaded." That night, Wazana and Eliyahu Tubul returned to the officer's house. Tubul, who could not rid himself of a sense of foreboding ("after all we were in Casablanca and the officer's wife was a world away—in France"), provided an extremely dramatic description of this meeting:

> We sat down and the officer asked Rabbi Ya'aqov, "How many months will it take to bring her here?" The officer didn't understand about those things. He thought Wazana would bring his wife by ship, and that it would take three or four months. Even the airplanes, those flying chickens, take two or three days. Rabbi Ya'aqov asked him the time and the officer replied, "Ten minutes to ten." Rabbi Ya'aqov then said, "At precisely ten o'clock your wife will arrive." The officer went into the next room and came back with his gun. He thought Rabbi Ya'aqov was making fun of him. But Rabbi Ya'aqov stayed calm and told the officer, "prepare a meal for her." When the officer was busy making the meal, Rabbi Ya'aqov took out some paper and wrote something, then he lit a fire, and suddenly the woman appeared.

It is easy to imagine the officer's bewilderment at the appearance of his wife. He hastened to photograph Wazana while muttering to himself, "He is my savior, I believe in him and I will pray to him." He immediately rang his equally astonished father-in-law, who reported the events that evening in Paris: "My daughter was in the house, with all the windows and doors shut, nothing could come in. Suddenly she disappeared. How did she get out?"

The educated member of the Wazana family, Rabbi Shmuel Suissa, who had also lived in Casablanca for a time, gave the story a more romantic flavor. In his elegant turn of phrase, he described a pair of French lovers—a French general's daughter, and a twenty-year-old nobody—"In those days there was something known as *noblesse oblige*, in other words, a general's daughter could only marry a general's son." Enraged at his daughter's involvement in this second-rate match, the father banned the union and removed his daughter back to France, leaving her lover languishing in Casablanca, "The boy was so desperately in love he wanted to die." The youth asked Wazana to intervene, and he agreed to orchestrate a clandestine meeting between the two. Through the power of his magic the girl was indeed snatched to Casablanca, for one last, brief reunion with her lover: "He saw her, he kissed her, and she returned to Paris. Vanished!"

For a short time, Wazana enjoyed resounding success in Casablanca. By helping to resolve romantic problems he acquired a reputation and riches, but his activities also exposed him to dangers undreamed of in his protected mountain home. All descriptions of this period stress the great secrecy under which he operated. His stay in Casablanca seems to have been marked by movement from place to place, hiding with people who helped conceal his identity. According to Eliyahu Tubul, "Rabbi Ya'aqov used to hide and do everything in secret." On one occasion Eliyahu himself fell prey to sorcery (skhur), and was forced to beg the woman hiding Wazana at the time to let him meet his friend. The secrecy under which Wazana worked is evident from the consistent way that the stories of his activities in Casablanca end. The French officer story, for example, ends with the delighted husband announcing Wazana's role in the affair to his outraged father-in-law, who had arrived hot-foot from Paris in search of his daughter. The general responded by publicizing his son-in-law's photograph of Rabbi Ya'aqov throughout Morocco, promising a handsome reward for information leading to Rabbi Ya'aqov. Even though the ending does not contain an explicit threat, the general's action bears every sign of a campaign to seize a wanted criminal. It appears that Rabbi Ya'aqov did feel threatened since from then on he took great care to conceal his activities.

The negative reaction to Wazana's activities is very plainly presented in another ending of the same story. This time the husband publicizes the story and the police chief of Casablanca quickly orders Wazana's arrest and imprisonment. However, the powers used by Wazana to deliver distant lovers also allow him to escape from under lock and key. The next day, when the guards came to open the cell door, they found their commissar inside, and Wazana nowhere in sight. In yet other versions, Wazana's power enables him to assume different disguises, and even make himself invisible in order to dodge his pursuers.

Why was Wazana hounded so relentlessly by the authorities in Casablanca? Perhaps the answer lies in the laconic statement made by the police commissar on Rabbi Ya'aqov's capture: "This sorcerer has the power to turn this country upside down!" Wazana is seen as wielding the power to bring turmoil to the social order with his supernatural activities, and as such, he is a liability to the authorities. The anarchistic tenor of his activities, with their disregard for the constraints of reality, whether in terms of the laws of nature or of social proprieties, is a thorn in the side of the government. Furthermore, for the first time it appears that Wazana was inside a framework which did not unanimously take his powers for granted. In far off Tifnoute, spells were fatalistically regarded as a basic, incontrovertible aspect of reality. In Casablanca, the French had difficulty accepting their usage, either from the Christian viewpoint, which regarded them as the dark power of Satan, or by the upholders of enlightenment and progress, who thought sorcerers peddlers of superstition spawned by ignorance. For all of these reasons, sorcery had to be uprooted. What is more, Wazana's activities touched on tension spots between Jews and Arabs whose expressions were far more rancorous than anything ever encountered in Tifnoute. According to the informants, Jewish families whose daughters had been kidnapped by Muslims used to commission Wazana to find them. And his success in this area drew down such fury from the Arabs that several plots were hatched against him.

We can therefore deduce that Wazana's presence near the center of government, and his conflict with the authorities, represented a predicament for both parties. In the end he was banished from Casablanca, a ruling he seems to have accepted, making no effort to return. In retrospect, his stay in Casablanca represents a transient and anomalous episode in Wazana's life. From that time until his death, he remained in the Western High Atlas, his native landscape. Yitzhak Peḥima, Wazana's close companion at the end of his life, described the blend of possibilities and trouble the city symbolized: "Wazana could have gone to Casablanca or to Marrakech. He could have gone anywhere and made millions—millions! But he couldn't. They made it so he couldn't work there—he could only work in his own area." As we later see, this dilemma, which is essentially about proscription and crossing borderlines, encapsulates the essence of Wazana's experience as portrayed by the informants who knew him.

11

"He Was Our Great Healer"

Wazana was surrounded by an aura of magic and mystery that was created by a combination of his performance of miracles, the unique nature of his personality, and his multifaceted identity. But we must look to his healing for the primary source of this aura, since that was the wellspring of Wazana's greatest fame, and it was toward this role that he had directed himself out of a clear sense of destiny and calling. In fact, every unusual aspect of his behavior and appearance was a by-product of his single-minded wish to become an all-powerful healer.

Wazana's healing techniques provide clear testimony to the Muslim roots of his training. There was indeed a great resemblance between Jewish and Muslim healing traditions in Morocco, which made it natural for those who sought relief from their troubles in either group to cross the ethnic boundaries between the faiths. As we have seen, even rabbi-healers did not disdain acquiring supplementary skills from local Arab sheikhs. Both groups believed that powerful words, capable of attacking the source of the problem, lay at the heart of healing. In fact, both had their own set of "holy" and "impure" names.[1] Holy names in the widest sense—names of God and of angels, and biblical verses (passages from the Koran for Muslims)—annulled curses and cured disease. "Impure" names, on the other hand, inflicted as well as neutralized mischief. Strictly speaking, the "impure" category contained names of demons, evil spirits, and other powers of the evil kingdom. Due to the religious tensions between Jews and Muslims, many Jews classified all Muslim healing formulae, regardless of their source, as "impure." This patronizing, ethnocentric stance, which needless to say had its analogy within the Muslim community, did not signify contempt or ridicule of Muslim names, but rather a specific moral position.

In discussing the demonic world, we learned that impurity was capable of accessing immense powers, which could be harnessed to healing. Essentially, in both the Jewish and the Muslim worlds the writing itself lay at the core of symbolic healing. The "complete" traditional treatment meant healing by eliminating the cause of the problem, and, equally important, by ensuring no recurrence of the problem (immunization). Two types of writing were therefore used. The first, to produce active healing, involved erasing the writing either by immersing the paper in water, or by burning it.[2] The second (immunization) involved hanging the writing (designated *qame'a*—amulet—in Hebrew) on the body, or wearing it as a defense against the forces responsible for the affliction. These techniques were sometimes supplemented with substances or incense comprised of healing herbs or minerals such as *ḥarmel, rota, casbur, pasokh, seb,* and *jawi,*[3] believed to keep demons and sorcery at bay. The various writing techniques and healing materials shared a single purpose: namely actual physical contact between the healing medium (holy or impure words, or incense), and the affected body part. Thus, depending on the problem, sufferers were required to wear an amulet next to their bodies, under their clothes, to protect them against demons or evil spirits. Alternatively, they might be required to rub the painful area with the solution containing the erased writing. Cases involving internal organs, or mental and emotional functions, required the patient to swallow the potion, or inhale the smoke produced by burning the writing. Sometimes the healing substance was thrown out in a particular place, or buried there to achieve a direct effect on the evil agent who resided there. For believers in this community, placing the healing substance next to the injured body part, or near the external source of the problem represented the highway to recovery.

Even though the origin of Wazana's interest in healing lay in his exposure to his father's book of names, it seems that he avoided Jewish healing traditions (based on kabbala) throughout his long career. In this he departed significantly from most rabbi-healers in Morocco and Israel. While a fair number of the latter used, and continue to use, Muslim names, none, as far as I know, base their expertise exclusively on these methods. For most of these healers, Muslim-based techniques were largely disregarded in favor of Jewish healing formulae. A good number of informants claimed that Wazana exclusively utilized "impure names" (Muslim names) for healing. It seems that he amassed these names during his training period in Sous, and later augmented them with others he discovered in Muslim healing books—much to the dismay of the local sheikhs. The sheikhs took great pains to force him to return the books to their owners, and threatened him repeatedly when he refused. However, Wazana's courage and boundless faith in his own powers usually enabled him to ignore these threats, though some acquaintances contended that the move from Agouim to Assarag, after his mother's death, was in fact a flight from the sheikhs' menace. Informants refer to the power held in Wazana's books with reverential awe. They are convinced that the books hold secret healing prescriptions for curing any affliction, cancer included.

Jointly, the power of the books and Wazana's covenant with the demons, which guaranteed their immediate assistance, transformed Wazana into the greatest healer in the mountains of southern Morocco. From Telouet to Ouarzazate, and from Tazenakht to the outskirts of Taroudant, Jews and Muslims swarmed to his door, staunch in their belief that only he could save them. Even the local rulers—French as well as Moroccan—occasionally used his services, thereby adding considerably to his prestige. The powerful Glaoui clan which governed vast tracts of southern Morocco,[4] and in particular Ḥaj Tehami, the autocratic pasha of Marrakech, and his kinsman, *kaid* Ibrahim of Telouet, took advantage of Wazana's skills in healing and clairvoyance.

Which ailments and problems did Wazana treat? According to the informants, his healing activities were those of any healer, and hardly seem to differ from those of the Jewish Moroccan healers operating in Israel today. What sets Wazana apart, however, from the others is the high percentage of witchcraft cases he treated. The most significant number of cases in this category involved pregnancy, childbirth, and fertility—primarily female infertility[5]—but also chronic miscarriages, difficult childbirth, and male impotence. The second largest group of cases were those related to interpersonal and romantic conflict, mainly in the marital context, but also problems that arose between engaged couples. In the third group were demonically caused afflictions (various manifestations of *tsira* and *aslai*), and children's diseases. Another main area of specialization, which other healers tended to avoid, was identifying thieves and retrieval of stolen property.

To appreciate the reason for Wazana's reputation in particular as an expert in sorcery, we need to be aware of the way *skhur* (witchcraft and sorcery) was perceived in traditional Moroccan society. Like demons, sorcery was often held responsible for ailments and adversity. However, as opposed to demons, which are supernatural beings existing outside normal existence, sorcery involved a human being who harnesses supernatural forces in order to inflict harm on another. *Skhur* is usually wrought by a kinsman or neighbor inflamed by envy, or motivated by a desire to avenge an old injury. To execute their malice, they commission a "writer" to create a formula of impure names, or, alternatively, they turn to a "wise woman" who concocts malevolent spells comprised of bones, bodily secretions, and dead animals. The use of articles of the victim's clothing, and, moreover, body parts (such as hair or fingernails), which are considered especially effective raw materials in the preparation of *skhur,* relies on the universal principle of contagious magic. Demons and sorcery alike are active either externally or within the victim's body. In the external case, the written formula or physical concoction is secretly buried in a desecrated spot such as a Muslim cemetery, while in the second instance—working inside the body—the *skhur* is introduced into the victim's food.

Tkaf is an important subdivision of *skhur* manifestation, and means binding, inhibiting, or preventing. Such magic is usually based on the principle of similarity.[6] Thus, it is believed that a woman may be prevented from conceiving by turning a key in a lock and hiding the key where it cannot be found. Alternatively, a needle can be heated and bent into a circle, the point inserted into the eye and the circle thus sealed. Such procedures are founded on the belief that a ritual act can produce a parallel outcome in reality due to the resemblance between the procedure and the desired outcome. Like produces like. Apart from infertility, impotence, and ensuring that someone never marries, which are believed to be typical *tkaf* effects, *skhur* can cause insanity, force a husband to become obedient and submissive, stir up conflict and dissent between close friends, cause divorce, or arouse uncontrollable love or hate.

The fact that removing spells was Wazana's primary specialization attests to his reputation as an expert in solving the hardest, most socially complex problems. Spells were believed to be a particularly serious matter because of the dual challenge they posed to the practitioner. The first challenge was that in order to terminate the *skhur*'s damaging effect, it was required to expose the spell physically and destroy its magical components. The second difficulty involved the delicate matter of accurately identifying the spell's perpetrator. Besides being a daunting challenge to the practitioner's skills, the second task was extremely delicate in terms of its social implications. As noted before, *skhur* was popularly believed to be commissioned by someone close to the victim. This meant that positive identification would in all likelihood lead to immense bitterness and animosity among kin or friends. Most healers I spoke to scrupulously avoided identifying the perpetrator for their clients on the grounds of not wishing to incite conflict and strife. Instead they were prepared to offer the victim a general but noncommittal account of the *skhur*'s origin.

From a skeptical point of view, it could be argued that this commitment to social harmony probably conceals a fear of identifying the source and suffering possibly embarrassing or far-reaching consequences. Compared with the vague indictment of a "demon" as the agent responsible for the crisis, resolving a *skhur* case meant accusing a specific, usually close-by, individual of a serious offense. The latter would naturally deny the accusation and would try to disprove it. If successful, the healer's reputation would be seriously damaged; if not, he ran the risk of the accused becoming a sworn enemy and of his own embroilment in a bitter quarrel.

Wazana's readiness to deal with problems resulting from sorcery and spells stemmed from his advantages over other healers, first in terms of the healing techniques at his disposal, and second owing to his standing within the community. The need to locate and destroy the *skhur* materials was fulfilled with the assistance of demons that hurried to his bidding. Instantly, the demons would deliver the spell, which in most cases they found in a remote non-Jewish cemetery. While other healers refused to perform the second aspect of *skhur* healing, in order to avoid bloodshed or recrimination, Wazana fearlessly named the spell perpetrator, being liberated from the constraints of social mores and obligations that bound others. His handling of *skhur* cases was typically to "go all the way," that is, he identified the sorcery and its origin without fearing the disruption of the delicate social fabric.

Another field in which Wazana gained renown was the identification of thieves. Both here and for exposing sorcerers he often employed *istinzal,* a distinctive ritual involving demonic collaboration that was considered both difficult and complicated (Bilu 1982). In this technique, the healer uses a boy or girl below the age of nine to mediate between him and the demons. The child is placed close to a source of light, in front of the healer, and a drop of oil or ink is poured into the palm of his hand. Substances enjoyed by demons are burned all around the child to attract them. The child is instructed to gaze into the liquid as the healer utters special invocations, enjoining the spirits to appear. The flickering light casts shadowy shapes on the burnished liquid pool in which the child sees the demons and communicates with them. Once the child indicates that figures are present in his palm, the healer issues a list of instructions to be transmitted to the demons. This is meant to summon as many demonic legions as possible, one after the other, until finally an individual or group of demons appears that can disclose the thief's identity, or help locate the source of the problem presented to the healer.

To induce large numbers of demons to show themselves, they were invited to feast in the child's palm. Usually the child could describe this in detail: the demons slaughtering the beef, cooking couscous, what they ate and drank. As soon as the demon able to solve the problem came into view, it was asked to make the perpetrator's image—whether a demon (in the case of demonic ailments), or a human (in the case of sorcery or theft)—materialize in the child's palm. At this juncture, the healer either negotiated with the demonic perpetrator to obtain the victim's release from the affliction, or enlisted the demons' cooperation in identifying the thief or sorcerer. With the conclusion of the ceremony, the child was instructed to dismiss the demons, and the oil or ink was wiped away.

The *istinzal* ceremony is a Moroccan variation of a common group of augury and divination techniques stretching back to the ritual practices of the Assyro-Babylonian world of the second or third millennium B.C. (Bilu 1982). The name given in the Talmud and other traditional Jewish sources for this type of technique is *sarei shemen* (princes of the oil).[7] In terms of the psychological experience, it appears that the common factor underlying techniques of this type is the ability to induce a state of altered consciousness in a "medium," the gazing child in this case, akin to a hypnotic trance. Such mental states are fertile ground for prediction and clairvoyance, which explains their widespread use and preservation over the years.

Istinzal was not perceived as a hypnotic technique in traditional Morocco. Nonetheless, the fact that during the ceremony the child-medium entered an unusual state of highly concentrated focus and total dissociation did not go unnoticed by witnesses. Several informants recalled occasions involving drastic resorts, such as slapping the child's face, or sprinkling him or her with water to restore normal consciousness. It is hardly surprising therefore that many parents were reluctant to allow their children to be used. Most healers were unhappy about the technique: in addition to the requirements of instructing the children and ensuring their emergence unscathed from the experience, they were expected to name the thief, with all the entailed social unpleasantness.

Wazana, we know, was indifferent to the social constraints that inhibited other healers. Moreover, *istinzal* was tailor-made for his capabilities, both due to his intimacy with the demonic world and control over its inhabitants, and his special way with children of all ages. It is therefore no surprise that *istinzal* became his apparent "trademark." He usually worked with Muslim children as most Jewish parents were averse to allowing their children to be exploited in this way. Given this, I was therefore fortunate to meet informants who had served as an *istinzal* medium for Wazana as a child. Yitzhak Elmaliakh clearly recalls the time his brother fell ill on returning from the local spring. Wishing to disclose the source of the affliction, Wazana used Yitzhak as his medium. In this case the procedure proved abortive: Yitzhak failed to see any images in the liquid, no matter how hard he tried. Despite the fact that Yitzhak's young brother was extremely sick with a life-threatening septic abscess in his throat, Wazana remained calm and joked with the redheaded boy. "Those from under the ground don't like you because you're a redhead," Elmaliakh recalls Wazana saying, "he just kept laughing and laughing, fit to split his sides. . . . He sat down, said to me 'I want some tea.' I replied, 'But my brother is dying,' to which he replied, 'I am in charge.' He drank the tea and picked up his books." In the end Wazana repeated the ceremony with another young boy who named the demon in the spring as the one responsible for the assault. Yitzhak's brother recovered his health when a fitting prize—food enjoyed by demons—was cast into the spring.

Chapter 11

Several times as a boy, Rabbi Shalom, Wazana's former disciple, acted as an *istinzal* medium for him. This is how he described his "initiation":

> There was a woman who had an expensive silver teapot which disappeared one day. So Wazana made a fire of coals and charcoal and kept adding *kusbar, jawi,* some *kusbar,* some *jawi,* onto the fire; and the fire jumped and smoke rose up like from a cigarette. Then he put ink into my hand. The first time I was scared. He asked me: "What can you see?" I said, "My nose" [reflected in the ink]. He did this three times, on the fourth time he asked, "Do you see anything?" I replied, "I see a man in a chair." He said, "Tell him, we haven't feasted for a long time; it is time to bring a sheep and slaughter it and make couscous and share it with the others." Straightaway the man did what I said. When the meal was prepared they celebrated and feasted and their king appeared and they brought him here and started dancing. I saw it all in my hand—just like watching television.
>
> Finally Wazana asked, "Have they finished eating?" I replied, "Yes." They were divided into groups on the beach, some wore red hats, some wore blue, there were different kinds of them. Then Wazana said, "Tell them to bring the Torah Scroll." They did and then he said, "Tell them they must solemnly swear to tell the truth." I did this and they swore. It was like a film. But no voices. I just saw what they were doing.
>
> Wazana said, "Tell them to fetch whoever stole the teapot—now!" They brought a woman. I knew her! It wasn't one of their women. They brought her into the ink, it was one of us, a neighbor. I said, "Mother, mother, it's so and so." Wazana said to me, "Shut up," and he laughed. Then he said, "Tell them to beat her until she gives back the teapot." Before he said this he asked me where she had hidden the teapot. I said, "She has hidden it in the oven, and covered it with ashes and coals." Then Wazana said, "Tell them to go in peace." I said good-bye to them and everything vanished. After that, Wazana went like this . . . and took the dye away. That's all.

Both ceremonies reflect Wazana's unique personal style. In the first, he is calm and self-assured, unruffled despite the gravity of the child's illness; in the second, he has no qualms when faced with the unpleasant task of naming a member of the community as the thief. From the story, he seems to have found the situation entertaining, his ebullience reflecting this enjoyment. The richness of the detail in Rabbi Shalom's narrative is quite rare. The experiences of most of the informants who had served as mediums were expunged from their memories upon resumption of their normal state of consciousness. This amnesia reinforces the hypothesis that the children were induced into hypnotic trance.

Perhaps the most famous of the many *istinzal* rituals Wazana conducted was the one which resulted in the restoration of the mighty sheikh's stolen dagger. This event "hit the headlines," due both to the sheikh's pre-eminence and the enormous value of the ornate silver-and-gem-studded dagger. On this occasion, Wazana summoned the demonic cohorts into the palm of a young Muslim girl, and making them swear on "Sidna Suleiman's [King Solomon's] Book," successfully brought about the thief's capture and the dagger's recovery.[8]

Another time, Makhluf Ben-Ḥayim, Wazana's longstanding host from Agouim, asked the healer to treat Aisha, his wife, who persistently gave birth to stillborn children. By means of *istinzal*, Wazana raised the she-demon responsible for the deaths of the couple's offspring. The she-demon, it transpired, was Aisha's demonic double who had punished Aisha for (unwittingly) injuring her demonic children. Through the medium—again a young Muslim girl—Wazana negotiated with the demon over the compensation Aisha must pay to end the deadly pattern. The demon demanded that two white female camels be sacrificed, and their blood mixed with Aisha's. After protracted haggling, the demon conceded to moderating her terms, and accepted an alternative white sacrifice of lesser value—two decorated eggs. In return for the eggs, Wazana made her solemnly swear never to harm Aisha's children again. When the ink was wiped from medium's hand, she, like the others, lost all memory of her experience. Wazana then ordered the girl to be paid twenty rials and sent her home. From that time on, Aisha gave birth to live, healthy babies.

Ḥana Buskila, Wazana's kinswoman, was the only female informant Wazana repeatedly used as a medium. "When I was young, before I married into his family, he did things in my hand and read things over me, with his hand on my head; then I saw them [the demons] in the palm of my hand." Like Rabbi Shalom, Ḥana Buskila can recall the ceremonies she participated in, enacted for locating sorcery. She claims that during *istinzal*, the demons unearthed the spell object and delivered it, moist and muddy, into her left hand (her free hand; the other contained the liquid), to be destroyed, and its force terminated. Only once were the demons unable to reveal the source of the spell. On that occasion, the case involved Ḥana's kinswoman, a woman whose fourteen-year marriage had been childless. The demons told Ḥana, who was six at the time, "There is no cure, she shouldn't waste her money, she will never have children; an Arab grave has been used so that she won't bear children." This case is very interesting since, upon learning the demonic verdict from Ḥana, the man divorced his wife. He remarried some years later and his new wife successfully bore him children. The new wife was none other than Ḥana!

Although an important and central technique in Wazana's repertoire, *istinzal* was not the only technique he employed to reveal secrets. Even in robbery cases other techniques were applied; for example, the Muslim book of secrets, which he successfully employed to expose the guilty. The next case, a story told by Yosef Knafo, the former goldsmith from Ouarzazate, is one such example.

One day, the town was abuzz with the news that 270,000 rials had disappeared from the French administration vault (Ouarzazate was one of the administration's centers in the south of Morocco). The acting governor, a French officer, was inconsolable. In his distress, he asked the goldsmith, his friend Yosef Knafo, for assistance. Knafo suggested that they drive to Agouim and find Wazana. In Agouim, the governor remained hidden in the car while the goldsmith went to look for Wazana. Knafo explained, "He [the governor] was so well known, he was afraid someone would recognize him." Wazana's reaction was typically understated: "Is that all?" he queried dismissively on learning how much money had been stolen, and promised to return the money forthwith. The distraught governor promised Wazana the earth if he succeeded: "If you find the money, you will be mayor, and you will be able to do whatever you like."

The three drove back to Ouarzazate. In the "bureau," the governor's office, Wazana consulted the book he had with him, and told the governor to follow the goldsmith. "He will give you the money." Wazana gave his friend certain signs that would lead him to the money: "Go to the tree by the roadside, there you will find a white mark. I will mark it for you. Just dig in the earth and remove the sack." The goldsmith did as instructed, and easily found the hidden loot. Now much calmer, the governor insisted that Wazana identify the thief. This time, the fearless healer, who usually had no qualms about naming culprits, seemed bothered by this request. The reason became transparent once he named the thief. The culprit, it transpired, belonged to an exceedingly distinguished Arab family in the employ of the administration. Under torture, the Arab confessed to the crime, whereupon Wazana was instructed to pass sentence on him. This climactic twist wherein Wazana is cast in the role of sentencing judge seems like wishful thinking on the informant's part. In fact, by ascribing the upper hand to the usually powerless Jew, the story completely reverses the traditional Jewish-Muslim roles: "The officer asked him, 'What is the sentence of this Arab?' Wazana answered, 'Burn him! Tell all the inhabitants of the town to come and stand while this Arab burns.' That was his decision. Forty or fifty thousand people came. They piled up the wood, bound the Arab, set it on fire and threw him onto the pyre. They all stood watching . . . Arabs and Jews, children, even girls, until he had gone up in smoke." Even if the story is no more than wishful thinking prompted by the circumstances of Jewish inferiority enforced by the Muslims, the fact is that the narrator chose Wazana, as the Jews' omnipotent representative, to seal the fate of a high status Arab. Not for the first time we find testimony to the endless power ascribed to Wazana by his fellows. According to this narrator, the event carried far-reaching consequences concerning the community's confidence and security: "After that, in our town, you could leave your gold on the sidewalk and no one took it. They didn't dare touch it—didn't even dream of it—because of what happened." Even though Wazana's special expertise lay in catching thieves, he was most famous for his acts of healing. Through several personal stories related by former clients let us examine his healing activities, special style, and the powers imputed to him. Between the lines of the various narratives emerges the powerful emotions underlying the memories of these grateful people.

Aaron Biton of Ouarzazate sought Wazana's help when a problem of some intimacy threatened to destroy his marriage. Beginning with his wedding night, and for four years after, Aaron Biton had been tormented by impotence. Hoping that Wazana would be able to restore his virility, he hiked for three days through the mountains and up the steep banks of the Tifnoute River in order to reach Assarag, home of the great healer. Wazana, radiating his typical air of confidence, confirmed Aaron's suspicions that "they had closed him up," that is, that he was victim to a *tkaf* spell. To discover the perpetrator, Wazana lit a fire and handed the informant a blank sheet of paper, ordering him to cast it into the flames. To Aaron's astonishment, instead of burning, an inscription appeared on the page and was immediately deciphered by the healer. The writing blamed a vindictive woman called Ḥana for the attack, confirming Aaron's suspicions. Ḥana was his neighbor in Ouarzazate, who bore him a grudge for refusing to marry her daughter.

Not content with merely naming the source of the spell, Wazana proposed transporting the woman to them: "Do you want her to come? She will be here in ten minutes, straight from her house, no, five minutes." Shaking with fright, his young client adamantly refused to countenance this, begging the healer to destroy the spell and be done. Wazana shrugged and read something, whereupon a gust of wind dropped a bundle wrapped in rough thread directly into Aaron's hand. Inside, Aaron discovered bones, black stones, clumps of hair matted with blood, and several seeds. He dropped the package, aghast, but Wazana soothed him: "Look what she did to you, this is from an Arab grave; we will get rid of it and it will all be over." This was indeed so and Aaron went home to his wife, and the couple lived "happily ever after."

This story exemplifies Wazana's uniqueness as a healer, both by his confident manner and his willingness to "go all the way." Not only is he prepared—in contrast to other healers—to identify the spell's originator, but he shows readiness (declined by the client) to transport the woman in a flash from Ouarzazate to Assarag to face her victim. Although never explicitly said, informants believe that Wazana's demonic servants made it possible for him to spirit people from place to place, or materialize spells out of nowhere.

A further case involving *skhur* was reported by Eliyahu Tubul, like Wazana, from Assarag. At the age of nineteen, Eliyahu fell in love with a young kinswoman from Casablanca and obtained her parents' permission to marry her. The engagement proceeded despite the fact that the girl had another boyfriend at the time. At the time of the engagement, Eliyahu lived in Rabat, and visited his beloved in Casablanca at every opportunity, eagerly counting the days to his wedding. However, as the happy day drew closer, the young man's joy turned to perplexity. While begging him to visit, his beloved treated him with indifference once he arrived, offering strange excuses to avoid spending time with him. Two years passed, and Eliyahu, spurned, grew desperate and lovesick, losing twenty kilos in weight. Finally, his errant fiancee informed him that she now loved her former boyfriend. On hearing this, Eliyahu knew that Wazana was the only one capable of restoring his beloved to him. Fortunately for him, Wazana was in Casablanca at the time, and despite the obstacles involved in gaining access to the healer, who was living underground, the two finally met. Wazana sympathized with his young friend's sorrow, insisting on going to see the girl immediately. The two went to see her in the afternoon, and were told she was working and would only be home in several hours. Wazana, who disliked being kept waiting, used his powers to transport her home directly. He then proceeded to account for her puzzlingly evasive behavior. The couple were the victims of an Arab sorcerer, who had been commissioned by her first boyfriend to create a spell. Wazana described the spell used in detail: "He [the sorcerer] wrote seven charms, each time using the blood of a different impure animal: a mouse, a snake, a lizard, etc. The inscriptions were affixed to a Muslim grave, and the girl could not marry until the corpse rose from the dead. When would this occur? On the ninth day of Av" [in other words, never].[9] Wazana sent Eliyahu to the Muslim cemetery to remove the spell from the grave. He provided him with explicit instructions regarding the tomb's location. However, the informant was afraid that Arabs would discover and punish him, and was reluctant to go. Wazana accepted this, and agreed to nullify the spell without its removal from the grave. He compiled a list of forty-three kinds of *tabkhar* (incense ingredients in whose smoke the client immerses his body), and told Eliyahu to purchase them in a particular store. On reading the list, the storekeeper was amazed, and implored Eliyahu to reveal its origins. Eliyahu refused, worried that this might lead to Wazana's discovery and prosecution by the Muslims. The storekeeper then declared that "whoever asked for these items must be a Jew and an Arab (at the same time). The *skhur* masters of Casablanca do not know these things." Finally, Eliyahu admitted that Wazana was the source. The storekeeper's reaction testifies to the fame Wazana had attained while in Casablanca: "The man was stunned, he stood up, and sat down again [in agitation]. 'How do you know Wazana? How have you got the money to pay him? Everyone knows Wazana costs a fortune.'"

Among the substances Eliyahu delivered to Wazana were *seb, pasokh, ḥarmel,* a rat's tail, and parts of a lizard, which Wazana threw onto a pan of live coals. He instructed the couple to stand one on either side of the pan, and covered them with a cloth. The smoke enveloped the pair completely, and when it dispersed, the girl gazed at the informant, her husband-to-be, and after that never sought to avoid him. The last service Wazana performed was to write an amulet guaranteeing Eliyahu protection from sorcery in the future. Moreover, he promised his young friend that the long-awaited marriage would take place within days— during the ten days separating Rosh Hashana (New Year) and Yom Kippur (Day of Atonement). And so it was. Before the week had ended, Eliyahu and his beloved were married in Casablanca.

Wazana not only treated adults. His success with children's diseases was particularly important in view of traditional Morocco's high infant mortality rate. Rabbi Shmuel Suissa, Rabbi Ya'aqov's kinsman, described how Wazana saved both his sister and niece. His stories are as follows:

> One day, my father, may he rest in peace, came home to find my three-year-old sister completely paralyzed. One moment she was fine, walking and talking, the next she was completely paralyzed. She couldn't even sit down. I was five or six at the time but I've got an excellent memory. My father wanted Wazana to see her, so he went and brought him because we are kinsmen. Wazana was in Assarag, we lived in Idirghan, almost in Sous. It is more than a day's walk. I remember Wazana [very emotional], I can still see him coming up the stairs. He wrote something on a plate and said to my father: "By Sunday she will sit, on Monday she will stand, on Tuesday she will speak. One hand will always be paralyzed." And so it is, still paralyzed. He cured her, she spoke, it all happened just as he promised. She is still alive and lives in Ashdod.
>
> In Casablanca he also did amazing things which seem completely illogical. My sister's little daughter was sick with typhus. The doctors all said she wouldn't live, that there was nothing they could do. They called Wazana again. For family he did a lot, he came especially, all the way to Casablanca. When he came he wrote something for her. He said, "I will put this cup next to her. If the cup jumps up and spins around

the room and nothing happens to it, she will rise tomorrow. If it smashes, there is no hope." The moment he finished writing [on the cup], it started to spin around the room, and then went back to its place. Then next day she felt better, as if nothing had been wrong. She is still alive and lives in Rishon le-Zion.

In both instances the treatment involved writing on a utensil. This was a popular technique that entailed writing names inside a plate or cup, then filling the vessel with water to erase the names. The patient either drank the solution or it was smeared over the afflicted body part. The technique described in the second story is highly unusual since the names Wazana wrote on the cup were supposed to work directly on the patient without being drunk or smeared on the body, the only condition being that the cup did not smash as it flew around the room. This case not only provides an outstanding demonstration of the powers ascribed to Wazana, but clearly depicts the dramatic quality of his treatment. This tale also reflects his kind devotion toward members of his family. Masouda Buskila, whose late husband had been Rabbi Ya'aqov's nephew, describes this aspect of Wazana's behavior very emotionally. Her poor language skills do not detract from her description of the climactic event in which Wazana's dogged determination rescued her from the jaws of death.

> I was staying in his house in Assarag and I was sick. They give me poison [this presumably means she fell victim to sorcery]. When I was so ill I had two children. A woman threw something into my food. . . . Rabbi Ya'aqov was in France [Casablanca] and I lay on the floor [not functioning because of her illness] for three years. Nobody would take me, my parents were very far away [in Tamzersht]. Don't remember a thing. Others took my children. No medicine, no doctors.
>
> Then he came back from France and stayed in a place called Tidili. My husband went there at night. "My wife is a lot sick, going to die." Then he came, of blessed memory. . . . [here began a lengthy digression concerning how Wazana sent large numbers of patients home so that he could be at her side].
>
> Then he did what he did. Held my hand, and read and read. And me, twins in my belly, seven months [pregnant]. He gave me medicine from France. They told him, "Maybe she will die because of this medicine." He said, "No, she won't die, she has much time left, but she will be sick, even die [may seem to die] in the next twenty-four hours. Do not take her to the cemetery." And the woman that did it to me [the spell] was near me! [a relative], jealous. He said, "What's got in her belly died three days ago, that's why the woman [herself]

100

is nearly dead." He gave me medicine, may he rest in peace, and what was in me, was going out [reference apparently to a miscarriage]. Afterwards the poison fell out [left her]. It was like a big yellow flower. This is what my mother told me. I don't remember.

Then the Jews said the Shema, and I was going into another world. And people went and dug a grave ready for me. I just remember that they got a bucket of water and some soap [they ritually washed her body] and sewed [her shroud]. Then two Jews said to the *tsaddiq*, "Give us the woman so we can take her to the cemetery, if you don't we will bring the police." Then a policeman came, and said to Wazana, "Give them the Jewish woman who died yesterday so the people can go home." But Wazana cannot be pressured. He answered, "I will not let them take her. They will not take her. She is my nephew's wife. Tell the people to go home. Tomorrow she may be dead, then I will take her to the cemetery alone." He didn't let them [take her body away].

But one of the Jews did things against him [accused him of wrongdoing], he said to him, "put her down" [leave her alone] so her soul can depart." And what did he do? He put on his *jellaba*, it was winter. Then all the dirt that was inside me came up inside him as well—it reached him up to here [pointing to her throat] and he didn't eat or drink for twenty-four hours. Just prayed. That is a saint [she sobbed]. Then somebody came in and Wazana said, "Go and get a small chicken, a chick." I don't remember that, my mother told it to me. They did all his things [everything he asked], they made food, and he gave me three drops in my mouth [of chicken soup]. At four in the afternoon I opened my eye, only one, not the other. [I was ill after that] maybe for a month. Then everyone was happy, and the man who said the saint did wrongdoing didn't go out for a month, then he died. He was walking along, met what he met, and fell down. That's why every year I make his feast.

On the one hand, the dramatic force of this story arises from the critically ill condition of the woman who is believed to have died, and on the other, from Wazana's devotion and his resolute determination to restore her to life. The healing story is literally a struggle between life and death, which ends positively despite the initially hopeless prognosis. Not only does Wazana battle the illness that brings the young woman to her deathbed, but also the people surrounding her, who treat her as though she were dead, and try to force him with combined threats and appeals, to hand over her body for burial. Wazana's determination, his courage and absolute commitment to the dying woman, to the point of physically identifying with her ("Then all the dirt inside me came up inside him as well—it reached him up to here [pointing to her throat] and he did not eat or drink for twenty-four hours") could hardly be more explicit. Wazana actually restores his young kinswoman's life, and it is therefore no surprise that, to her, Wazana is indisputably a saint. Later we see in detail that Masouda is utterly certain that Wazana continues to guard and protect her, in Israel, even in death. In the stories pertaining to the deaths of Wazana's parents we already touched on the problematic matter of attempting to restore life to the dead. This issue recurs once more in the story of Rabbi Ya'aqov's own death. Wazana's tremendous healing power seems at its zenith in the story cited above: he successfully revives someone believed to be dead, whose body has even been prepared for burial.

The fact that Wazana was sought out by the great and the grand of Moroccan society further testifies to his potency as a healer: "Great ones came to him for help, governors, el-Pasha Glaoui, Ḥaj Tehami from Marrakech, and his kinsman, *kaid* Ibrahim of Telouet. Who didn't know him?" queried David Ben-Ḥamo of Agouim, but also hastened to add, "not in Casablanca, or in the North." In other words, Ben-Ḥamo wishes it to be quite clear that Wazana was nevertheless a distinctly local hero. The stories of several informants recount how Wazana saved Ḥaj Tehami, the most powerful man in southern Morocco prior to independence, from death by poisoning.[10] As a reward, this ruler, who was renowned for his brutality, honored Wazana by granting him an audience whenever he desired, "like one of the family." Another version states that the pasha was doomed to die of a serious illness but Wazana cured him and extended his life span several more years. We referred earlier to how Wazana assisted representatives of the Muslim and French law-and-order establishment, capturing thieves and recovering stolen property on their behalf.

Although the dominant note in the healing stories is Wazana's boundless omnipotence, a few let slip here and there that Wazana's powers were not unlimited. One example of this involves the story of a woman on the verge of death "owing to a snake in her belly." Upon turning to the healer, Wazana's unequivocal response was: "Sell your cow and go somewhere where there are doctors. I cannot get it out." Rabbi Ya'aqov's candid answer, acknowledging the limitations of his power as compared with conventional doctors, was exceptional among the body of stories. Instances where Wazana failed to prevent death are slightly more common, but on the whole, their negativity is mitigated by the fact that he could either accurately predict the time of death, or else postpone it.

Alu Yifrakh, formerly of Timjdut, reported that once her uncle asked Wazana to treat his sick wife. Wazana consulted the demons in an *istinzal* ceremony and was told that the woman's fate had been sealed: "They will bear her away on a stretcher." Rabbi Ya'aqov appealed, pleading: "Can anything be done?" but the demons replied, "Nothing can be done. It is over. Maybe today, maybe tomorrow [she will die]." Rabbi Ya'aqov had no recourse left but to beg an extension of three days to enable the dying woman's family to travel from Marrakech. This petition was granted. The family assembled round the patient's bed, and there was time for her to divide her property and state her last requests.

Shlomo Gabai of Amassine recounted that his mother had been taken to "an American doctor" in Marrakech who informed her that she was carrying twins, "one alive, the other dead." The doctor assessed her chance of not surviving cesarean surgery as "99 percent." According to Gabai, when the family heard the terrible odds they carried the woman to her father's house in Tidili and called Wazana to come. Wazana performed *istinzal* with a six-year-old Arab boy who was instructed to ask, "What lies in store for this girl? Is she for this world or the next?" The child medium described the activities of the demons in his palm: "They feasted, they slaughtered sheep and a calf and they said blessings." Suddenly, the boy reported seeing a white cloth in the picture. "It's over," announced Wazana, realizing that the cloth symbolized a shroud. Indeed, shortly after that the woman died. The fact that Wazana could not save his patient's life was in this case mitigated by his ability to predict her fate through *istinzal*, and by his affirmation of the doctor's dire prognosis for her condition.

Besides *istinzal*, there were other techniques at Wazana's disposal for determining whether a patient would live or die. When the infant daughter of his friend David Ben-Ḥamo of Agouim fell sick, Wazana took two eggs of equal size, wrote names on them and placed them in a scale. When one of the eggs came to rest lower than the other, he delivered the verdict: "It's over, you can forget the child." That day, the little girl died.

The few stories which refer to Wazana's inability to save desperate cases are dwarfed by the larger, overall portrait of a successful, self-confident healer who never balked at challenge or danger. "Wazana healed the serious cases," stated his pupil, Rabbi Shalom. "He did not need to write very much; just like antibiotics, the sickness went in no time at all." The depiction of effortless efficiency was reiterated by informants who recalled that Wazana tended to dismiss problems presented to him lightly: "Is that all?" he quipped derisively when asked by the governor of Ouarzazate to help find the 270,000 rials stolen from his office. "Only children?" he bantered when someone considered divorce after seven years of childless marriage. "Fear not. Do as I say and you will have so many children you won't know what to do."

If we do not strain to hear, we risk missing the rare but important mention of his failures amidst the loud fanfare of his many successes over the decades. As we see, great though Wazana's power was, it was not boundless. In a rare display of candor, Rabbi Ya'aqov explained to Yamna

Gabai of Amassine his inability to cure her mother of the illness that killed her. "I must do everything my friends down there tell me." In the case of Gabai's mother, the demons had forbidden his intervention, forcing him to obey for fear of losing his own life. Once again we witness the limits of Wazana's powers. With respect to the demons, Wazana appears to have been as subordinate to them as they were to him. Although in the clear majority of cases Wazana's demonic covenant granted him vast powers of divination and healing, a forbidden area beyond his grasp was always present. The few illustrations of the limits of his reach define this area clearly. Even Rabbi Ya'aqov was forbidden to rescue someone sentenced to die. An intimation of this limit may already be present in the stories of his parents' disinterment which, as we have said, possibly reflect his frustrated wish to bring them back to life. In Masouda Buskila's tale in which Rabbi Ya'aqov saved her from the burial party following ritual purification and preparation in shrouds, we reach the extreme edge of Wazana's healing abilities. In the story of restoring the life of the sheikh's daughter, which caused his death, he crossed this "red line."

12

The Move to Agouim

Many of the informants who observed Wazana's powerful attachment to his mother regarded her death as the principal reason for his move away from Assarag. They maintain that Wazana was unable to tolerate his life in the empty house, close to his mother's fresh grave, and therefore left his native village, never to return. From that time until the end of his life, Rabbi Ya'aqov never had a home of his own. He roamed the villages of the Western Atlas from his new base in the village of Agouim on the Marrakech-Ouarzazate highway, some ninety kilometers east of Assarag and the Tifnoute Valley. Judging by Wazana's stricken response to his mother's death, it is indeed likely that the trauma of her death contributed to his leaving Tifnoute. However, informants also offered alternative explanations for his move, linked to other aspects of Wazana's life—particularly his multifaceted identity. Apart from those factors that prompted Wazana to uproot from Assarag, we need to understand his reasons for selecting Agouim specifically as his base.

Several informants contend that other reasons, unconnected with his anguish at the separation from his mother, drove Wazana from his village. His great intimacy with the Muslims, on the one hand, and with the demons on the other, caused complications that even this usually fearless man had difficulty handling. His problem with the Muslims involved the dark jealousy of powerful sheikhs, healers, and men of religion who could not bear that a Jewish healer had achieved such renown through arts acquired from them. They were especially infuriated by the fact that Muslim holy books had fallen into the hands of an unworthy infidel. More than once Wazana's life was threatened in forceful attempts to retrieve the books. Perhaps the combination of threats and the deterioration in

Chapter 12

Muslim-Jewish relations in the latter half of the 1940s also encouraged Wazana to leave his birthplace.

Another explanation was offered by a few informants who saw his departure from Agouim as flight before demonic retribution. They believe that Wazana defied his allies from beneath the ground by engaging in forbidden healing. This rare interpretation is of great importance to understanding the figure of Wazana as shaped by the informants, since it once again makes allusion to the limits of his control over the demons. As we see later, Rabbi Ya'aqov's obstinacy in healing someone the demons had forbidden him to cure caused his downfall. The demon-related explanation for his departure from Assarag thus indicates that the seeds of this stubbornness were present already in Assarag.

To the various levels of explanation—the personal (mother's death), the Muslim, and the demonic—should be added a further factor, one which perhaps carries the most weight in accounting for his abandoning Assarag. During the second part of the 1940s, even before the period of mass emigration to Israel, an acceleration in a demographic trend which had started in the early part of the century occurred. The Jews of the mountain and desert regions of southern Morocco emigrated en masse to the large coastal cities (especially Casablanca), drawn by improved economic opportunities under French rule. This internal migration was particularly marked in the post-Second World War period due to episodes of drought and famine that struck the area. Even the remote Tifnoute region was affected by this trend, its Jewish communities gradually dwindling and dying out. For the gregarious Wazana, life in Assarag emptied of its Jews had little to recommend it. Even prior to his permanent move, he began staying away from the village for increasing lengths of time. The *mellah* (Jewish quarter) in Timjdut, for example, was one place he often visited. A native of Timjdut recalls, "He would come from Assarag and live with us for a month or two at a time because there was nobody to talk to in Assarag." Agouim folk had a similar explanation for Wazana's arrival in their village: "There was nobody to sit with in Tifnoute, no Jews for him. How many were left there? Two families?"

In contrast to Assarag, the Jewish community of Agouim still numbered a few score families. Wazana naturally favored this village because his sister's son, Ya'aqov Buskila, lived there. Agouim was also notably the nearest Jewish *mellah* to the tomb of Rabbi David u-Moshe. We cannot know whether the shrine also drew Wazana to Agouim, but we do know that after his move, he often visited there. Many informants recall meeting him inside the impressive shrine, participating in feasts and entertaining visitors with his magic. From that time, Wazana became a familiar figure among the villages and towns near Rabbi David u-Moshe's tomb—Timestint, Tidili, Ouarzazate, Skoura, Imini, Amassine, Sour, and Tezort.

Rabbi and pupils in the synagogue of Agouim, ca. 1950

Some informants stressed that Wazana's behavior underwent dramatic transformation after his move to Agouim. According to their reports, the man with the multiple identity, who prayed both "Arab prayers and Jewish prayers," shed his Muslim identity and once more became a Jew in every sense. If these descriptions indeed denote a genuine transformation, and not merely the informants' wish for Wazana to repent before his death, then his frequent visits to the tomb of the nearby *tsaddiq* might have been a contributing factor.

Even though his nephew lived in Agouim, Wazana chose to make his home with Makhluf Ben-Ḥayim, whose relationship with the Wazana family stretched back many years. Makhluf believed that his own birth was owed to the power of Rabbi Avraham Wazana's prayers. When Makhluf's wife repeatedly miscarried, and the couple were threatened with childlessness, Rabbi Ya'aqov made it possible for them to have children. It is no wonder that in gratitude Makhluf gave Rabbi Ya'aqov the use of one room and treated him with great devotion. Makhluf's house served as Wazana's home throughout his years in Agouim. It was from there that he set out on his travels around the Western Atlas and it was there he also died.

13

Death of Wazana

Wazana's death was abrupt and untimely. People from Agouim recall that before the fateful Friday when, at the age of fifty, his condition started deteriorating, "Wazana was the same as usual. There was nothing wrong with him; he gleamed like a mirror—so strong and healthy." A minority version claims that several days before his death gray streaks appeared in his hair, and his eyesight dimmed slightly. Makhluf Ben-Ḥayim, Wazana's benefactor in Agouim, blamed these changes on a ruling by the authorities that forced many Jews, including Wazana, to work on a strenuous road construction project. However, someone else claimed that Wazana himself made these early signs of aging appear, to gain a discharge from the backbreaking work.

Whatever the case, all agree that the sequence of events that led Wazana to his death began when he cured the daughter of a local shiekh, and defied a categorical prohibition of the demons. The sheikh's daughter, a member of a prosperous and distinguished family, became mortally afflicted one day after she stumbled upon several snakes (which were actually demon progeny), on her way to the river, and smashed their heads. Furious at the death of their young, the demons counterattacked so viciously that the girl's features became contorted, her head twisted around backwards, and she fell unconscious. According to accounts provided by other informants, the demons were not content with physical punishment, but penetrated her body and possessed her. Whether this was *tsira* (demonic assault) or *aslai* (demonic possession), the girl appeared mortally ill; she lay on her bed, "unable to speak or move—she was dried up [paralyzed]."

Her family did not summon Wazana immediately. Accounts emphasize her father's frantic efforts to find relief for her before, in despair, he finally turned to Rabbi Ya'aqov: "They took her to a doctor, they took her to an Arab, they took her to rabbis. . . . There was nowhere in the world they didn't go—and nothing helped!" The girl's family was dismayed at having to ask a Jewish healer for help even though Wazana had been recommended by Arabs who tried to treat her. In the end, however, having exhausted all their options, they reluctantly begged Rabbi Ya'aqov's assistance. The size of Wazana's fee depends on the scope and richness of each informant's imagination: it ranged from a sheep or goat, to "two sheep, a mare and a suitcase filled with gold and silver"—it even reached as high as "three or four million rial." Most likely, the size of the reward is an indication of the informant's preconceived ideas regarding Wazana's motives for defying the demons. Those who exaggerated the payment consider the reward itself the incentive ("the sheikh bribed him"), while those who downgraded his reward regarded Wazana's courage, his tendency to take risks, and his coolness in the face of difficulty, as the motivating factors.

At any event, not a single informant claimed that the great healer went to his death ignorant or innocent of his action. The demons, whether members of Wazana's demonic clan or otherwise, all cautioned him against healing the girl, and even tried sabotaging his efforts, overturning his inkstand as he prepared the amulet for her and wildly shaking his quill. Nevertheless, Rabbi Ya'aqov refused to surrender, and "forced himself" to continue until his work was done.

Informants phrased the demons' admonitions in authoritative, urgent language which included explicit threats against Wazana's life: according to an informant from Agouim, the demons warned him, "Go away, go away—if you treat her you will surely die." Wazana's kinswoman excitedly recalled the demons' pleas: "It is forbidden! Take care, we come to this girl from heaven. She killed our children." Another remembered, "They cautioned him: 'Watch out, you are at the limit!'" Those who believed the girl's affliction to be caused by *aslai* (possession), placed the demonic warnings within the victim's body: "Beware Wazana! If you come to drive us away, you will not leave here alive. . . . Do not interfere with us. . . . You must do what we tell you!" In another version, "He [Wazana] said to them: 'Leave her!' and they answered: 'We will not leave. Someone is going to die! Better this *goyah* [non-Jew] dies than you!'"

Apart from the obvious and recurrent explanation involving "restitution," according to which the fate of the sheikh's daughter (or the fate of whoever treated her) was sealed the moment she killed the demons' offspring, there is another explanation, namely, that the sickness came not from "under the ground" but from "heaven." It was the will of God, and the demons were merely fulfilling the role of executioners. "We have descended through seven firmaments, we are from heaven," declared the demons, desperately trying to prevent Wazana from crossing the girl's threshold. "Do not enter, Ya'aqov," they cautioned, "if you do, you will die in her place. We must take her because she slew our children." But, Wazana, as we know, was deaf to their warnings, and continued on his fateful way across the threshold of the room.

Several people maintained that Rabbi Ya'aqov was forbidden to interfere in this case since the demons the girl had killed belonged to a special breed over which he had no control. One informant claimed that Wazana was aware of such an eventuality and had considered its implications. Thus, the informant claimed, when asked to heal the sheikh's daughter he replied, "I will go to her; if she is sick because of the demonic people I lived with, I will be able to heal her, if not, I cannot promise anything." When he crossed the threshold to the sickroom, the demon inhabiting her body addressed him through her mouth: "Wazana, we are not the same kind that you lived with. Know that if you enter, it is at your own risk. Beware."

Another informant couched the demons' stance and warning in political terms: "Let us suppose you are the United States, and you've got seven hundred million [people]. They belong to you. We are the Soviet Union and we don't belong to you. We are not the people you rule over. Beware of us. This girl killed one of our kind, we will avenge ourselves on her. We must take her soul. If you choose to fight us, it will cost you dearly." The clear unequivocality of the demonic interdiction tells us that even a healer of Rabbi Ya'aqov's stature was not omnipotent: his activities were proscribed by certain constraints, few though they might be. There were demonic legions outside his sphere of influence, and he was not entitled to meddle in their affairs.

Wazana's response to the demonic threats was confident, intransigent, and presumptuous. He answered their final warning: "I will save this girl—no matter the cost. If you do not leave her in a few seconds, I will set fire to this cloth and burn the whole lot of you."[1] When the demons explained that "the girl's sickness was from heaven," and not from under the ground, his insolent reply was, "Even if it comes from higher still, I must save her, I am not afraid." When the demons cautioned him, saying, "You are not one of us, we are not your kin, you do not rule us," he ignored them, "continued writing" (preparing the amulet), and drove the demon out of the sick girl's body.

The repeated use of expressions denoting entry and exit, plus the positioning of the confrontation between Wazana and the demons on the threshold of the girl's sickroom, seem natural to this event, the purpose of which was to force out demons who had penetrated the human's body, in order to drive them away and send them back whence they came. At the same time, these phrases focus attention on the quintessential problem in this particular case: transgressing boundaries and invading unauthorized territory.

The moment the demon (or demons) were exorcised from the girl's body, her recovery came swift and complete, to the extent that Rabbi Yitḥak Peḥima reported catching sight of her that very evening returning from the river in the company of the village girls, a large jar on her shoulder. According to versions which designated the girl's sickness as *tsira* (external demonic attack), as opposed to possession, she needed to place the amulet Wazana had prepared in the Arab cemetery, next to a Muslim grave. Having done this, she was miraculously cured.

Healing the sheikh's daughter is therefore the most impressive evidence of Wazana's healing powers: he restores life to a mortally sick and doomed individual. However, even Wazana could not remain wholly unruffled by the demons' threats. Ḥana Buskila, a young girl already married to his nephew at the time of Wazana's death, recalls the state of stress Wazana appeared to be in on his return from healing the girl. According to Ḥana, the girl was seven months pregnant when her father summoned Rabbi Ya'aqov:

> He came to me and said, "Ḥana, make me a cup of tea."
> I made it for him and he said, "Go and see her, someone must die today." I went and saw her. She had given birth to a dead baby. I went back to him and said, "Rabbi Ya'aqov, she gave birth to a baby that died." He sighed deeply and said, "So be it, now bring me *arak* and something to eat." The poor man ate while holding his head in his hand. "Come here," he said to me, "I will tell you what I did today. . . . The Arab gave me eight thousand lira because she was going to die. They warned me someone must die today. Now her son is dead and there has been atonement."

If the thought ever crossed Rabbi Ya'aqov's mind that the infant's death might save him from the demons' wrath, then the events of that Friday afternoon on the winding road into Agouim would have told him that healing the girl was no more than an illusory victory—the opening scene in the run-up to his death. Many of the residents of Agouim could describe these events in detail, providing notes of personal involvement, as though they had witnessed or actively participated in the proceedings. For example, Yitzḥak Elmaliakh, a trader from Agouim, recounted that Rabbi Ya'aqov sat with him in his shop by the main road that Friday before taking his leave and climbing the hill to the village. From the doorway of his store Elmaliakh watched Rabbi Ya'aqov halt abruptly on the bend next to the Muslim cemetery, then glance back as if searching for something. "He didn't see anyone, so he sat down, and thought and thought. In the end he went home." Some described this scene from different vantage points in the village. Rabbi Yitzḥak Peḥima claimed to have accompanied Wazana when he cured the Arab girl, and to have been at Wazana's side for that last walk into the village.

> On Friday when his death was near, I went down with
> him to the main road. He bought three candles for the syn-
> agogue [according to more down-to-earth versions, Wazana
> bought either cigarettes or *arak*]. There is a path leading up the
> mountain, and I climbed up with him. Suddenly he went like
> this [cupped his ear, as if listening], and looked back. He asked
> me, "Do you hear anything?" I said, "I don't hear anything."
> He said, "There's something wrong with me today, I don't
> know what it is." The sweat poured out of him like a stream,
> and he kept wiping it, but it kept on pouring.

Only later Peḥima, Elmaliakh, and the rest of the watchers learned that Rabbi Ya'aqov heard a voice calling out his name from the Muslim cemetery. In traditional Morocco it was held that disappearing, disembodied voices—especially those originating from cemeteries (favored demon haunts)—belonged to demons.[2] Wazana himself, who was closer than anyone to "those from under the ground," once explained to the Yifrakh family when visiting their home in Timjdut that if something invisible ever called their name, "You mustn't say yes; you mustn't answer, until you hear it call three times. After the third time, they won't do anything." Yet, Wazana himself, who knew better than anyone else how to behave in such a situation, could not resist answering, and responded to the call hastily. When his answer was ignored he understood that he was doomed. During his final hours, he expressed his sense of impending doom in a number of ways. Perhaps the most poignant of all was his short conversation with Asher Azoulai, then a child of three or four, whose family lived close to Wazana. Due to the insufferably hot summer, people used to lie outside on the roof, where sleep came more easily in the cool night air. The sociable Wazana used to tease young Asher and chat with him before sleep overtook them on their adjacent roofs. That Friday however, when the child struck up conversation with Rabbi Ya'aqov, Wazana lay silent for a long time without answering. According to a neighbor who overheard, he finally whispered, "Asher, the story is over, go to sleep."

The transformation that took place in Wazana during his final hours was most noticed by Makhluf and Aisha Ben-Ḥayim, with whom he lived in Agouim. As noted earlier, the relationship between Ben-Ḥayim and Rabbi Ya'aqov was a long and emotional one: "The Wazana family helped my family from time immemorial," noted Makhluf. When Makhluf's father had no male children for many years, Rabbi Avraham Wazana blessed him, and Makhluf himself was born—the only boy in a family of four girls. We have related the story of how Rabbi Ya'aqov helped Makhluf's wife Aisha, whose seven babies died before their first birthdays, by performing *istinzal* and summoning the she-demon responsible for their deaths. After compensating the she-demon with some boiled eggs, Aisha's subsequent children all survived. When Aisha gave birth after the *istinzal* ceremony, Wazana joined the Ben-Ḥayim household, living with his friends for the last eighteen months of his life. Makhluf clearly recalls that Rabbi Ya'aqov ordered Aisha to wean the son born as a result of his intervention because she was pregnant once more. At exactly that time, Wazana was working on the roads which made his hair show signs of gray, and he was called by the sheikh to heal his daughter. His death followed eight days after these events.

According to Makhluf, during Wazana's final hours he completely changed: his memory became unreliable, and he dropped things. Furthermore, he became fearful that robbers were coming to steal from him and begged not to be left alone. The Makhlufs therefore offered him a bed in the corner of the room where the family slept. Because of his condition, he missed the Sabbath services in the synagogue. "I am unwell today," he told his kinswoman, Ḥana Buskila, "I feel I am in another world." All of her efforts to discover what had happened to him were in vain. He kept to his bed, where Makhluf nursed him. Sweat gushed from his body. His strong nerve, the foundation of his reputation, deserted him completely, leaving him overwhelmed by a rising tide of dread and terror.

At first, Wazana refused to accept his fate. He asked his friends, the healers Rabbi Makhluf Biton and Rabbi Yitzhak Peḥima, to come to his bedside, and even tried dictating some healing formulae. It was commonly held by the informants that both these healers were also victims of demonic vengeance for trying to cure Rabbi Ya'aqov. Rabbi Makhluf Biton died within a year, and Rabbi Yitzhak became blind in one eye. Even Wazana's last, desperate attempt to heal himself failed: "He managed to get to his room, and picked up his pen, but he couldn't hold it, and it dropped from his hand. He said: 'If I could just write one letter, I could be in control (of the demons).' But he could not write even one letter. They already had him." After this abortive attempt, Wazana seems to have accepted his fate, and struggled no further. His former neighbors reported hearing him muttering feverishly in the darkness to unseen beings. Some conjectured that this was when he took his leave of his demonic spouse and children.

Wazana died on 27th of the month of Tammuz, in the hours between Friday and Saturday, in fact, during the Three Weeks (Bein Hametsarim).[3] Before drawing his final breath sometime between three or four in the morning, he let out three blood-curdling screams that could be heard from one end of the village to another. His shrieks, reminiscent of "an animal being slaughtered," pierced the dreams of the people of Agouim lying asleep on their roofs. They ran to him, only to discover his lifeless body sprawled across the floor. Blood was spurting from his throat, spattering the whole room.[4]

The powerful impact of these events on the Jews of Agouim can be measured by the story that reached the ears of one informant from Tamzersht: "The neighbors heard him screaming the loudest sound you have ever heard: 'AAAAGGGHHH' [he demonstrated], three times, like that. They went in, and found him like a burned body, like he had been hit by a bomb. They found his throat completely burned." All who knew Wazana were convinced that his death was caused by the demons he had defied.[5] "If you betray them, they get you," was the popular verdict.

Due to the fact that Wazana died between Friday night and Saturday morning and could therefore only be buried on Sunday (according to Jewish law, burial is forbidden on the Sabbath), his blood-soaked room filled with a ghastly stench, and the swollen, fetid body stank terribly. In the burning heat of the end of August, his friends from Agouim bore his heavy corpse—he was, as we know, a tall, well-built man—up the steep hillside to the village cemetery where they buried him. Although none of the informants had returned to their former home in Morocco, they nevertheless assured me that Wazana's grave is dutifully tended by a Berber woman he once cured of childlessness by removing a spell.[6]

Some informants were inclined to deduce lessons of distinctly moral nature from the circumstances of Rabbi Ya'aqov's death. One popular lesson related to a person's prescribed place within the universal scheme and the dire consequences of deviating from it. Expressions such as "they set limits for him," or "they gave him a limit and he crossed it," were frequently voiced. Whether implicitly or explicitly stated, these informants see the events surrounding Wazana's death as a punishment for crossing the red line and trespassing on forbidden territory. We have already noted the recurrent use of such phrases as "going into," "leaving," "do not enter," "keep out," and also the demarcation line of the threshold to the house where the demons tried to prevent Wazana from entering.

Not unrelated to this is the way some informants portrayed the risk of a too great proximity to the demons' menacing world. Their conclusions were unequivocal. "Whoever plays games with snakes, gets bitten in the end," said Rabbi Yitzhak Pehima, while someone else compared Wazana's intimacy with the demons to "playing with fire." Apart from the obvious risks involved in messing with snakes or fire, these are images particularly associated with demons. Demons often disguise themselves as snakes, and we have seen the snake motif appear in the story of the sheikh's daughter who, by killing the demons disguised as snakes, sparked off the train of events which ultimately cost Wazana his life. Demons are attracted to fire, and, according to one explanation, fire is one of the elements

Author with a piece of broken tombstone inscribed with the word, *Tammuz* (Wazana's month of death), in the ruined Jewish cemetery in Agouim, September 1993

from which they are formed. One informant who discussed the problem of having too close an association with demons offered an interesting analogy taken from family life: "If a wife betrays her husband, he must divorce her. You betray them [the demons], they do away with you." It is interesting that in this analogy, the husband, that is, the man, represents the demons, while the wife stands for the men, who, like Wazana, consort with the demons. In Wazana's case the complete reverse is true, since he, the male, took the she-demon for a wife. Does the reversal implicit in this analogy allude to the "femininity" of the men who preferred a wife from "under the ground" to a normal, human woman? This question will be discussed shortly.

Another object lesson Wazana's acquaintances considered as they related the story of his death concerns the relationship with neighbors "above the ground"—the Muslim Arabs and Berbers among whom the Jews lived. The informants were clearly aware that the chain of events leading to Wazana's tragic death was set in motion when he healed the sheikh's daughter against the demons' express wish. The possibility that he had been coerced into healing the girl was never explicitly raised. The opposite in fact was true: all versions highlighted Wazana's enthusiasm and determination to carry out this act. It should be recalled, however, that in the past, Rabbi Ya'aqov had been forced to treat the sheikh of Talouine's son (resulting in his unfortunate absence from home at the time of his mother's death). In recounting the case of the sheikh's daughter, some informants implied that the generous reward, "the bribe," offered him by the girl's father was a form of pressure. The story of Wazana thus seems to contain a lesson on the perils of being too intimate with either the demonic world or the surrounding Muslim environment. These dangers are embodied in the phrasing used in some stories, in which a twofold explanation for Wazana's death is offered: that "the demons slaughtered him at night," and that "the Arab girl killed him."

Indeed, the inversion in the story of Wazana's demise, whereby the sheikh's daughter "arose from her sickbed and was restored to health, while Wazana became sick and died," is greatly emphasized in the tales. The reverse symmetry is highlighted both in the moral issue of retribution and restoration of balance embedded in the core of the plot (the death of the demonic children cannot be ignored, therefore, their killer or the girl's savior must forfeit his life: "someone must die"), and in the popular Moroccan belief in "affliction transference."[7] The possibility that the sheikh's daughter "transferred" her affliction to Rabbi Ya'aqov is especially appealing in the light of the promise by the demon possessing her that he would avenge himself on the healer for expelling him. This would mean that the demon who attacked her was also the one who dealt Rabbi Ya'aqov the mortal blow. Even if the sheikh's daughter was not afflicted by *aslai* (possession), in which case Wazana certainly did not exorcise the attacking demon from her body, the option of affliction transference remains valid. One version of the healing mentions that the girl recovered after throwing the charm Wazana had written for her into the Muslim cemetery in Agouim. Presumably this charm was designed to attack the demon responsible for her disorder, who resided in the cemetery. Indeed, the disappearing voice heard by Wazana at the bend in the road, which everyone regards as signaling his doom, came from that very cemetery.

A number of Wazana's friends, keen to mold his figure along the lines of the family *tsaddiqim* who had preceded him, minimized the extent of his association with the Arabs. They chose to emphasize Wazana's devotion to his calling, which led him to sacrifice his life for the Arab girl. This picture of courageous self-sacrifice emerged, for example, in the discussion that took place at the home of David Ben-Ḥamo in Atseret, in which many of the family, young and old alike, participated. David recalled: "She [the Arab girl] killed him, because he was forbidden to heal her." A neighbor added: "He was forbidden to do it, but he was prepared to sacrifice his life to save her life." "And did he save her?" queried David's wide-eyed, young grandson, "Yes," answered the family in chorus, "and that is why he died."

The presence and personal involvement of the informants are more conspicuous in the story of Wazana's death than in any other event of the healer's life. It appears that dozens of eyes followed his progress that Friday, documenting each step on his final journey. Rabbi Yitzhak Pehima accompanied him to the sheikh's home, and is at his side when Wazana heard the voice calling his name. In the evening, when Pehima came to supper with him, bringing with him an ox liver from the slaughterhouse, he found him confined to bed, his condition critical. Yitzhak Elmaliakh and other Agouim store owners observed his last walk to the village. Makhluf Ben-Hayim nursed him on his deathbed at home, and Hana Buskila, Wazana's kinswoman, did the same. Other Agouim residents recall emotion-laden details connected with the events of that fateful Friday (we have noted already the farewell exchange with the neighbors' young son, Asher). Even people whose homes lay far from Agouim claim to have been in the area prior to his death. His kinsmen Ya'aqov and Shaul Wazana, from far-off Ouarzazate, met him near the shrine of Rabbi David u-Moshe (outside Agouim), and heard the story of healing the sheikh's daughter from his own lips. It seems that all roads led to Agouim in those late summer days. All were gathered there, watching in wonder and fascination as the events of Rabbi Ya'aqov's death unfolded. The pervasive and profound sense of identification with the figure they describe is most evident in the dramatic and distressful descriptions of his death. Involvement draws them closer to the events, and by amplifying the

Shrine of Rabbi David u-Moshe near Agouim (Western High Atlas Mountains)

details with personal, subjective volume, an affective note of participation is added. Perhaps we should see this as a fantasy wish on the part of the informants, who, when all is said and done, are merely background figures, extras in the spectacular plot they have laid out before us. They appear anxious to immortalize their own place in the story of Wazana's life, to push forward onto center stage, which, for one last transitory moment, is lit, before the curtain falls on the story of Wazana's life.

14

"Nothing of His Remains"

"**H**e was an enigma, everything about him was mysterious," asserted Wazana's distant kinsman, Rabbi Shmuel Suissa. This eloquent, educated informant was doubtlessly referring to Rabbi Ya'aqov's unusual lifestyle, the wondrous feats he routinely performed, and his impressive capacity to heal people. Greatly contributing to the riddle that these elements entail, and to the mythical halo surrounding the figure of Wazana, is the fact that memories of him lack any concrete basis linking him to reality. "Nothing of his remains. He left nothing behind," his Moroccan friends declare wistfully.

The lack of momentoes is best explained by the fact that material possession was a low priority for Wazana, and his belongings were commensurably few and poor. However, there were certain articles that he valued beyond all others: the *bordo* that belonged to his father, and his mother's robe from which he was never parted, and the copper ring, the magic mirror, and the amber beads—the "tools" of his trade. And what happened to his perfectly white clothes whose cleanliness signified so much in his life: the *jellaba,* the *chamir,* the *farajiya* and the *salam,*[1] and the red *tarboosh* he invariably wore, into whose lining, rumor had it, were sewn amulets to protect the wearer from harm? And what became of his famed healing books—those of his forefathers and the ones he acquired deviously from the Muslim wise men—the most prized of which remained with Wazana so much that "he slept with it, ate with it," and kept it on him [under his clothes] so that no one would take it?

According to several informants, all these vanished into thin air because Wazana had no wife, children, or brothers to claim his property. It has been noted that his room was looted when he died, whether out of greed or people's belief that they would be blessed by possession of these objects. Makhluf Ben-Ḥayim, in whose house Wazana lived throughout his stay in Agouim, insists that he took none of the deceased's belongings. Whatever he found he handed over to Wazana's nephew, Ya'aqov Buskila of Agouim, who died in Be'er Sheva in the early 1990s. However, the response of Buskila's widow to questions regarding Wazana's property was unequivocal: "Nothing; not a trace of anything that belonged to him!" Her brother added: "If there were brothers, to sit *shivah* [seven days of ritual mourning] for him, they would have kept something." He does not rule out, however, the possibility that the disappearance of Wazana's personal effects was divinely orchestrated, either as a means of ensuring that they did not fall into unworthy hands, or that this was Wazana's punishment for abusing the powers he was blessed with.

Wazana's friends were especially intrigued by the disappearance of his books. They are certain that some books reached Israel and there are various theories explaining their whereabouts. The prime suspects are three rabbi-healers, Wazana's former associates, whose denials of guilt are scoffed at. The latent potential of these volumes continues to fire the imaginations of informants.

Above all, the "matter of his pictures" deepens the blur that Wazana left behind. As one informant put it, "No pictures of him. Not one. When someone who had pictures of him went to look for them, he suddenly couldn't find them. The pictures vanished. No one knows who took them. Finished. Nothing. Nothing at all was left, nothing."

Without photographs or any kind of tangible evidence, the figure of Wazana becomes increasingly hazy as it is gnawed by the passage of the years and kneaded into shapes by the informants' fantasies and needs. That Wazana had no heir heightens the sense of loss, the finality of it all. "Rabbi Avraham had twelve children. All of them died. He was the only one left. It is a sad thing for the family. Everyone in that family died, may God have mercy on them," bemoaned Rabbi Shalom of Agouim. Thus a tragic veil falls on the Wazana family of Assarag, as if a sentence had been passed that no descendants would carry the memory onward through time. Even their property was destined to vanish without a trace, leaving only the memory that has become legend.

15

Wazana in Israel

More than a generation has passed since Wazana died. The period immediately after his death marked the onset of a massive wave of emigration from Morocco to Israel, which finally drew the curtain on Jewish life in the Atlas Mountains. Wazana's circle found a new reality, a very harsh one, awaiting them in their new home. Some fared better than others, but by now all are immersed in life in Israel of the present. Behind them, entombed in another place, in another time, Wazana is extremely remote from the here and now. Nonetheless, despite the expanse of time and space, Wazana's figure lives on with vivid intensity in the memories of many of his former acquaintances. They often hark back to him, in the *moshav* settlements or development towns where they now reside, disturbed by his unconventional personality, wistful at the loss of his healing powers. Some are sure that he continues to help them in times of troubles even today—a belief reinforced by the fact that he appears regularly in their dreams. At least three people commemorate the anniversary of his death with a festive meal (*se'udah*). It is doubtful whether this book would have seen the light of day if Wazana had less prominence in the current lives of the informants.

Some of his acquaintances ponder what would have happened if Wazana had lived to emigrate to Israel. A few like to dwell on the special position he could have enjoyed, drawing the obvious comparison with the Abu-Ḥatseras and their most popular scion in Israel: "If he lived in Israel, he would have been like the Baba Sali [Rabbi Yisrael Abu-Ḥatsera]." However, most prefer fantasizing about his marvelous powers and their usefulness. Time has in no way reduced these powers; on the contrary, they have been considerably magnified. His friends believe he would have been

121

able to cure any disease, including cancer. His powers of divination could have been harnessed to Israel's internal security needs, "if he had joined the police, or the security services, or the Department of Investigations," or alternatively to the foreign security services, where he could have helped eliminate the Arab threat. Interviewees referred to Wazana's power to transport people from place to place instantaneously, suggesting he could have seized Arafat and thus ended Palestinian terrorism. As we have seen, many insisted that all of Wazana's possessions and healing apparatus had disappeared after his death. Nevertheless, against such claims that "nothing of his was left," rumors abound that several of Wazana's books were somehow brought to Israel. The object of such rumors is the tiny clique of rabbi-healers intimately associated with Wazana in Morocco. These individuals, however, deny all knowledge of the books. Only two of them, Rabbi Yitzhak Pehima and Rabbi Shalom Ben-Hamo, reluctantly and with great protestation, semi-acknowledged that they indeed had something once belonging to Wazana, but refused to divulge any more than that. Rabbi Yitzhak maintains that he does not use Wazana's book since "the writing is smudged" and illegible. Nevertheless, a patient of his reported that when seized by anxiety attacks following a grenade explosion at her *moshav* which claimed several lives, Rabbi Yitzhak offered her "Wazana's book" to sleep with at night. At first, Rabbi Shalom claimed that Wazana's book was held by another healer, Rabbi Moshe Tubul, of Hadera. He then asserted that "Pehima had taken the books and copied from them day and night, and after that he was attacked, and became so scared he would not use it any more." Finally he confessed that he too had such a book: "I only use it in the worst cases [as a last resort], I never take it out; it is a holy book and I am afraid of it." According to his statement, he has the book concealed nearby in his old mother's house, buried under her clothes, to lower the risk of thieves breaking into his home to steal it. The benefits of owning Wazana's books are so obvious that we need to treat this point very cautiously.[1] However, even if we accept that some books reached Israel, it is clear from the admissions of those involved that they are hardly ever used, either out of concern for being injured or from lack of knowledge as to how to apply them.

Most informants claiming that Wazana helped them in Israel made no reference to his books since the nature of the late Rabbi Ya'aqov's intervention in their lives has been unmediated and instantaneous. Immediately after his death in Morocco, the prototype of his "afterlife assistance" was already in evidence: "He had a kinsman. . . . He always promised that his kinsman's wife would become pregnant, but the couple had no children before he died. Then Wazana died suddenly and there was no time to arrange this for them. So when he died he came to the woman in a dream and told her: 'Get up and take the plate in the corner, there is writing on it,' he instructed her what to do with it, and she had a baby boy she called Ya'aqov in his honor."

Wazana's apparitions in friends and acquaintances' dreams enables them to reap the benefit of his amazing powers even after death. It is thus hardly surprising that we heard of such dreams mostly from informants who had benefited considerably from Wazana's assistance in the past. For them, his regular nightly appearances offer some compensation for the void in their lives left by his sudden death. For example, during Wazana's life, Makhluf and Aisha Ben-Ḥayim, his hosts in Agouim, tended to seek his help whenever problems arose, in the same way Makhluf's parents had sought the blessing of Rabbi Ya'aqov's father Rabbi Avraham. Because the advent of their first children was predicated on Wazana's intervention, after the healer's death the Ben-Ḥayims' feared no more children would be born. However, Rabbi Ya'aqov's appearance in Aisha's dream dispelled this concern. According to Makhluf, Wazana appeared to his wife disguised as a snake,[2] which encircled her body three times, and asked her with each twist: "What are you afraid of? Maybe you have got a son you can name Ya'aqov." A boy, the last of the couple's children, was indeed born a year later, and naturally was named Ya'aqov. Several other young men in Israel also bear Rabbi Ya'aqov's name.

David and Rachel Ben-Ḥamo of *moshav* Atseret, and Masouda Buskila, Wazana's kinswoman from Be'er Sheva, all scrupulously celebrate Wazana's memory with a festive meal on his death anniversary. Their stories provide clear evidence that Wazana's place in their lives is no less after death than it was in life.

David first came to Wazana for help after a seven-year-long childless marriage, determined to divorce his wife should the healer's intervention

Shrine of Baba Sali in Netivot, Israel

Chapter 15

prove unsuccessful. The marriage was saved when Wazana removed the spell (*tkaf*) producing barrenness in Rachel, David's wife. The child born as a result, Reuven, was portrayed as a short-tempered, nervy boy, because "he was born by force." According to Reuven's young wife, when Reuven was born Wazana held him in his arms, lifted him up, and announced to his mother, "This boy is half yours and half mine." The informant explained this declaration of paternity as reference to the fact that "he had no children of his own, only under the ground." Rabbi Ya'aqov then released Rachel from the clutches of an evil spirit illness (*aslai*) that had affected her on and off throughout her marriage. In light of this, it is hardly surprising that a powerful bond formed between the young woman and the celebrated healer: "They were like two fingers on the same hand," said Rachel's daughter-in-law; Rachel rejoining, "I helped him and did his laundry; he loved me like a daughter. He always reassured me by saying, 'Don't worry, I will guard you and your children, nothing bad will ever happen to you.' If I went to the stream, for example, to wash clothes, he would throw me apples or tangerines."

When Rabbi Ya'aqov died, Rachel began commemorating the anniversary of his death with a festive meal, first in Agouim, and later when she moved to Marrakech. Prior to the family's emigration to Israel in the early 1960s, Wazana appeared in Rachel's dream, beseeching her to continue celebrating his *hillula* in the new country. The couple indeed complied with this wish, and were quickly rewarded. They are convinced that Rabbi Ya'aqov saved both them and their children from all kinds of difficult and strange situations. In particular, they highlight the way Wazana helped Reuven, the son born as a result of his intervention. One night during Reuven's army service as a driver, he was involved in a serious accident on the road to Be'er Sheva. That same night, Rabbi Ya'aqov appeared, lamp in hand, in Rachel's dream and called out her name. Aghast, the woman screamed, "But Wazana, you are dead!" The healer ignored this, and informed her that he had just saved her son from a fatal accident. He ordered her to purchase a candle similar to the one in his hand and to donate it to the synagogue in gratitude to him for saving her son's life. At precisely that time, Reuven was struggling to free himself from the twisted car wreckage. Moments earlier, as the wheel went out of control he had screamed Rabbi Ya'aqov's name, and seen the healer appear before his eyes. On arriving at the scene, the police were amazed to discover Reuven, alive and well, waiting near the debris of his car.

Wazana continued keeping an eye on Reuven, "his child," even after his army service ended. When the young man's romance threatened to break up after the girl he loved became more interested in another man, Rabbi Ya'aqov appeared in her dream, informing her that she was under a spell commissioned by Reuven's rival. On learning this, the girl came to her senses and married Reuven. These visitations by Wazana in the guise of savior at important crossroads in Reuven's life, starting with his birth, and ending in his marriage, have earned him the place of patron saint of the young man and his family. Indeed, Wazana is the family *tsaddiq* for all the Ben-Ḥamos, and all turn to him for help. "Whenever I have a problem—if the children are sick or things like that—I ask him to help me and he does instantly," said Reuven's mother, Rachel. Even the younger, Israeli-born generation, who never knew Rabbi Ya'aqov, enjoys his protection. For example, one of Rachel's daughters-in-law told the story of how her four-year-old daughter had been seriously injured in the head after tumbling from a great height and lay comatose for three months in the hospital. One Friday, she recalled, Rachel lit a candle for Wazana, and prayed to him for help. That night Wazana visited her in a dream, promising to restore her granddaughter to health. His promise was fulfilled, and the child recovered within a short time.

Children in the family are intimately familiar with Rabbi Ya'aqov. "We don't know Rabbi David u-Moshe," said one girl, "but Wazana?— someone who lives with you, who used to live with our parents. Sometimes we all gather for the festivals and you hear about him. It's a family experience. On the ninth of Av we hold a memorial service at home in his honor." Another girl added, "We truly believe. Our parents brought us up that way." Indeed, the name Wazana is regularly heard on the family's lips: "If you forget something, you must say 'Rabbi Ya'aqov Wazána' near the candles and whatever you lost will come to you. . . . We ask his help all the time." When Reuven fills in his lottery coupon he speaks the *tsaddiq's* name: "They taught us in the family, its just like with the Baba Sali."

The young people in the family grumble sometimes at being drafted to help in preparations for the *hillula*. Their groans are silenced, however, by their mother's timeworn rejoinder: "If not for him, you wouldn't be here [would not have been born]. How come we're here? Because of Wazana." The feeling among members of the family that their very existence is owed to Rabbi Ya'aqov makes him a basic and natural part in their lives.

Masouda Buskila is someone else who has Wazana to thank for her life. It will be recalled that Wazana fought grimly to restore her to life when the rest of the village gave her up for dead and began preparing her body for burial. A number of years after that incident, when Masouda was still a young woman, her leg became infected when a sharp splinter of wood pierced it and could not be removed. Wazana effortlessly removed the splinter, saving her limb from threatened amputation. When her infant son lay dying, once again it was Wazana who cured him. Given such a history, it is no wonder that Wazana's death failed to terminate his connection with Masouda. Masouda is more than grateful for all Wazana's efforts on her behalf and regards Rabbi Ya'aqov as a *tsaddiq*: "He raised me, he saved me, he is a *tsaddiq*, he saves me time and again. . . . I would have died

Chapter 15

forty years ago if not for him. . . . Nobody is like Rabbi Ya'aqov. No one in the world, He gave me back my life!"

An ongoing dialogue exists between the two, the climactics of which are no less powerful than the story of Wazana saving Masouda's life back in Morocco. Wazana regularly appears in her dreams to offer advice and assistance: if necessary he chides her. When Masouda dedicated a Torah scroll in memory of a son who died while on military reserve duty, she needed to limit the scope of Rabbi Ya'aqov's feast, due to the high cost entailed in sponsoring the scroll. That year the couple arranged for a modest meal to be held in Wazana's honor at their local synagogue, and not, as was customary, in the comfort of their own home: "I baked just four *ḥallot* [braided loaves], and roasted two chickens, there was a bottle of *arak,* four bottles of juice, a few apples and some bananas," listed Masouda candidly. However, it was not just the modesty of the meal, but the guests' behavior, that detracted from the festive atmosphere: "They didn't bother with grace before meals, simply didn't bother, they did this [she mimed snatching and gobbling food], they just grabbed whatever they could!" The following night Wazana visited Masouda. She was overjoyed: "Just yesterday, Rabbi Ya'aqov I made your feast." Wazana scowled at her, "You made me nothing!" Shocked, Masouda sought advice from a well known rabbi, who told her to make the meal at home in the future— never again in the synagogue.

Perhaps the tiny amount spent on the feast is a reflection of Masouda's repressed feelings of bitterness toward Rabbi Ya'aqov for failing to safeguard her son. An allusion to her trauma is evident from the forthright question she put to Wazana when he reappeared in another dream: "Rabbi Ya'aqov, why did you love Felix [the son Wazana saved in infancy], and not Rephael [the son who died while on military duty]?" Wazana's rejoinder, however, dispelled all her doubts: "Is that what you think? Were it not for my protection, that boy would have had no life at all." In other words, Rabbi Ya'aqov told her that he had lengthened the life of Rephael, who should have died at birth. Whatever the case, Masouda's manner of relating to Wazana testifies to the personal quality of the connection between them, and to the moral responsibility ascribed to him as the family saint ("family" in every sense of the word, since Masouda and Rabbi Ya'aqov were related). This responsibility reached its peak one Lag Ba'Omer night in the mid-1980s when, over forty years after he rescued her from the clutches of the burial party, Rabbi Ya'aqov again rescued Masouda from death.

One evening, Masouda's husband was at the local synagogue, attending a *hillula* honoring Rabbi Shimon Bar-Yoḥai. Their youngest daughter and a grandchild were in the house, but they too left for the synagogue, leaving her all alone. At one in the morning Masouda experienced a revelation:

126

I went like this [she mimed astonishment], it was the *tsaddiq* coming. I saw him with my own eyes—Rabbi Ya'aqov. He told me: "If you don't want to die, don't answer the door. Don't open it. Three people will come." I saw him in a dream or maybe not in a dream, I don't really know. He came and said to me: "Get out of bed," so I got up. Soon somebody knocked at the door. Thieves—three men. I asked, "Who's there?" He answered, "Your brother." I said, "Reuven? Braham? David?" He said, "Your brother." I said, "Look Reuven, I won't open the door. I am nearly dead. When I saw the *tsaddiq,* my hands, my feet, my whole body went dead." Then he said to me, "Open the door!" I said, "I won't open it, go to David the neighbor, sleep there, I'm sick, I can't even lift myself up."

Then I said to myself, "How could I say to my brother I won't open the door for him. How?" I got up and fell down— here [next to the door], again, I got up and fell down. Only my hand kept going to open it, but couldn't feel it, I couldn't open the door, there was no feeling. It still hurts me. So I was sitting by the door. There was a light. Then the thieves went away. They went into the religious people's apartment downstairs, my neighbors. Then they called the police, and the thieves ran away. They escaped into the next neighborhood. They got into a poor old man's house and killed him. Now they're in jail, for the rest of their lives.

In Assarag Wazana saved Masouda from the burial party; in Be'er Sheva he saved her from herself as she tried desperately to reach her front door to open it for someone pretending to be her brother but who was in fact a dangerous thief. To save her, Rabbi Ya'aqov struck her to the ground, paralyzed. The dramatic struggle culminates with Masouda prostrate, shocked, and exhausted, at the doorway as the robbers, their plans thwarted, ran off and took another person's life. The trauma scarred Masouda, "I was sick for maybe three months, I couldn't speak, why, because I saw the *tsaddiq.* It was hard. Very hard, so hard." However, this incident only intensified the bond between Masouda and Wazana. "Whenever something is about to happen to me, he comes to tell me. He must come. Rabbi Ya'aqov must tell me. He is my guardian."

For Makhluf Ben-Ḥayim, Rachel Ben-Ḥamo, Masouda Buskila, and others like them, the healer continues to be very near; actively protecting them and their loved ones. Despite the fact that Wazana belongs to an increasingly distant era of their lives, his figure is nonetheless engraved in their minds, present in their memories, alive in their dreams. However, we should bear in mind that very few people carry these intensely vivid memories of him. As we know, even in Morocco, Wazana was a distinctly local hero, his reputation hardly extending beyond the mountainous hinterlands of the south of the country. Within the Moroccan community in Israel too, Wazana's friends and admirers represent but a tiny minority. Even among the adherents of the Wazana family *tsaddiqim,* there are many who barely know of Rabbi Ya'aqov, who is in any case ranked far lower than figures such as Rabbi Avraham "the Great" or Rabbi David Wazana. We have seen that, generally speaking, the status of the Wazana family has deteriorated greatly in Israel, in stark contrast to the groundswell of adulation enveloping the Abu-Hatsera dynasty. When interviewed, the Wazana family insisted that in Morocco, "*ait* Wazana was the same as *ait* Abu-Hatsera, no difference," although they too are aware of the enormous discrepancy between the reputation of the two families in Israel. The main celebration honoring Rabbi Avraham "The Great," organized by his blind descendent, Shaul, in a hall in Natanya draws several hundred followers from all over the country. However, this event is dwarfed by the thronged *hillula* for Rabbi Yisrael Abu-Hatsera (Baba Sali) held in Netivot, and that of his brother, Rabbi Yitzhak (Baba Haki), in Ramle. Having said that, even the *hillula* in Natanya seems an impressive public event when compared with the modest family celebrations held in Rabbi Ya'aqov's name.

Each summer, toward the end of the month of Tammuz, the home in Atlit of Makhluf Ben-Hayim of Agouim, with whom Wazana spent the last part of his life, serves as the venue for a festive meal in the healer's honor. I attended such a feast and it was interesting to see that beside the family and their children, there were only seven guests including myself. Only two people, one formerly of Agouim, the other from the nearby village of Imini, had known Wazana in the old days. The ceremonial part of the evening preceding the meal was conducted by two rabbis—neither of whom knew the healer. In chorus, guests read portions of the mystical Book of the Zohar, the *kaddish* (mourning prayer) was declaimed in Wazana's memory, and the men said the evening prayers. Having completed the prayers, salads, alcoholic drinks, and soda were laid on the table, and a main course of beef, chicken, quiche, and rice was set before the guests. The meal was organized in two sittings: the guests ate their fill first, as the Ben-Hayim family, apart from Makhluf and a son-in-law, waited in an adjacent room, or busied themselves serving food. As the wine took effect, spirits rose and the level of laughter increased. However, I noted that Rabbi Ya'aqov, the sole reason for the feast in the first place, was conspicuously absent from the abundance of stories, learned discussions, and Torah tidbits that filled the air. Makhluf himself hardly spoke during the entire meal.

Less than two hours after their arrival the guests departed, the table was again set, and the family finally sat down to enjoy their meal. Makhluf's children, four sons and three daughters, all married, surrounded their elderly parents with their spouses and children. Wazana's presence was far more real during the second part of the evening. As noted, the birth of the Makhlufs' eldest son Yehuda came after Makhluf's previous seven children had died in infancy, following Rabbi Ya'aqov's intervention. Wazana had given Yehuda his blessing at birth, and the family believes that his spirit still abides with Yehuda. Sometimes, they say, he stuns them with his ability to predict the future and to locate missing objects. They are certain that Rabbi Ya'aqov endowed him with these powers in his blessing. As noted, the Makhluf's youngest son Ya'aqov was named after Wazana. According to Makhluf and Aisha, they both recovered from serious illnesses after asking Wazana to cure them in order to organize his feast in time. Indeed, Aisha's movements still bore the signs of the stroke from which she was slowly convalescing. "He came to see me in Carmel Hospital," she told me. "He said, 'Don't worry about anything,' and touched my body and my head [she indicated the places]. 'In two or three days you'll be back at home,' he said."

The meal in Atlit was the last time I participated in an event associated with my quest for material on Rabbi Ya'aqov. The picture that remained with me when I left the house truly captures Wazana's role of domestic *tsaddiq*. There was wrinkled, bearded Makhluf, beret on head, seated happy and proud in his armchair, his latest grandchild cradled in his arms. Surrounding him, the richness of his family—sons, daughters, sons-in-law, daughters-in-law, and their offspring. And the name of the baby he held so proudly—Ya'aqov of course!

16

The Song of the Sirens:
The Psychology of Wazana

The story of Rabbi Ya'aqov Wazana's life, through the eyes of the informants, illuminates a figure that even within the context of the traditional culture from which he sprang, appears highly anomalous. Can one reasonably expect to understand the psychological drives underlying Wazana's strange personality and peculiar lifestyle? Any answer seeking to assign Wazana some defined psychological typification will inevitably be fraught with problems. How can one possibly penetrate the psyche of a figure who is swathed in the mists of legends, and molded as much by the twists and turns of memory as by the reality of his life? However, while such questions obviously need to be addressed (and will be in the next chapter), the intriguing nature of Wazana's life makes it difficult to resist delving into the hidden recesses of his personality.

It is difficult to ignore Wazana's unique relationship with his parents as we search to understand what drove him and what lay behind his practically limitless healing powers? The roots of his attachment obviously stem from early childhood when, apart from a younger sister, he was the only child, all other siblings having died in infancy. His father's death at a young age, and the feelings of bereavement and helplessness generated by the sudden loss, were exacerbated when circumstances not only dictated his absence from his father's side at the hour of death, but kept him from both his father's funeral and burial as well. Naturally, Rabbi Ya'aqov's conviction that his father would have lived longer had he been there only aggravated his pain, perhaps even feeding the guilt sparked by his absence at this critical time. The sense that Rabbi Abraham's death left Wazana indelibly scarred is supported further by reports of his aversion toward Amassine, where his father died, and his steadfast refusal to set foot there. This apparent "phobia" appears even more significant in view of the courage and daring that generally characterized the healer.

The strongest expression of Wazana's inconsolable loss is the strange story of unearthing his father's grave. This story encapsulates the son's incapacity to accept the father's death, and his consequent desperate attempt to restore him to life. If this is indeed the wish behind this taboo act, it is presented through the narrative as an attainable goal, but though the unearthed body is miraculously complete and unravaged by time, Wazana's goal is ultimately unfulfilled. His father is left lying in his grave and Wazana remains agonized by the separation, his yearning unalleviated. The first inclination that his anguish and longing for reunification might be translated into the power to heal (we deal with this point later) appears in the story of Wazana's visit to the cemetery, when Rabbi Avraham, having awoken in his grave, grants his son the power to heal.

With his father's death, and his sister's marriage and departure from home, Wazana's mother, Esther, is the only close person in his life. On the point of the deep connection between mother and son, the informants were very clear. Here however, let us just reiterate that Wazana, who never established a home with a human spouse, preferred living with his mother until her death in his forties. Even when she died, Wazana stayed completely bound to her memory and was painfully bereft, as evidenced by the poignant daily ritual with her robe. The ritual, which has been described by a close friend, seems so very personal and laden with sorrow and longing, that we are impressed with a sense of having witnessed a rare, unmediated glimpse into the healer's inner world. At any rate, it is tempting to explain his long-term unmarried status as the result of a psychological inhibition arising from his incapacity to detach himself from his mother emotionally.

From the psychological point of view, it is interesting that the identical set of adverse circumstances that transformed the death of Wazana's father into such a painful episode recurs in the story of the mother's death three decades later, only this time with even greater impact. Again, informants report Wazana's absence from home at the time of his mother's death, and once again, their stories indicate a desperate longing for reunification after her death, and in short, a desire to restore her to life. Guilt associated with the death of a parent, which was more or less latent in the father's story, appears here in explicit form, at least in some of the stories, according to which Wazana was away indulging himself in the sheikh's home as his mother lay on her deathbed.

It seems that the stories of both deaths seek to emphasize the level of pain experienced by Wazana and his inability to accept the loss. His father's cane and mother's robe, the two concrete reminders of his parents that Wazana always kept at his side, are far more than objects compensating for their absence. They actually symbolize his inability to free himself from his parents' memory.[1] The stories of opening the graves to reveal the corpses, which may denote his fantasy of restoring them to life, is the ultimate expression of this. Does the unremitting pattern he exhibits of "going all the way," gazing at what is forbidden, retrieving the irretrievable, hold the key to understanding Wazana's unique modus operandi?

Indeed, it was the very "visible" and public expression of his divination and healing techniques that marked Wazana's uniqueness as a healer. He raised demons from the depths of the earth—in contrast to the parents underground he could not raise—and these mysterious, elusive beings became his closest allies and family. In this sense he was set apart even within the "demonic culture" of traditional Morocco, where the prevailing attitude toward demons was avoidance whenever possible (within the constraints dictated by the cultural perceptions of the behavior of the demonic world). Note that demons in Morocco were known as "the invisible," and people avoided uttering their name explicitly for fear of incurring their wrath.[2] Wazana's penchant for exposing that which is best left unseen and unexplored can also be seen in his actions against sorcerers. Of all the healers, only he dares to identify them, only he delivers the harmful materials they have concocted from Muslim graves where they are buried, to be destroyed.

This leads us, perhaps, closer to the psychological drives underpinning Rabbi Ya'aqov's healing powers. His extraordinary style, with its characteristic audacity, indefatigability, and firmness of mind, and his uncompromising pursuit of his objectives, was perhaps an outgrowth of his painfully hopeless effort "to heal" first his dead father, and then his dead mother, and bring them once more to life. These personal qualities enabled him to treat *almost* every kind of affliction, with complete disregard for the surrounding circumstances. In this sense it is highly significant that Wazana's rare failures involved patients who were fated to die. Apart from the remarkable case of his kinswoman Masouda Buskila, whom he delivers from the clutches of the grave diggers, the stories of his failures repeatedly indicate that even the greatest healer of them all was not omnipotent. Even he lacks the power to bridge the great divide separating the living from the dead. Translated into the language of yearning and desire, one might say that the ambition underlying his desire to heal—the fantasy of reviving his parents—was beyond Wazana's reach.

Considered against this background, the healing of the sheikh's daughter represents the dramatic climax of Wazana's life narrative. In this story he defies the demons, transgressing the only restriction imposed on his healing activities, and brings a condemned patient back to life. Thus, Wazana retroactively fulfills his lifelong ambition, and finally attains symbolic compensation for his beloved parents' deaths. His triumph is short-lived, however, as he forfeits his own life by restoring that of the sheikh's daughter. Besides the important matter of redressing the balance between the worlds that his death entails (see next chapter), there is also the sense that his life force begins to ebb the moment he fulfills his lifelong goal of compensating for his parents' death by restoring another human life.

Any psychological analysis of Wazana is incomplete without reference to his relationship with the demonic world. This, however, is not the place to discuss in any depth the significance of demons in traditional Moroccan society, since in this society the demonic world was regarded as a very real and primary aspect of everyday life. If we accept the premise that demons and sorcerers, as well as saints, as culturally constituted, could provide a mechanism that allowed individuals to mold and articulate their inchoate emotional experiences, then it would certainly be appropriate to question how these elements functioned in Wazana's life. What needs and desires was Wazana able to satisfy through his association with the demonic world?

A relatively straightforward answer would emphasize the power that domination of the demons was capable of bestowing. By their choice of healing as an occupation, people attracted to this vocation, whatever their personal motives, demonstrate a distinct need for power and control, since they naturally become the focus of great dependency on the part of those requiring their services. What is the origin of the powerful urge for control that drives certain people to train as healers? And could it be that a healing career offers compensation for some privation or loss during childhood? In Wazana's case, the premature loss of his father and the painful circumstances surrounding that event again come to the fore. The fact that it was his father who bequeathed him this pursuit immediately after his death, when Wazana first visited his grave, increases the likelihood that the choice of healing as a career was some sort of compensation for being deprived of his parent. It is worth reiterating that the association between the loss of a parent and the healing vocation is not unique to Wazana. Most of the Moroccan healers I found in Israel also lost their fathers at an early age.

Thus Wazana's excessive intimacy with the demonic world offered him a means of controlling his world and subordinating it to his will. If he indeed sought to compensate for the loss of his parents through the powers of his demonic servants, as argued above, then it is particularly significant that those powers resided in beings who, like his dead parents, were under the ground, but who, unlike his parents, he did have the power to bring to the surface. The correlation between recurring loss, especially of parents, and mystical experience involving the apparition of supernatural beings with whom a compensatory relationship is established, has been dealt with extensively in contemporary psychology literature.[3]

Chapter 16

Within the spectrum of Wazana's diverse interactions with the demonic world, the most arresting is his marriage to a she-demon. It is tempting to regard this strange relationship, which was uncommon even by
Moroccan standards, let alone among rabbi-healers, as connected to the
explanation above regarding Wazana's single status "above the ground."
On the one hand, he was incapable of detaching himself emotionally
from his mother and of forming a relationship with another woman; on
the other, he was subject to pressure, mainly from his mother, to settle
down and raise children. His ineffectuality in coping with these conflicting
pressures may have led him to choose the demonic option, an option that
looks to be "imaginary" from the extra-cultural perspective, but which is
nevertheless a viable, though perhaps marginal and unusual, alternative
in intra-cultural terms. The psychological profile of Muslim men of the
Moroccan Ḥamadsha sect, who are supposedly coerced into marriage by
she-demons, has been extensively documented by anthropologist Vincent
Crapanzano (1973, 1980). Crapanzano explains that the choice of a
demonic spouse, and the incumbent unmarried status in the human world,
denotes a response to a failure to live up to the typical male role required
in traditional Moroccan society. Marriage to a she-demon therefore provides an acceptable cultural outlet for men who cannot establish normal
relationships with women due to deep-seated feelings of inadequacy and
weakness, nourished perhaps by latent homosexual tendencies.

Of course, we will never know the truth behind Wazana's attachment
to his mother. Nevertheless, it is relevant to note the difference between
Wazana and the sect Crapanzano studied. Crapanzano's study took in a
specific group of socially inferior Muslim males who exist in a state of
miserable poverty on the margins of Moroccan society. In stark contrast
to the Ḥamadsha's personal and social plight, Rabbi Ya'aqov Wazana
was perceived by his peers as a courageous and respected individual.
There are abundant stories showing him radiating power, control, and
self-confidence in his work and emphasizing a behavior style that is
outstanding in its boldness. Even if Wazana and the Ḥamadsha share
similar emotional conflicts, Wazana's strategy for coping was more effective than theirs and shows plain evidence of compensation, or even
overcompensation. Thus, Wazana's healing exploits and extraordinary
lifestyle may be regarded as a vehicle used to convert his handicaps and
weaknesses into reservoirs of energy and strength.

With respect to the demonic factor, Wazana and the Ḥamadsha sect
differ in so far as the Ḥamadsha present themselves as victims forced into
marriage after falling prey to the seductive powers of the she-demons.
Wazana in contrast is portrayed by informants as actively, and of his
own initiative, seeking the union with a she-demon. Readers unfamiliar
with traditional Moroccan society will regard either behavior as denoting
emotional disturbance. However, from a culture-sensitive standpoint we

cannot but be impressed by Wazana's talent for exploiting the demonic re-lationship as a legitimate idiom for articulating his emotional distress and inner conflict. Similarly, his creativity in establishing a surrogate family—complete with demonic offspring—as an alternative to that he lost and the human family he failed to raise, can only be cause for admiration. Thus Wazana created for himself a unique and highly remarkable lifestyle that was culturally acceptable, and in many respects meritorious, despite its marginality (cf. Obeyesekere, 1981, 1990).

In this chapter we have attempted to present one interpretation of the riddle of Wazana's life, based on his yearning for his father, whom he lost at an early age, and his close attachment to his mother, which drove him to a union with a she-demon rather than a human spouse. We can perhaps see in the incident that immediately caused his death—his failure to keep silent and ignore the voice calling him on the bend in the road near the cemetery in Agouim—a significant life juncture, the confluence of all of the driving forces and desires that shaped and influenced his personality and behavior. His reckless response to the demonic voice demonstrates his undeviating loyalty to that unreserved, bold attitude that characterized all his actions, an unfettered gesture even in the face of an explicit prohibition. Just as Wazana never balked at entering the dark realms of the demonic and the magical, and unearthed and examined that which he should have left hidden, here too he responds to the challenge flung down by the demonic call, fully aware of the risk to his own life. On the other hand, if we remember that by saving a person condemned to die, Wazana had effectively accomplished his lifelong ambition, then the possibility should be considered that his response to the voice attests to resignation and acceptance on his part—a mortal weariness after interminable years of sorrow and pining after his parents. It is almost as if the voice of his demon brethren, crying out his name from the depths of the earth, is the very voice of his yearning for his parents who, just as the demons, reside in the dust of the cemetery. Thus for Wazana, the demonic summons may be seen as the song of the sirens, beckoning him to the nirvana he strived toward all his life, to unite with the beloved parents whose absence he could never accept.

17

Without Bounds:
Wazana the Symbolic Type

A s tempting as it may be to try to comprehend the psychological bases
for Wazana's personality, this approach is seriously problematic.
Its attraction can be partially ascribed to the contemporary tendency to
focus on the individual's inner reality with its contributory psychological
forces and to regard these as the determinants of behavior. This tendency
to "psychologize" however cannot obscure the fact that the figure we
contemplate here belongs to another place and time and therefore cannot
possibly be studied directly. Our impressions of Wazana are mediated
by the informants, and rest exclusively on their evaluations and interpretations. In a way, the attempt to plumb the inner reality that forged
Wazana's behavior is more than a little presumptuous, insofar as it over-
looks past dialogue between Wazana and the informants, and ongoing
present-time dialogue with the figure in their memories. Given the lack
of complementary sources of information, we cannot be sure that the
explication presented here reflects either Wazana's inner world or that of
the informants.

This fundamental problem directs us down a different avenue—
one that does not entail a psychological, but rather a cultural-symbolic,
analysis. This avenue does not disregard the numerous layers separating
Wazana from the researcher: on the contrary, it shifts the focus away from
Wazana's psychological reality and onto the social reality of Wazana's
interaction with the Jews of the Western Atlas. The suggestion is that the
informants' portrayal of Wazana is replete with evaluations and interpretations no less than with facts; and that, moreover, these evaluations

and interpretations are shaped by shared cultural assumptions and moral standpoints to no less an extent than by the matrix of a particular informant's unique psychological background and life circumstances. Viewed from this position, the collective-cultural portrait of Wazana appears to be molded to a significant degree by those quintessential aspects of his lifestyle that provoked in his acquaintances an ambivalent response of attraction and repulsion, admiration and fear, esteem and condemnation. The informants' perception of Wazana is of someone whose position on the edge of the social order stems from his exhaustive exploitation of his society's cardinal cultural resources, and from his persistent defiance of their constraints. Such antinomian behavior, I wish to show now, while it generates a tremendously liberating and healing power, is at one and the same time sinister as well as terrifying to others.

This ambivalent attitude toward Wazana hardly emerges in the stories of his life. We did encounter, here and there, a note of condemnation for his strange ways and his tendency to overstep the bounds of acceptable behavior. However, this tone, which was evident, for example, in the rather disparaging opinion of Wazana held by his blind cousin Ya'aqov Wazana, and in Rabbi Yosef Abu-Ḥatsera's overt aversion toward him, was almost totally dwarfed by the swell of adoration and gratitude displayed by the vast majority of informants. The only set of narrated events reflecting a plainly negative moral stance toward Wazana is the story of his death. The negative attitude, enfolded in the different versions of this story, is all the more acute if we juxtapose the plot of his death with that of his father's death. The two death stories are totally antithetical, and it would be understating the disparity to say that Rabbi Ya'aqov suffers by comparison. We now turn to an in-depth examination of the two death narratives.

First, Wazana's father, Rabbi Avraham, dies in holiness and purity, having prayed in synagogue and recited the Shema. Rabbi Ya'aqov's death, on the other hand, is the consequence of over-intimacy with the demonic world, and follows a demonic assault adjacent to a Muslim cemetery. Antithetical elements of sanctity and impurity that are defined in space (synagogue, place of Jewish worship, versus Muslim graveyard, favored habitation of demons), are further reinforced by the different time lapses between death and burial for each protagonist. Rabbi Avraham died on Thursday night, and despite the great distance between Amassine where he died and Tamzersht where he was buried, he is given the honor of burial on Friday, immediately before the commencement of the Sabbath. Wazana, on the other hand, was attacked by demons on Friday afternoon, died on Friday night, and was buried on Sunday. In temporal terms, the father's death corresponds to a recurring pattern found in the death legends of saints—ability to miraculously change the normal passage of time to avoid profaning the Sabbath; whereas Wazana's death occurred on the Sabbath itself, thereby "desecrating" the holy day.[1] What is more, Rabbi Avraham serenely accepts his imminent death, whereas Wazana is overwhelmed by terror, has difficulty accepting his fate, and tries in vain to forestall it. The father's body felt as light as a feather, and was carried, quickly and easily, over many miles, whereas his son's body weighed so much that a supreme effort was needed to carry it even the short distance to the local cemetery. Rabbi Avraham's body did not decay even in his tomb, while the stench from Wazana's corpse still hung in the air a month after his death. Contrasting the honey, symbol of bliss and abundance, that flowed from Rabbi Avraham's mouth, Wazana's mouth gushed with the blood relished by demons.[2] The role of the Muslim in the death stories also changes and is reversed: the Arab's attitude is transformed in Rabbi Avraham's story from contemptuousness and hostility to respectful deference, while the Arab sheikh who appreciated Wazana's powers and is helped by Wazana, indirectly causes his death by persuading him to perform a forbidden act.

The seasons themselves, constituting the temporal backdrop for the death accounts, completely contrast one another. Rabbi Avraham dies in the month of Tevet, in mid-winter, "in the coldest place in the world," as one informant hyperbolically put it. The deep drifts of snow and the freezing cold temperature fulfilled, it will be recalled, an important role in underscoring the miraculous nature of the death event, since they did not interfere with the miraculous transportation of the body "in a flash." Wazana, on the other hand, dies at the height of summer, on a sizzling day in the month of Tammuz, and we find glinting among the details of his death and burial the burning sun, the sweat, and the stench of putrefaction that characterized the accounts of these moments. The sharp contrast between summer and winter in the mountain hinterlands of southern Morocco accentuates the divergences of cleanliness and purity (cold and snow) in the one story and filth and defilement (heat and sweat) in the other. Another layer of contrast with respect to time is embedded in the meaning ascribed to the dates of the two deaths within the Jewish calendar: Rabbi Avraham died during Ḥanukka, a festival of Jewish redemption and rejoicing, crowded with miracles. His son, however, as many informants stressed, died during the inauspicious Three Weeks (Bein Hametsarim) period, a time of mourning associated with catastrophe and destruction.[3] Indeed, in their descriptions of Rabbi Ya'aqov's death, informants referred to the customs of mourning observed during this period such as abstention from eating meat.[4]

To summarize: the death story concerning Rabbi Avraham, the mystic who dedicated his life to study but who was not very active during his lifetime, is replete with miracles, while in Rabbi Ya'aqov's story they are completely absent, despite the fact that acts of wonder were a matter of course in his lifetime. The atmosphere surrounding his father's death denotes power and self-realization, whereas the messages emanating from the son's death convey weakness and non-fulfillment.

There is a transparent moral embedded in these stories: he who lives an upright life, within the limits of the social order, and does not abuse his *zekhut avot* (ancestral privileges), will die at a ripe old age, preserving and even adding to the aura of saintliness associated with his image. The profligate son, however, who abuses his inherited powers and violates the boundaries of social order, will die a sudden, premature, and violent death.

The discrepancy between the messages embedded in the death stories of Wazana and his father becomes even clearer when these stories are compared with those of the earlier Wazana family *tsaddiqim*. The description of Rabbi Avraham's death legend appears to be a later version of the death legend of the greatest of the family *tsaddiqim*, Rabbi Avraham "The Great" [el-Kebir]. As we know, the dynasty founder died in the midst of a festive meal attended by learned men, after reciting the afternoon and evening prayers. Foreknowledge of the time of his own death, a typical element of the death stories of *tsaddiqim*, made it possible for Rabbi Avraham to instruct his followers to say the Shema and recite passages from Psalms until midnight came. Wazana's father died in a similar way, although in his story, the scholars are exchanged for a synagogue congregation. Besides foreknowledge and acceptance of imminent death allowing for proper arrangements to be made, both stories entail the appearance of the *tsaddiq* in a dream, his burial somewhere other than the location of his death, the miracle of traveling great distances in "a flash," and the involvement of an Arab horseman in the funeral. The clear correspondence between the death descriptions of the founder of the dynasty and his descendant, Wazana's father, is hardly surprising given that both originate in the recurring narrative matrix of saints' deaths appearing in the corpus of Jewish Moroccan saint legends (Ben-Ami 1984: 61–63). The narrated plot of Rabbi Avraham "The Great" 's death was presumably a venerated family model, duplicated in the stories of the deaths of other *tsaddiqim* in the family. The family model further accentuates the deviation from the norm of Rabbi Ya'aqov's death narrative.

We turn now to a comparison between the narrative logic found in the death story of Wazana and some of the miracles concerning Rabbi David, son of Rabbi Avraham "The Great." The first miracle, as noted, occurred just prior to his marriage, and involved the transformation of the *kaid*'s daughter into a hen as a punishment for stealing a pet chick belonging to a young Jewish girl. At the end of the story, the *kaid*'s daughter is restored to human form by the *tsaddiq*, but at the cost of her mother's life.

We can view this story and the death of Rabbi Ya'aqov as contrasting versions of the same deep structure. While we find in the death legends pertaining to Rabbi Ya'aqov and his father numerous antithetical elements, the "chicken miracle" legend and the account of Wazana's death in fact share a recognized narrative pattern entailing disruption and subsequent restoration of the natural order. The pattern is composed of a series of five analogous steps. The contrast is embedded in the specific content of each step, steps that will now be examined in detail.

At the heart of these stories lies the traditional belief that order and harmony between the world's inhabitants—Jews and Muslims, humans and demons—is a desirable goal which it is imperative to maintain.[5] In terms of the narrative, the first step described below is that which destroys the status quo:

High status Muslim girl kills living creature

The significant difference between the story of Rabbi David and that of Rabbi Ya'aqov relates to the identity of the creature killed. In the case of Rabbi David, the *kaid*'s daughter causes the death of a chicken, a kosher animal, raised by a Jewish child. In contrast, in the story of Rabbi Ya'aqov's death, the sheikh's daughter is responsible for the death of impure snakes, moreover, demons in disguise. Both times the natural order needs to be reestablished, and indeed, the second stage of the narrative pattern entails restoring the order.

The victim's representative strikes the perpetrator

The "restitution" principle is brought into play. Rabbi David, representing the Jewish girl, transforms the covetous Muslim child into a hen, whereas in the story involving Rabbi Ya'aqov, the demonic kin of the dead snakes strike the perpetrator (the sheikh's daughter) intending to slay her. The individual who first disrupted the order pays a high price. The suffering of these people and their families acts as the catalyst for the next stage.

Jewish healer brought to heal the perpetrator-cum-victim

This stage, if completed, upsets the newly restored equilibrium. This plot juncture suspends the action, heightening the tension. The options available to both Wazana healers are: not to intervene, thereby preserving the newly restored balance, or help the Arab girl, reintroduce disorder, and then pay the price. Both choose the second option.

Jewish healer cures Muslim girl

Rabbi David transforms the *kaid*'s daughter back into human form, and Rabbi Ya'aqov brings the condemned daughter of the sheikh back to life. In both stories, the punishment for disrupting the reestablished order is heavier than the punishment for the wrongdoing that set the sequence of events in motion.

The accessory to the perpetrator pays with his or her life

The victims of the disruption of order, or to be more precise, those sacrificed to achieve its final restoration, are, on the one hand, the *kaid*'s wife, who pays for slaughtering the pet chicken, and Rabbi Ya'aqov on the other, for healing the sheikh's daughter. In stark contrast to Rabbi Ya'aqov's story, not only does Rabbi David emerge unscathed from the affair, but weds the girl he championed.

The shared narrative pattern and identical sequence of steps serves to emphasize the differences between Rabbi David and Rabbi Ya'aqov. In the story of Rabbi David, the tension originates in Jewish-Muslim relations, whereas in the story of Rabbi Ya'aqov's death, the axis of conflict flows between humans and demons, though the Muslims play a vital role in the plot. Rabbi David dispenses retribution on the Muslims, further entrenching the boundary between the two communities. Rabbi Ya'aqov, in antagonism with the demons, demolishes that boundary by executing the forbidden act of healing the sheikh's daughter. The former is successful since his actions are in keeping with Jewish social traditions; the latter fails by deviating from them. It is particularly interesting to contrast the victims in the last stage, in which Wazana emerges as the counterpart to the *kaid*'s wife—a Muslim woman. Could the purpose of this be to draw attention to the issue of Wazana's "Muslimness" and "femininity"?

Before we examine another legend about Rabbi David, it is important to note that the story of Rabbi Ya'aqov's death bears a strong resemblance to that of his mother Esther. Here, the shared narrative structure is not antithetical in content but strikingly similar. The mother's death almost seems to presage some of the themes that reverberate through Wazana's death story. As we know, his mother's story opens with a summons to Wazana to heal the son of a local sheikh at the time his mother lay dying. Both the opening, and the predicament it establishes, remind us of the phases in the run up to Rabbi Ya'aqov's death. Furthermore, in both cases, Wazana adopts a similar approach to settling the dilemma— he heals the patient. In both stories, the sheikhs "bribe" him generously, motivating him to press on, ignoring the inherent risk. In the first case, the price is his mother's life, which is exchanged for that of the child; in the second, however, his own life is forfeit for the life he gives. The only significant discrepancy between the two stories is the role of the demons. In the first story, they are Wazana's loyal and obedient servants, who help him to disinter his mother, in the second, they turn against him and slay him.

We return now to Rabbi David to examine another legend in which he appears, the story of saving the Jewish girl snatched by the river demon who took her for his wife. The comparison begged here is not with the story of Wazana's death, but with the story of his marriage. In both cases, the basic pattern is a human-demon marriage. However, in each of the stories, the common structure is overlaid with such differing elements that total antithesis is produced. The first point of comparison is the human's gender—a young girl in the first case, and a man (Wazana), in the second. Again, this may be an allusion to Wazana's latent "femininity." The complementary point of comparison is the gender of the demon, that is, a male demon counterpart to the she-demon. In both cases, the union is sought by the male partner, but the eagerness to enter the marriage on the part of the human is altogether different. In the river demon legend, the Jewish girl is abducted and forced into a union by her captor. This contrasts with Wazana's deliberate effort to find a demonic spouse and his voluntary marriage. In terms of similarity of action, in initiating the marriage, Wazana in fact mirrors the male river demon's position. Ultimately, however, the resolution of each plot is wholly antithetical: the demonic marriage is annulled, and the human bride's marriage fulfilled in the legend of Rabbi David. Wazana, on the other hand, never marries a bride of his own kind "above the ground," preferring instead union with a she-demon.

In this legend too, Rabbi David appears as an enforcer of boundaries: in the story of the kidnapped bride, the climax clearly conveys a redefinition of the dissolved boundary between the human and demonic worlds. Rabbi Ya'aqov's actions, as we have seen, are conducive to eliminating these boundaries. Thus the one preserves the social order while the other repeatedly disrupts it.

The divergence between Rabbi Ya'aqov's death legend and the legends of his sainted ancestors, from dynasty founder Rabbi Avraham el-Kebir, through his son Rabbi David, to Rabbi Avraham, Wazana's father, reinforces the sense of Wazana's deviancy. The narrative structures underlying the stories of his marriage and death present an aberrant pattern of binary opposition and tension with the normative saint legends. As indicated, while these oppositions may assume different guises, their recurrence is impressively systematic.[6] The divergent patterns of structural inversion bear a clear moral message: censure for Wazana compared with his forebears, an implicit condemnation for a man with no respect for boundaries, a man who unhesitatingly violated the social order, who willfully misused the privilege he inherited from his saintly ancestors. However, the reproof of Wazana inherent in his death legend, and which the comparison with the family *tsaddiqim* heavily underscores, was almost entirely absent from the informants' personal evaluations. The emotions that colored their memories were nostalgic and affectionate. Like the legends, their personal stories related primarily to Wazana's uniqueness and remarkability: the assertion that "there was no one like Wazana anywhere in Morocco," was heard more often than any other, but the tone of voice in which it was spoken expressed wonder and esteem rather than disapprobation.

It seems that Wazana's unusual marginality and dismissiveness of the regulations of the social order were responsible for the plainly ambivalent attitude toward him (as reflected in the tension between the affectionate personal recollections and the harsh tone of his death legend). On the one hand he was perceived as alarming and dangerous; on the other, the unlimited healing powers ascribed to him made him into a vital communal resource. To appreciate Wazana's special place within the Jewish community, we must examine the meaning of that dangerous but therapeutic marginality.

Wazana's exceptionality owed to the fact that cohabiting in his persona were different, mutually exclusive social elements normally perceived by traditional Moroccan society as fundamentally antagonistic. In his uncompromising push toward extremes, the roots of which we have attempted to analyze in the previous chapter, Wazana did away with the strict demarcations that normally separated these categories, providing a bridge between them. The alchemic nature of his activities and his very essence was manifest on many levels: Within a cosmology that allocates humans and *jnun* clearly distinct (though juxtaposed) worlds, Wazana crossed the ontological border by marrying a demonic wife who produced demonic offspring. In a society in which Jew and Muslim belonged to sharply differentiated social categories, he shattered religious-ethnic lines by adopting a mixed Muslim-Jewish identity. In a world that placed, as all religions do, the sacred and the profane at conflicting ends of the social order, he destroyed the moral-theosophical divide, in that he was (by virtue of his role as rabbi-healer) empowered both by the piety and sanctity of his ancestors as well as by impure agents (the demons).

Furthermore, basic social roles were left unoccupied by Wazana. Without family, he never assumed the roles of "husband" or "father"—at least not "above the ground." He never cared for material wealth and was free of most mundane concerns, having amassed no possessions—not even his own home. In a society highly segregated by age and sex, he befriended women, children, and layabouts in a reckless manner, unconcerned with his own status and prestige as a healer. Even age categories were inapplicable to Wazana in the usual sense. His acquaintances contend that his age was a mystery to them, since his appearance seemed unmarked by time until the day he died.

What is the significance of this formless, slippery alchemic quality that dissolved boundaries, defied norms, and challenged the social order? And why does it gather, story by story, in an increasingly thick cloud around the figure of Wazana? The answers apparently lie in the tremendous stores of energy released by discarding the oppressive impositions of social constraints, allowing flexibility and creativity to surge from beneath the rubble of the social order, and in the fertile power of the forbidden coupling of normally sharply differentiated fundaments and categories.

Anthropologist Mary Douglas (1966) offers some excellent insights into the sources of the power and inherent dangers of blurring boundaries and mixing the contents of social concepts and categories. Douglas emphasizes that the wish to apprehend the world represents a primal, pan-human drive expressed through the imposition of order on natural and social phenomena, and by their organization into divisions and taxonomies. This drive to gain understanding by means of structuring, which is conceptualized differently depending on the culture, offers society members a cognitive map with which to interpret their reality. The map however can never be complete and there will inevitably remain a residue of deviant phenomena that refuses to be classified since its components belong to categories perceived by the cultural order as incompatible, irreconcilable, and contradictory. Such phenomena are indefinable since they cross the conceptual boundaries recognized by the culture. From this inability to conceptualize, certain phenomena evoke feelings of puzzlement, disquiet, and revulsion. Thus we find in both tribal and complex societies a distinct tendency to steer clear of aberrant phenomena, which the society views as dangerously powerful. This may be seen, for example, in the Jewish dietary laws (*kashrut*), and in the myths and rituals of the Lele group in Zaire (Douglas 1957). The former forbid the eating of certain "deviant" animals, such as those that do not chew the cud and do not have cloven hooves, or fish that lack fins and scales. The latter see the pangolin—an anteater resembling a fish with its tail and scales, other mammals in its limbs and habitat, and humans in certain aspects of its behavior (for example, it does not flee from hunters like other animals, but rolls into an armored ball and freezes)—as an object of fear and veneration purported to possess tremendous fertility powers. With a stretch of the imagination, can we find a resemblance between Wazana and the pangolin?

Insofar as we are discussing borders, it seems that the resemblance indeed exists. The illimitable Wazana, like his comrades the demons, was able to assume and discard disguises. Like demons, he could become formless and invisible—in this way he evaded capture in Casablanca—and in his healing activities, he could break down the constraints of time and space. By being both human and close to demons, a Jew and a Muslim, young and old, holy and profane, masculine and feminine, he commanded forces totally unavailable to normal mortals trapped within their rigid boundaries of age and sex, position and status, religion and ethnicity, and harnessed those powers for the benefit of others.

The above analysis captures Wazana as a mediated figure, with a non-static, but fluid and flexible place in the world. He is not classifiable or definable in terms of definitive social categories, being usually located on the threshold between them, wandering their edges, drawn to the brink of the social order, defying and challenging its constraints. In fact, he appears as the quintessence of liminality (Lat. *Limen,* meaning "threshold"). Anthropologist Victor Turner (1967, 1969, 1974)[7] has explained liminality as an elementary though latent social process, primarily typified by absence of order, elimination of structural divisions, ambiguity, and openness. It manifests itself for circumscribed periods of time, in highly ceremonial social events, when differentiations of extraction and socioeconomic status melt away. Consequently participants in such events— for example, adolescent participants in a tribal initiation ceremony, or pilgrims flocking to a shrine—meld into a single, homogeneous, egalitarian grouping sharing a sense of fraternity and common destiny. When structure is eliminated through the temporary suspension of the social arrangements that regulate daily existence, a unique opportunity arises for social change and cultural regeneration. While the resultant anti-structure acts to threaten and endanger the existence of the social order, it also furnishes fertile ground for the emergence of a new kind of order.

How can we apply the concept of liminality, which actually refers to the social process of dissolving structural demarcations, to a human figure such as Wazana? Among all the various efforts to define as "liminal figures" such social actors as beggars, clowns, saints, and other types of "strangers" whose lives actualize emancipation from the constraints of social order, the suggestion put forward by Don Handelman (1985, 1991) seems the most apt. According to Handelman, certain cultural figures (human or mythological) are believed to possess extraordinary charismatic powers that carry the liminal process into the fabric of social life. These figures, which he labels "symbolic types," have such undeviating fidelity to their inner truth that they are unwilling to compromise whatsoever with social order constraints. Furthermore, their emancipation from social and cultural frameworks empowers them to mold these contexts in their own image. Symbolic types often embody the basic social dilemmas, contradictions, and paradoxes perceived and articulated by their cultures. This gives them an inner complexity that licenses them as agents of social change but also vests in them the power to restabilize the social structure. As such they appear as intermediaries between different levels of order and disorder embedded in social life. Can we view Wazana as a symbolic type?

If it is possible to apply the term "symbolic type" to certain healers, including Wazana, this is mainly because they harness the cultural contradictions and paradoxes they personify, the disorder that lies at the very heart of their natures, in order to restore order. Sickness, like many other human afflictions, is perceived, in the broadest sense, as deviation from equilibrium and harmony—an assault on the normal course of the social order. This perception is most evident in such traditional societies as the Jewish community of southern Morocco. According to the penetrating analysis advanced by anthropologist Barbara Myerhoff (1976), healers in such societies, particularly those we recognize as shamans,[8] derive their healing powers from their ability to seize the edges of the universe and provide a bridge between different worlds. The main challenge of their role is to preserve the state of balance between the opposites they have bridged.

Myerhoff recounts her utter amazement at the daring acrobatics performed by the Indian shamans she met. She describes the way Domenico, a healer of the Luiseno tribe in southern California, performed hair-raising balancing feats every Friday afternoon on the roof of his house. Elsewhere, she recalls her amazement at Ramon, of the Huichol tribe in northern Mexico, who executed similar feats on a towering cliff high above a plunging waterfall. It took a while for the researcher to realize that through these acrobatics, the Indian shamans were demonstrating their skills in balancing and mediating between worlds. Their expertise allowed them to correct and heal distortion, in other words, to restore order to the world. Can we then compare Wazana to Domenico and Ramon, the Indian shamans?

The fact that Wazana was the quintessential embodiment of his culture's contradictions afforded him the tools for "bridging between worlds." His activities involved dissolving boundaries, best reflected in the act of summoning the demons to assist him in this world. He served to rectify divergence and restore the equilibrium when it was disturbed. As a symbolic, liminal type, Wazana enjoyed emancipation from social order constraints, "he could turn the country upside down," while contrastingly this very freedom enabled him to uphold the order of the world. This dialectic tension can be seen plainly in the types of problems Wazana treated: he enabled young girls to find spouses, while never marrying himself (that is, never "above the ground"); he helped the barren, while remaining childless "above the ground"; he restored sexual potency to other men, while his own sexual life was meager or nonexistent.

Indeed, many informants saw Wazana as a defender of order. One even remarked that all thefts and burglaries had ceased when Wazana came to Agouim: "no one dared steal anymore." According to another, "in our town, you could leave your gold on the sidewalk and no one took it—they dared not touch it." So deeply rooted was the image of Wazana as the guardian of order and harmony that some informants even connected Wazana's death with the upsurge of terrorism in Morocco![9] It is an interesting note that even Rabbi Ya'aqov's name embodies a reminder of his role as mediator and restorer of balance: in Arabic, *wazana* means to balance.

However, Wazana's capacity to restore order was contingent upon his capacity to preserve the balance between the opposites he bridged. Here, it would appear, lay the seed of the disaster that eventually led to his downfall. It lay in his tendency to "go all the way," to gaze into the forbidden, and to seek to retrieve the irretrievable. This disposition, which ultimately played havoc with his role as mediator and restorer of balance, may be explained on the psychological level as a reaction to the painful loss of both parents, and, on the cultural level, in terms of the inner logic of the symbolic type indifferent to external constraints running counter to his nature. Wazana balanced between worlds, but also ended up clashing with their various inhabitants. A part of him was Muslim, but the Arabs pursued him in Casablanca and threatened his life in Assarag, finally seducing him into using his powers on their behalf—at the cost of his life. He was partly demonic, but he transgressed the only prohibition imposed on him by the demons,[10] trespassing on forbidden territory to become their quarry. He was part saint, but he affronted God by seeking to alter the order of the universe and by saving a life destined for death, and, moreover, by proclaiming to God's emissaries, the demons, that: "Even if it [the affliction] comes from higher still, I must save her, I am not afraid." All these factors resulted in his downfall.

The story of Wazana's death, which is in itself an expression of the restoration of order between the human and demonic worlds, points to the dangers of a marginality that crosses accepted social boundaries, and to the heavy price paid when the bridging is excessive and far-reaching. In his tragic end, reinforced by the fact that "nothing of his remained," it is almost as if a cultural verdict has been passed on this remarkable and restless individual, who defied every norm and broke every rule in pursuit of freedom from limitations.

In light of this analysis, we cannot avoid feeling a sense of poetic justice in the fact that Wazana, the symbolic type of traditional Jewish society of southern Morocco, died in the early 1950s, before the mass emigration of Moroccan Jews to Israel reached its height. He was spared the sight of the passing of the way of life he himself embodied, and worse still, the installment of a disenchanted new reality with which he, a symbolic type, loyal to himself, could never have compromised. Wazana's absolute loyalty to the inner truth that drove him, whether driven by a unique mental constellation ("psychology") or by virtue of his cultural construction as a symbolic model ("culture"), is reflected in the timing of his death, no less than in the events of his life. That power of loyalty to his own nature has determined that his figure remains untarnished by time, growing brighter over the years, its enduring power and vitality transforming him into the legend before us today.

18

Wazana of the Heart

Where has our journey in Wazana's footsteps taken us? Here, at the end of the line, it seems appropriate to restate the cautionary remarks that prefaced this expedition. We have traveled to the heart of the High Atlas Mountains via the inner space of the minds of the informants whose image of Wazana has been formed by their personal desires and cultural cognitions. Our quest has taken us not on a time voyage back forty, fifty, and sixty years, to Wazana's youth and adulthood, but into the mists of human memories in which the past is evaluated from the perspective of life in the present. Wazana, whose death sealed the Moroccan chapter of the informants' lives, has become an integral part of that past life, his figure subjected to the informants' retrospective evaluations of the past.

Once we accept that the Wazana who lived and operated in the Atlas Mountains during the first half of this century does not await us at the end of the road, and that the stories we have gathered about him do not stand for snapshots of objective facts from which an accurate historical biography can be reconstructed, then it is clear that all that can be offered is a set of interpretations, suggesting possible (though not exhaustive) meanings for the memories and impressions of those who knew him in another place and time. This we have tried to do in the two preceding chapters. However, we cannot ignore the basic premise underlying this search, namely, that the informants' memories entail the fragments of a mosaic picture that when reconstructed offers a generalized, well-integrated portrait of Wazana. How does this reconcile with the notion that these are memories saturated with personal and subjective evaluations and impressions, or with the fact that the portrayals traced by the informants do not necessarily overlap, and sometimes even controvert each other?

The answer lies in the complexity and wealth of data embedded in the stories and in the multiple options for deciphering them. The informants' recollections are varied. Embedded in them are shared subjects, familiar to everyone, which keep recurring with minor changes, side by side with unique personal experiences and individual recollections, lending the impression that deep in the heart of each informant lives another Wazana. As noted, our starting premise was that a generalized picture might be constructed from the stories and therefore we have focused on the commonalities. Nevertheless, it is still appropriate to investigate the discrepancies, even though these may rattle the framework and crack the portrait here and there.

Let us return and reexamine the portrait while listening to *all* of the informants' voices together, including those that clash with the dominant note within the stories. Wazana is generally depicted as an unprecedentedly courageous person, with contempt for danger and delight in challenge; however, there are some who maintain that his behavior on critical occasions in his life was that of a coward who showed his back to intimidating opponents. His cowardice is clearest in the conflict with the Muslims who sought to harm him—his flight from Casablanca and move from Assarag because of the threats—and in abandoning his dying mother when pressured by a local sheikh to heal his dying son. At the moment of truth, as he confronted the actuality of his own death, he crumpled with fear and dread.

Many people dwelt on Wazana's sociability and his universal friendliness; however, there were those who described him as a lone wolf, a free spirit, someone who worshipped in the synagogue alone, an unusual practice among Jews. Some regarded him as a proud and avaricious man—we recall the "bribes" offered him by the sheikhs of Assarag and Agouim—while others portray him as a frivolous clown, a man who exhibited little concern for self-respect, for whom money and material possessions were low priorities. With hindsight, some of these contradictions demonstrate no more than behavioral divergences stemming from the circumstances of the informants' various encounters with Wazana; however, they also appear to reflect the individual informants' divergent personal perspectives.

Indeed, besides the differences of opinion with respect to his personality traits, it seems that the general portrait of Wazana undergoes significant transformations among different groupings of informants. At the "positive" end of the spectrum of images and evaluations, he emerges as an authentic family *tsaddiq,* no different from the others venerated by Moroccan Jewry except in level of popularity. Within this band of admirers, comprised mainly of family members and close friends from Agouim, we found narratives that seemed to whitewash certain problematic facets of his identity and lifestyle. Thus, for example, some categorically denied his Muslim side, or asserted hastily that he at least experienced a complete change of heart prior to his death. Some insisted that he gradually abandoned his association with the demons when his fame as a healer spread, and rejected the popular version of his death as a result of demonic revenge. The great efforts on the part of some in this group to ensure that Wazana's life fell more in line with typical saint legends suppress the intriguing qualities in whose absence close examination of his figure would be pointless. The Tubul couple, for example, among the extremists in the "whitewashing" group, maintained that Wazana did not miss his father's funeral at all. They are satisfied that angels carried him with great speed to Tamzersht, enabling him to attend the funeral. This minority version obviously undermines our argument regarding the motivation behind Wazana's desire to become a healer. The old couple even disputed the popular narrative regarding the time of Rabbi Ya'aqov's death, maintaining—to bring it in line with the orthodox format—that he was privileged to be buried on Friday, in time for the Sabbath.

At another extreme are the informants who treat Rabbi Ya'aqov with more than a pinch of disapprobation. Interestingly, the most critical of these were members of Wazana's own clan, who regard him as the black sheep of the family, a profligate son whose peculiar behavior bespoke an abuse of the privileges bequeathed by his forebears. Shaul and Ya'aqov Wazana, Rabbi Ya'aqov's blind cousins, carefully distinguished between Wazana and the earlier family *tsaddiqim,* and tended to minimize his stature. The adoring attitude of Masouda Buskila, married to Rabbi Ya'aqov's nephew, who refers to the healer as the "sainted Rabbi Wazana *el-Aziz* [the Beloved], the kindest person in the world," upon whom the divine presence rested, is very far removed from the reservations implicit in the speech of Wazana's blind cousin from Pardes Ḥana, who referred to the healer with more than a modicum of scorn as "that Ya'aqov."

Most informants fall somewhere between these two extremes. Their personal memories express admiration for a man able to relieve all kinds of trials and tribulations; however, their shared stories, especially those concerning Wazana's death, unwittingly convey a palpable sense of tension and unease at the memory of his irregularities and unorthodoxy.

The fact that divergent images of Wazana are discernible among the informants' narratives is not difficult to explain given the informants' differing degrees of closeness to him, and the circumstances of their encounters with him. However, it also seems that the informants' present-day circumstances influence their perceptions. In our nationwide journey in search of Wazana, we found that the diverse groups of "Wazana's people" had localized versions of his exploits which shared details either missing or different from stories in other localities. In a sense, this means that we may speak of a Wazana belonging to the people of *moshav* Makor, and another who lives on with his friends in Be'er Sheva.

To what extent does the informants' past and present personal lives affect their configuration of Wazana's image? Careful examination reveals that some of their memories involve a hybridization of past events, including their encounters with Wazana, with personal experiences in the present apparently unrelated to him. Our first example of this concerns the way Rabbi Shalom Ben-Hamo from Atseret and Rabbi Yitzhak Pehima of Kiryat Gat perceive Wazana's books, which are believed to be in their possession (both men grudgingly admit this to be the case). Both claimed that the books could not possibly be used now, but for different reasons: the urban healer, Pehima, was inclined to undervalue the importance of the book on the grounds that its contents were illegible ("the writing is smudged"), whereas Ben-Hamo, the healer from the *moshav,* insisted that on the contrary, he could not use the book because of the terrifying powers it held ("names that might destroy the world"). Pehima's reaction stems perhaps from the fact that he is cut off from his former community, that he lives among people who did not know Wazana, whereas Ben-Hamo, who lives among those who knew Wazana and admired his powers, and who is presently struggling to maintain his position in the *moshav,* feels it important to underscore the powers he allegedly can access. The evaluation of the efficacy of Wazana's instrument of healing is, in this case, colored by the informant's current circumstances.

At least in part, a fair number of informants have forged their portrait of Wazana on the anvil of their own predicaments. It is no coincidence perhaps that Yosef Abutbul, who is childless, chose to open his account of Wazana's exploits with the story of how Wazana cured his mother's childlessness which had been caused by a spell. He enthused excitedly over the way the great healer had shaken a lock over his mother's abdomen, unlocking and relocking it. "When you hear the sound of gunfire, she will give birth," Wazana had promised, and indeed this promise was soon realized. Judging by his enthusiastic tone of voice, it seemed that Yosef, who had fruitlessly consulted healers—Jewish, Arab, folk, and medical—up and down the country, yearns for the lock and gunfire that would give his wife the child of her dreams.

Rabbi Moshe Tubul was the only informant to claim that the sheikh's daughter in Wazana's death story had been barren. It seems that his version stems directly from the fact that it was for childlessness that he turned to Wazana. On the other hand, Hana Buskila, Rabbi Ya'aqov's kinswoman, reported that Wazana's last treatment was to an Arab girl, seven months pregnant, who eventually miscarried. It emerged that she herself had consulted Wazana many times regarding miscarriages and problematic pregnancies. Another kinsman, Rabbi Shmuel Suissa, who is handicapped in one leg, started his account of Wazana's life with the story of how the healer had cured his younger sister who was stricken with paralysis. In another example, blind, old Rabbi Ya'aqov Wazana claimed that his cousin had also been blind toward the end of his life.

Thus the informants seemed to connect Wazana with events and experiences in their own lives. Perhaps the most dramatic example of such transference concerns Rabbi Shalom Ben-Hamo of Agouim, now residing in Atseret. He provided the best description of the confrontation between Wazana and Rabbi Yosef Abu-Hatsera some forty years ago near the shrine of Rabbi David u-Moshe. With great relish he recalled that Wazana had made the roast beef prepared for Rabbi Yosef and his retinue disappear when the latter insulted him, ordering his seat to be placed away from the rest of the celebrants. It seems that not only Wazana, but Rabbi Shalom himself had experienced the wrath of that esteemed member of the Abu-Hatsera family. Rabbi Yosef Abu-Hatsera, who lived in France, had the custom of visiting his supporters in Israel, including those in Atseret. During one visit, he knocked at Rabbi Shalom's door, only to find that one of his kinsmen—a longtime enemy—was present in the house. At this discovery Rabbi Yosef stormed away in a fury, cursing host and guest vociferously. Some time later Rabbi Shalom's daughter died of pesticide poisoning, leaving the latter in no doubt whatsoever that her death resulted from Rabbi Yosef's curse. Rabbi Shalom made this grave accusation with total equanimity, commenting that ordinary mortals ought not to question the acts of *tsaddiqim*. Could it be that a thirst for revenge curdling inside him provided the raw material for his description of the confrontation between Wazana and Rabbi Yosef?

These examples support the assumption with which our quest began, and with which we will now conclude: that the figure of Wazana carried in the hearts and minds of his friends and acquaintances is to a substantial degree a private, personal, and subjective memory carved by the shifting sands of their current lives. The elusive character of this memory serves to magnify the enigma of Wazana's life, making it complicated to unravel. At the same time it imparts his image with sufficient mystery to justify the fascination he arouses in the informants, his friends, and not least, in this narrator, who has had the pleasure of recording their voices.

Epilogue: Wazana's Afterlife

Postmodern anthropology is informed by a social reality in which the boundaries between the ethnographer and the informant are being systematically eroded: the "native" as an object of analysis may become an analyzing subject (Rosaldo 1989) and the "other" may appear as a critical reader of the ethnographic account (Clifford and Marcus 1986; and Marcus and Fischer 1986). Under these circumstances, anthropologists have become more attentive to the reverberations of their fieldwork and particularly ethnographic writing in the lives and the social world of the people they study. The growing sensitivity to the political and moral-ethical aspects of the impact of ethnographic accounts on the communities studied has given rise to a new genre of reflexive works in which the complex relations between fieldwork, text, and audience are thoroughly explored (see, for example, Blackman 1992; and Brettell 1993). The essays in Blackman's edited collection, designated "The Afterlife of the Life History," focus on the postpublication of what is written as life history. "Afterlife makes the point that the life history continues beyond the crystallization of the narrative into text to encompass audience response to the published work, reflections on its construction as text, as well as its impact on the lives of its narrator and collector" (Blackman 1992: 2).

Issues related to the afterlife of ethnographic accounts are particularly pertinent in Israel. On top of the fact that most Israeli anthropologists are studying their own society, the small size of the country, the relatively open avenues of communication, and the wide exposure to the same few mass media agencies—all create problems of involvement with which anthropologists working in remote milieus are less bothered. This epilogue, in which I narratively chart the afterlife of Rabbi Ya'aqov Wazana following the publication of the Hebrew version of my book on his life, sheds light on some of these problems of involvement. Moreover, beyond the ethical problems of the "politics of the life story," amply discussed in Blackman's collection, Wazana's postpublication vicissitudes raise an intriguing epistemological question concerning the interplay between the ethnographic text and the reality it is supposed to represent.

My book in Hebrew on Wazana appeared in March 1993. Although it was published in a small number of copies by an academic press, it received relatively high media coverage. I believe that the concatenation of events that ensued was triggered by this media exposure (the credit for which should go to Wazana's colorful and intriguing character), and particularly by two lengthy pieces that appeared simultaneously in the weekend supplements of the two leading Israeli dailies.[1] I found out that the book, no less than its protagonist, was a mediated object of knowledge. But this time the filters through which Wazana's figure was conveyed to the public were newspaper and television reports in which his exotic and magical aspects were all the more accentuated.

In the beginning of April 1993, a thirty-five-year-old man named Yosef Waqnin[2] from the town of Be'er Sheva, an ex-barber who had recently gone back to study in a religious institution, called me at my office at the Hebrew University. Claiming that his parents had known Wazana in Morocco, he started to unfold, in a trembling voice burning with excitement, a series of dream encounters with the late rabbi-healer. While it is impossible to rule out the possibility that some of the dreams had preceded the publication, it became evident at the outset that the book, and particularly the attention drawn to it by the media, precipitated Yosef's decision to "go public" with the nightly messages from Rabbi Ya'aqov. Needless to say, Yosef's phone call engaged my attention instantaneously. In recent years I had studied the symbolic transfer of Jewish saints from Morocco to Israel and their reinstallation in the new country (Ben-Ari and Bilu 1987). This translocation was based on the spontaneous initiative of simple devotees of Moroccan background, men and women alike, who erected a shrine for a Maghrebi *tsaddiq* in their homes following an inspiring dream-series in which the saint urged them to do so.[3] These dreams were usually promulgated as "Announcements to the Public" which they circulated among Moroccan-born Israelis. I designated these individual entrepreneurs "saint impresarios" in order to convey their relentless efforts to develop their shrines and increase their popularity. Much of my work with the saint impresarios centered on their personal narratives and life stories (see, for example, Bilu 1990; Bilu and Hasan-Rokem 1989). As articulated by the saint impresarios, these accounts, always concluding on a positive note with the saint's apparition and the enduring liaison with him, are based on life events that pave the road for the transformative visitational dreams. Was I witnessing the emergence of a new saint impresario, whose vision to promote and "glorify" Rabbi

Ya'aqov Wazana was triggered by my book? The undertaking seemed all the more intriguing given the antinomian character and deviant lifestyle of Rabbi Ya'aqov, the black sheep of the Wazana family, who abused the powers of his venerated forefathers. In life and death, Wazana could hardly be seen as a worthy candidate for wide-range enshrinement.

I suggested a meeting in Be'er Sheva so that I could record or write down verbatim Yosef's dream accounts. He wholeheartedly agreed, but said that to expedite matters, he would send me the written version of his nocturnal experiences with Wazana. One day later, a handwritten account six pages long of six dreams reached me through the department's fax machine. Only after I read the dream report did I start to realize the scope of Yosef's vision and my expected role in it: as Wazana's biographer (or, from Yosef's point of view, as Wazana's hagiographer), I was assigned the role of Yosef's confidante and adviser in his attempts to promote and give publicity to the name of the legendary but relatively unknown healer in Israel.

In the introduction to the dream accounts Yosef praises the greatness of Rabbi Ya'aqov and the holiness of his great forbears. Then he asks: "How did it turn out that precisely now, fifty-one years after the death of Rabbi Ya'aqov Wazana [in fact, only forty-one years had passed since Wazana's death], it was decided to erect this holy site which bears the name of these *tsaddiqim*?" In his answer, he highlights the miraculous cures that Wazana lavished on his family, but then moves on to give credit to my work:

> Professor Yoram Bilu . . . [here my academic title and position, as presented on the back cover of the book, are specified] traveled through the whole country in his attempts to inquire about the greatness of Rabbi Ya'aqov Wazana. And he found out that many were the people who had known Wazana and his miraculous achievements. This journey in the footsteps of Wazana he described in a book [titled] The Life and Death of Rabbi Ya'aqov Wazana. And he certainly deserves a credit for his wonderful work and commitment.

In an unmistakable allusion to Joseph, the great biblical dreamer, the dream series was titled "The Dreams of Yosef." It represents a coherent narrative sequence in which the drama of the multiple encounters with Wazana picks up until its final resolve. In the first dream report, Wazana reveals himself to Yosef and asks him to erect a site for him and his forefathers for celebrating their *hillulot*. The pattern of the reported nocturnal interactions between the dreamer and the healer that ensues is indistinguishable from that reported by other saint impresarios in describing their emergent alliance with their patron-*tsaddiq*. Like them, Yosef initially assumes an ambivalent, if not a reluctant, position, doubting his ability to pursue the calling imposed on him by Wazana. But the latter, like the saints in the dreams of the impresarios, gradually disarms Yosef of his resistance by showering him with messages of encouragement and promises for help.

In the sixth and last dream, dreamt also on Sabbath night, these affectionate gestures are transformed into specific instructions: "Yosef my son, my blessing on your head, count three days from today and go to the government's [municipality] house. There someone will cross your way, and everything will turn all right." The pursuit of these instructions shows how easily visitation dreams spill over to waking reality. After waiting a long time, Yosef prays for Wazana's help, and, sure enough, he bumps into an acquaintance working in the municipality who is stunned to hear Yosef's story. "The guy's face turned white and he said to me, in tremor and amazement: 'You should know that I didn't mean to come here. I was drawn to you like a magnet; and on your right I saw a *tsaddiq* looking like an angel.' He started describing the *tsaddiq* but I stopped him and asked: 'Did the *tsaddiq* wear a white *jellaba* and a red *tarboosh* on his head? Was he holding a walking stick in his hand?' 'Yes,' he replied, and the *tsaddiq* asked me three times: 'help him, help him, help him.'"

As a result of this acquaintance's intercession, Yosef finally got hold of a huge public shelter not far from his home. His account ends with "a passionate appeal to the public" to make contributions for remodeling the shelter and transforming it into a shrine. In subsequent phone calls he tried to recruit me too, begging me to look for potential patrons for the site in Israel and abroad.

I soon found out, however, that Yosef was concerned with "remodeling" Wazana's figure no less than with remodeling the shelter. Our first meeting took place in Be'er Sheva at the end of May 1993, just a few days after I discussed Wazana in a literary program on Israeli television. Once again Wazana's deviant character was in the spotlight, but this time Yosef could not disregard it. He was devastated by the idea that his idol, for whom he was seeking to establish a sacred site, was presented in the program as a deviant healer, partly Muslim and partly demonic. In his despair, he even suggested we eliminate all the copies of the book from the bookstores and write a revised version together, after gaining the proper rabbinical approval. He withdrew his suggestion only after I made it clear that it was precisely the subversive side of Wazana that made me write down his life story.

This was, in fact, our one and only confrontation. Still, Yosef could not resign himself to the unorthodox aspects of Wazana, and did all he could to decrease their salience. In his discourse, he was cautious not to mention Wazana's name without juxtaposing it to his pious forebears, thus seeking to envelop him, as it were, in their saintly aura. When Wazana's oddities nevertheless came to the fore he was adamant to remove their sting by positive reframing. Thus he would often resort to mystical causes, presumably incomprehensible to ordinary people, in accounting for Wazana's alliance with the Muslims and the demons.

Yosef's efforts to deprive Wazana of his uniqueness and to recast him in the mold of a stereotypical Jewish Moroccan saint added a measure of unrelieved tension to our relations. Nevertheless, the dialogue between us could be maintained because it was based on a certain degree of symmetry, reciprocity, and interdependence. As a university professor keenly interested in the figure Yosef sought to idolize, I could serve as a source of legitimization and respectability for him in his efforts to popularize the new site.

But Yosef was no less important to my work, since I was determined to document and study the intriguing "resurrection" of Rabbi Ya'aqov Wazana which he initiated. To some extent, my professional career was dependent on Israelis of Moroccan background like Yosef—folk-healers, traditional patients, saint impresarios, and other devotees—whose knowledge, beliefs, visions, and misery I transformed into scholarly work. In the case of Wazana, the contribution to my academic standing that I took for granted was augmented by narcissistic gratification. The idea that my book was conducive to Wazana's reemergence in a saintly guise was so captivating that I was determined to investigate exhaustively the cultural phenomenon I had helped create. In a curiously symmetrical way, each of us managed to overcome or contain the problems posed by the other— for Yosef, the deviant aspects of Wazana emphasized in my book; for me, Yosef's attempt to replace these aspects with saintly ones—recognizing the potential contribution of the other to one's own goals.

The uneasy complicity between Yosef and myself was tested already on my first visit to Be'er Sheva. In fact, I scheduled the visit on the same day I was supposed to discuss my book on Wazana with students at Ben-Gurion University in Be'er Sheva. In doing this, I was well aware of the two levels of discourse, pertaining to different epistemological realms, that I juxtaposed, yet I was confident and even took delight in the fact that I could maneuver between the two readings of Wazana—as object of enshrinement and veneration and as object of skeptical inquiry. Unlike the protagonist of my book, with his shamanic power of bridging between worlds, I sought to compartmentalize the two realms of discourse. But Yosef interfered with my plan. When I tried to take my leave, after visiting the shelter-turned-into-a-shrine, he insisted that I should stay overnight at his place and I had to tell him about my other commitment. He immediately put forward his wish to join me and dismissed all my alarmed attempts to dissuade him from doing so. Even though I made it clear to Yosef that the students might be particularly interested in those aspects of Wazana's lifestyle he sought to silence, I felt quite insecure when we entered together the lecture hall where the meeting took place.

Epilogue

Despite my apprehension, the evening was quite successful. Sitting quietly among the students, Yosef followed attentively my introductory remarks and the lively discussion that ensued (in which, as I expected, the bizarre side of Wazana was a central topic). Toward the end of the meeting one student raised the issue of relevance: is it possible that people living in Israel in the 1990s are still moved by Wazana? To answer the question, I invited Yosef to the podium, on the spur of the moment, to tell his story. Delighted to have the arena for himself, Yosef unfolded the sequence of events that led him to erect the shrine to the Wazana family. I was amazed by his articulate and poised performance, which left the audience speechless. For one enchanted moment the two realms of discourse mingled after all.

Elated by the impact he had had on the students, Yosef felt very grateful to me for giving him the opportunity to tell his story in a setting he considered very prestigious. Much later, I was puzzled to find out that he had recorded the whole affair on a small tape recorder which he carried in his bag. I do not know how, if at all, he used the recorded material, but the measure he had taken further reduced the traditional gap between ethnographer and informant. The prerogative assumed by the researcher to isolate and objectify data extracted from the other, rendering it amenable for processing and analysis, was thus seized and employed by that other.

My turn to use a tape recorder (and a video camera) came several weeks later, in mid-July 1993, when Yosef invited me to "the first *hillula* of Rabbi Ya'aqov Wazana in Israel, commemorating his forty-first death anniversary," at Yosef's home in Be'er Sheva. Since some members of the Wazana family were also among the guests, I was a bit concerned about possible negative reactions to the book, but to my relief no one mentioned the anomalous aspects of Wazana. Moreover, from the compliments they bestowed on me for promulgating the life story of their kin, I came to the conclusion that not one of them had read the book. From my perspective, the high point of the modest, domestic *hillula* was an ornate speech delivered by a local rabbi, a remote kin of Rabbi Ya'aqov and one of the most respected descendants of the Wazana family, which was sealed as follows: "Rabbi Ya'aqov Wazana has made many wonders in his lifetime and in the afterworld, but his greatest miracle was to make a distinguished professor at the Hebrew University write this book."

Yosef also delivered a speech in which he elaborated on my association with Wazana. He deconstructed my name, Bilu, an acronym for the biblical verse *Beit Ya'aqov Lekhu Venelkha* ("House of Jacob, let us go"), as indicating my eagerness to go from house to house of would-be informants in pursuit of Rabbi Ya'aqov.

Note that in both speeches the two realms of discourse on Wazana were combined again, but this time it was the traditionally privileged social science perspective (Wazana as an object of investigation) which was appropriated and used to account for by the mystical perspective (Wazana as sainted figure). Of course, the process did not end here, since my ongoing attempts to document it constituted some form of reappropriation reflected, among other things, in this epilogue. The video camera, in particular, gave me an edge over Yosef. Operated by André Levy, a doctoral student of mine, it enabled me, by "freezing" the events of the *hillula,* to transform them into an objectified topic of study, amenable to multiple analyses and deconstructions. In subsequent months, however, Yosef added a video camera to the ever-more-advanced arsenal of tools he had been using in his attempts to promote his venture. The extent of his organizational efforts and sophistication became evident to me in the next public event he initiated for promoting the shrine, which took place in May 1994.

This time the celebration took place in a synagogue in Be'er Sheva. From the invitation to the occurrence I learned that the new shrine was designated the "Glory of the Ancestors—The Wazana Dynasty." The gathering was depicted in the invitation as "An evening dedicated to the Torah" in which many religious functionaries and political figures, from the chief rabbi of Be'er Sheva to two deputy-mayors, were supposed to address the attendants. My name too appeared among the local dignitaries. I was surprised to find out that I was "a member of the presidential body of the Hebrew University," and even more so that I was nominated "a member of the presidential body of [the sanctuary of] The Glory of the Ancestors—The Wazana Dynasty." The symmetry between the two designations, and particularly their juxtaposition, were lucid demonstrations of how deeply engulfed I had become in the "sacred discourse" about Wazana which Yosef cultivated. Aside from my name, my attention was also drawn to an enigmatic statement in the invitation announcing that "the sacred book of the saint Rabbi Ya'aqov Wazana will be presented in the synagogue." I found it hard to believe that this is how Yosef would designate my book, but given the hyperbolic language of the invitation I could not (perhaps I did not want to) altogether deny that possibility.

The evening was well organized. Food and beverages were distributed to the 150 congregants, and a local band played popular religious music. An articulate master of ceremonies presented the speakers and a professional team of photographers, with all sorts of cameras including video, documented the affair, including the speech I was asked to deliver. André, my student and colleague, also videoed the event, and this dual documentation, in which each side was captured and filmed by the other side, further blurred the boundaries between reality and its representation. Realizing the delicacy of the situation, I decided to circumvent in my speech the issue of Wazana's oddities and limit myself to the genealogy of the Wazana family and the way in which I had collected the material for the book. I was well aware that in so doing I was acquiescing to Yosef's attempts to sanctify Wazana, but in the ceremonial atmosphere that prevailed I did not feel I could act otherwise. I comforted myself that my temporary "betrayal" of the protagonist of my book was a necessary price for maintaining the privilege to study a phenomenon I had inadvertently helped set in motion. Moreover, there was something exciting, though at times upsetting too, in documenting the very process into which I was drawn as a key participant.

Listening to the other speeches, I could witness once again how my academic involvement with Wazana was mobilized in the service of mythologically rearranging his figure. Thus, I was amazed to hear that my voyage in the footsteps of Wazana was conducted in the remote areas of the Atlas Mountains, where I withstood many a predicament, rather than in Israel. This way the voyage (and by implication the figure that propelled it) was made grander and more heroic. Another speaker informed the impressed audience that in seventeen universities throughout the world research on the Wazana family was currently being conducted! A common thread in many of the speeches was that my fascination with Wazana could not be incidental. Rather, it was mystically informed and ought to be taken as another indication of Wazana's great stature.

Yosef, respectfully designated "Rabbi Yosef" by the master of ceremonies, was the last of the speakers. After unfolding the concatenation of events that led him to erect the shrine, he came to the highlight of the evening. He related how, following clues he received from Wazana in a recent dream message, he was able to secure, after an arduous odyssey, one of the healer's enigmatic books. To appreciate the excitement that this disclosure stirred in the audience, it should be recalled that Wazana's former associates consistently pointed to his old, handwritten books, replete with magical incantations and esoteric formulae, as a major source of his power. However, most of them also contended that Wazana's few possessions, including these precious books, had all mysteriously disappeared after his sudden death (see chapter 14). Despite persistent rumors claiming that one or more of the books had found their way to Israel, no one admitted to having seen them.

Following the public auction of gigantic colorful candles designed to collect money for the shrine, an indispensable part of such celebrations, Yosef presented the book to the congregants. As far as I could see, it was indeed a genuine book of medicine, handwritten in the distinctive Judeo-Maghrebi discursive writing (Bilu 1978: 364). The unmistakably Jewish origin of the book was incongruent with the recurrent claim that Wazana had exclusively relied on Muslim traditions in his work, but the participants were not bothered with questions of authenticity. Bustling and swarming they congregated around Yosef, trying to touch

160

the book in their hands and kiss it. It was clear that in their eyes the book, a sort of metonymic extension of the great healer, was endowed with great therapeutic powers that could be absorbed through physical contact. Having anticipated this enthusiastic response, Yosef circulated special forms among the congregants in which they were asked to write down the names of relatives and friends "to be blessed by the book of the saint." This initiative proved very lucrative, as indicated by the pile of envelopes filled up with forms and money that was aggregated on the podium at the end of the evening.

The discovery of the book adds an ironic twist and a sense of narrative closure to the preparatory part of Wazana's resurrection. The symmetry of the two realms of discourse between which I was precariously navigating and which had been formerly manifested in parallel employment of documentation means (such as tape and video) had been extended to the domain of the text—formerly the cherished prerogative of the researcher. I could not escape the egocentric notion that the book of healing attributed to Wazana was brought to the fore, among other things, as a counterweight to my own book. The ethnographic writing, an initial booster but also a potential obstacle to the sanctification of Wazana, has been replaced with a sacred text, more suited to the folk-religious idioms of the believers. At the same time, the two books appear complementary rather than exclusive, as Wazana's afterlife trajectory, paved to some degree by my book, gained a remarkable boost following the discovery of 'his' healing book. With a devoted, indefatigable, and creative impresario like Yosef, with a shrine commemorating Wazana's and his ancestors' names, and with a book that contains his healing power—with all this Wazana was transformed, more than forty years after his death, from a deviant healer into a venerated *tsaddiq*.

Several years have passed since the first presentation of Wazana's healing book, but the plot of his afterlife (or, no less important, of his promulgated life story) is still being developed. During these years, Wazana's emissary, Yosef, has also been transformed. When we first met, I saw before me a small man with penetrating eyes, short unkempt beard, and black skullcap. Like many other North African newcomers in the 1950s and 1960s, his family was not spared of the predicaments of absorption into Israel. His father, a successful merchant in Morocco, had to find his living in Israel as a manual laborer. The family lived in a transit camp in Be'er Sheva before moving to a working-class neighborhood. Eleven years old when the family moved to Israel, Yosef drifted between various low-level educational institutions and later became a barber in Netivot. When Rabbi Ya'aqov started to appear in his dreams he was in his mid-thirties, married with three little children. While never entirely divorced from religion, he became more observant before the revelation and began open-ended study in a local yeshiva—a move that made his wife, a kindergarten's caretaker, the family's breadwinner. As a participant-observer in Yosef's undertaking, I saw him growing as his project expanded; but I missed the critical year—1995—in which his popularity began to soar, as I was out of the country on sabbatical. In that year Yosef made Wazana's healing book the cornerstone of his enterprise. Starting in Israel's urban periphery but later extending his visits to the main cities, he organized public meetings in synagogues, hotels, and private homes at which he told his story, solicited contributions for the shrine, and promoted Wazana's book as a panacea for all sorts of life problems. The surging popularity of the book, which he masterfully cultivated through local media avenues (radio, television, and newspapers), made Yosef a well-known healer.

After my return to Israel, Yosef invited me to watch videotapes documenting some of these public gatherings. Only then could I appreciate the change he had undergone. The audience gathered at these meetings waited for him for a long time, animated by music and stories of his spiritual stance and healing miracles. When his entrance was announced, he was called Rabbi Yosef Waqnin *Shlite* (an acronym for "May he live for many days and years"), the *tsaddiq* of Be'er Sheva. Escorted by two yeshiva students on each side, he would step in, and with his prayer shawl over his head and the holy book clenched in his hands, he was welcomed by the ululations of the older women. Many congregants would rush to him to kiss his hand and receive his blessing. I was amazed to find out that Wazana's hallowed status, which Yosef worked so hard to establish, was now enveloping Yosef himself.

The program of the gatherings was quite uniform. It would start with an introductory presentation by Yosef depicting Wazana's grandeur and therapeutic feats, then move to a festive meal punctuated by the public auction of colorful candles and pictures of saints, and end with a healing ritual focusing on the book. Yosef's rhetorical style and eloquence, which had impressed me in the past, became more pronounced by his new assets: confident authority, soft-spoken parlance, and tenderness and empathy in his interactions with the supplicants. I had to admit that he knew how to address people in need, how to listen to them and cheer them up. His appearance too had changed. With his beard full-grown and the prayer shawl wrapping his head and shoulders throughout the meeting he appeared now immersed in spirituality.

Despite my absence, I found that my place in Yosef's project had been maintained. In his talks, he continued to use my work to glorify the Wazanas, "a family that won the attention of scholars all over the world, headed by professor Yoram Bilu, my dear friend, who is now in the United States, presenting his work on Wazana in American universities." He told his audience that I have been working on this topic for the last twenty years, "dedicating days and nights to this sublime end, taking pride at the holy family, and about to finish a new book on this subject." I also found that Yosef incorporated episodes from our encounters into his speeches. He described the presentation at Ben-Gurion University as follows: "I told this story [on a miraculous healing by Wazana] at Ben-Gurion University; a large audience, ordinarily removed from this domain, was present at my lecture. They remained there until late at night; and these are people engaged in research. They sat there and listened attentively. And it was all recorded. Professor Yoram Bilu, the chairman of the Hebrew University, who invited me to this lecture, was present too."

The climax of the meetings is when Yosef uses Wazana's book for blessing and healing. Altogether ignorant of the mystical procedures for diagnosis and healing specified by the book (which are based on elaborate word permutations and the writing of esoteric formulae), he has turned it into a magical object. For divination, the client is instructed to randomly open the book and look for any reference that could be associated with the problem. Healing is strictly mechanistic. After uttering a blessing, in which the names of Wazana and his ancestors are embedded, Yosef gently taps the client's forehead with the book. What renders this simple act therapeutic is the strong faith of the supplicants in the magical quality of the book and the good rapport Yosef establishes with them. Yosef's account of his recent success reflects his growing confidence and self-appreciation: "I talk [to the clients] from heart to heart, no connection whatsoever to religion, no coercion, in a gracious and open way. I am using my knowledge in a tolerant, prudent manner. I don't know how to call it, perhaps it's psychology. But it works!" Judging from the videotapes of the gathering I was watching, this self-characterization is not groundless.

The basis for Yosef's growing popularity has not gone unchallenged. Members of the Wazana family in Israel, and particularly the children of Rabbi Ya'aqov's blind cousin Shaul, view him as a usurper encroaching on their turf and depriving them of their *zekhut avot* (cf. Marcus 1985). In the *hillulot* of Rabbi Avraham el-Kebir, the founder of the dynasty, celebrated in Natanya, the Wazanas emphasize their exclusive right to the saint's blessing and smear and vilify Yosef's enterprise. Their malicious defamation does not seem to affect Yosef's popularity, however, since the book in his possession that ostensibly encapsulates Wazana's bliss keeps drawing large numbers of people to his gatherings. Rather than attacking his vilifiers, Yosef fosters a subdued and magnanimous stance, showing his appreciation and respect for the Wazana offspring. But at the same time, he uses my book to highlight the disparaging view that many of Rabbi Ya'aqov's kin took of his deviant lifestyle. In contrast, Yosef's own family in the Western High Atlas took good care of the healer until his last day and thus obtained the right to enjoy his blessing. He justifies the "expansionist" designation of his project (the "Glory of the Ancestors—The Wazana dynasty") by asserting that the title merely refers to the family line of Assarag. Rather than the great founder of the Wazana dynasty, Rabbi Avraham in this line is Ya'aqov Wazana's father, a *tsaddiq* without heirs.

In a further attempt to mitigate his image as usurper, Yosef started to claim recently that his family and Rabbi Ya'aqov's became related through intermarriage. Judging from his relentless efforts to transform the deviant healer into a popular *tsaddiq*, he may indeed be seen as a spiritual heir of Wazana. That he genuinely views himself as the inheritor of Rabbi Ya'aqov's blessing becomes apparent from the way he describes their critical encounter in the fifth visitational dream that sealed their alliance: "In the dream he [Wazana] put up his stick. He told me: 'hold this stick.' He drew me to him, covered me with this mantle, and started to pray and bless me with holy names. His hug made me happy and joyful. He kept blessing me: 'go on, go on, you will prevail, I will always be on your side.' I felt that his power had penetrated my body, that I was not the same Yosi [nickname for Yosef] Waqnin anymore." Yosef's moment of initiation is presented as a classic conversion in that the *tsaddiq*'s special power enters his body and irrevocably changes his identity.

In the fourth visitational dream Rabbi Ya'aqov explicitly assured Yosef: "I hereby submit to you all the powers of my forebears and me." This transmission, repeatedly announced by Yosef in his public meetings, indicates that the apprehension of the Wazanas is not unfounded. Notwithstanding Yosef's conciliatory approach toward them, in traditional Morocco the blessing or *zekhut* of the family was viewed as a limited good that cannot be replenished when expropriated by a contender (see Bilu 1988). If indeed Yosef identifies himself in fantasy with the biblical Joseph, this ascription may include the latter's descent. Since Joseph's father was no other than Jacob (Ya'aqov) the patriarch, Rabbi Ya'aqov's opening remark in the last visitational dream—"Yosef *my son*, my blessing on your head"—is not so metaphorical. It is possible that this dream blessing was modeled on the biblical prototype of Jacob's blessing to Joseph and his sons, which was granted "on their head" (Genesis 48: 14–18).[4]

The story of Rabbi Ya'aqov's afterlife is still being developed. Yosef's project is quickly expanding. The institutions of the "Glory of the Ancestors—the Holy Wazana Dynasty" now boat a yeshiva and *beit midrash* (religious school), separate Torah classes for men and women, and a welfare foundation for helping the needy. The institutionalization of the charisma is manifested, among other things, in a call for the monthly contribution, using automatic deposit, to the bank account of the "Glory of the Ancestors"; in distributing registration forms for blessings; and in holiday parties for women organized by Yosef's wife. A nice illustration of "the holy book" adorns all the forms, letter sheets, and envelopes of the institutions. The last expansion of the "Glory of the Ancestors" is a matchmaking agency headed by Yosef and an energetic aide, designated "general manager."

The close associations Yosef was able to forge with journalists in Be'er Sheva propagated a salvo of items praising his achievements in newspapers in southern Israel, with titles such "The Miracle Maker," "The Holy Book of Rabbi Ya'aqov," "The Wonders of Rabbi Yosef Waqnin," and "The Cat-Scanner of Be'er Sheva."[5] Excerpts from "The Cat-Scanner of Be'er Sheva" illustrate the enterprising self-marketing of the ex-barber turned "*tsaddiq* of Be'er Sheva" (cf. Weingrod 1990).

> Rabbi Yosef Waqnin *Shlite* takes over Be'er Sheva and
> its periphery, particularly Shderot and Netivot. Those who
> know Rabbi Waqnin hasten to dub him "The Cat-Scanner of
> Be'er Sheva" because of the amazing skills of diagnosis and
> consultation that this modest rabbi exhibits. I heard many
> stories from people who were miraculously helped by the
> Cat Scanner. Examples are endless: cancer cured, marriage
> affirmed against all odds, marital discord turned into harmony.
> Businessmen report positive changes in their activities, follow-
> ing the Rabbi's famous blessing for business, given in a special
> atmosphere of kindness and peacefulness. . . . Thousands and
> tens of thousands of women report an amazing improvement
> in their lives following the Rabbi's renowned blessing that
> gained recognition in Israel and the world. An article in a local
> communication media described the rabbi as a miracle maker
> of unusual stature; he simply entreats the holy book, and the
> latter complies. Soon the rabbi will star on the front page of a
> national daily and in several radio programs which will expose
> him to the entire population. Hence, our tip to you is: hurry
> to the Cat Scanner and get his blessing at once. I promise you:
> You will come back stunned.

To sum up, the vicissitudes of Wazana's afterlife—how Yosi Waqnin became Rabbi Yosef Waqnin *Shlite*, the Saint of Be'er Sheva, and how I became unwittingly involved in the process—points to the undermining of the authority of "ethnographic realism" (Marcus and Cushman 1982) in three areas. The "natives" as an object of analysis may become analyzing subjects, capable of manipulating the ethnographer to their ends (Rosaldo 1989); the ethnographer is not a detached observer, dissociated from the process of knowledge production; and, most pertinent to this case study, the ethnographic text might have strong impact on the community studied (cf. Blackman 1992; Brettell 1993). When the researcher keeps studying this impact, and the subjects keep responding to his presence in the field, the ethnographic arena turns into a hall of mirrors. The blurred images reflected in these mirrors stand for a postmodern ethnographic reality: kaleidoscopic, elusive, and constituted by its own documentation. In the narrative sequence I depicted, the moment most emblematic of this complex reality occurred in the celebration in Be'er Sheva when both sides, researcher and subjects, stabilized and framed each other with their video cameras. Fixating the observer in the lenses of the observed reflects the narrowing of the gap between "modern" and "traditional." The "traditional" subject, using advanced technology, attempts to appropriate the so-called scholarly product of the researcher and bask in its prestige. The researcher reacts by drawing away, resorting to a "postmodern" discourse, replete with contradictions and self-irony.

This process of distancing highlights the fact that the boundaries between Yosef and myself were blurred but not entirely dissolved. Our preliminary mutual enthusiasm was later tinged with ambivalence and reservations, but we learned to cooperate and benefit from each other, neutralizing controversies and suspending incompatible expectations. Yosef's gains from our interaction were obvious. First, my book served as a trigger, if not as a source of inspiration, for his project. Second, he knew how to transform my interest in Wazana and his afterlife into resources of legitimacy and prestige. This he did by a major input of selection and processing which entailed excluding any extra-cultural analysis of Wazana offered by the book, denying the antinomian aspects in his makeup, highlighting his miraculous and healing feats, and augmenting them with features common to the stereotypical image of Maghrebi *tsaddiqim*.

My main gain from the awkward interaction with Yosef, very gratifying at certain moments but no less embarrassing at others, was the opportunity to convert it into some sort of professional good, including this epilogue. Needless to say, the monopoly I retained over the writing of this chapter significantly curtails the symmetry between researcher and subject I highlighted earlier. Yosef was not partner to the writing, his identity was disguised, and the emerging narrative of Wazana's afterlife represents my interpretation of the unfolding events. As in traditional ethnographic writing, the authority and "voice" remain mine. Note, however, that the textual representation of reality is but a partial and limited province of meaning within it. As made clear before, Yosef generated many arenas of self-presentation where his "voice" and interpretations loomed high. In the last analysis, it was his ability to appropriate the ethnographic text and to use it to his ends, in other words, "to tell me," which propelled me to add this epilogue about Wazana's afterlife.

From a credulous perspective grounded in the discourse common in Yosef's arenas of action, it is not difficult to show that the concatenation of all events in Wazana's afterlife constitutes further evidence of the legendary healer's endless powers. More than forty years after his death, this energy seems to activate the researcher no less than Wazana's former acquaintances and new followers. Given my skeptical point of view, this perspective is presented with a modicum of irony. But in a very serious vein we may conclude that what started as an attempt to document and present a dynamic reality evolved into an intricate interaction, epistemologically precarious, in which the ethnographic work became a building block in constituting this reality. In this process I have unwittingly became a popularizer and propagator of Wazana—an impresario of saint impresarios.

Notes

Chapter 1

1. The current work, focusing on the life story of a Jewish Moroccan folk healer with "shamanic" qualities, follows the tradition of using biographies to highlight a wider social reality, prevalent both among students of the Maghreb (see, for example, Crapanzano 1980; Munson 1984; and Waterbury 1972) and anthropologists interested in folk healers (for example, Edgerton 1971; Handelman 1967; Langness and Frank 1981; and Low 1988). The best known biographical account of a shaman, Castaneda's Don Juan (1968), raises serious questions of credibility (De Mille 1980).

Chapter 2

1. I would like to thank Edna Cheichel from the Israel Folktale Archive for affording me access to the stories. For a structural analysis of Abutbul's account of Wazana's death sent to the Archive see Jason (1976). The insightful analysis treats Wazana as a legendary figure.
2. *Hillula* is an Aramaic word designating "wedding celebration." In Jewish mystical circles the death of an especially pious man was viewed as leading to a mystical union between his soul and the Godhead (Deshen 1977: 110; and Weingrod 1990: 11).
3. On Rabbi David u-Moshe in Morocco and Israel see Ben-Ami 1981, 1984; and Bilu 1987.
4. A traditional Jewish Moroccan springtime celebration taking place on the day following Passover. On the origins of the Mimuna and its transformation into an ethnic renewal celebration in Israel, part of the national calendar of festivals, see Goldberg 1978 and Weingrod 1990.

Notes

5. On the Abu-Ḥatseras' impressive genealogy of *tsaddiqim* in Morocco and Israel see Ben-Ami 1984; Bar-Moḥa and Dor 1995; and Bilu and Ben-Ari 1992.
6. *Ait* in Moroccan Arabic denotes "family," "tribe," or "clan."
7. Lag Ba'Omer, a Jewish festival marked by bonfires, which is conducted on the thirty-third day of the counting of the barley (starting on Passover), is also the *hillula* day of Rabbi Shimon Bar-Yoḥai, the putative second-century author of the holy Zohar, the canonical text of Jewish mysticism. Rabbi Shimon's *hillula* in Meron is the largest pilgrimage in Israel, drawing up to two hundred thousand celebrants.

Chapter 3

1. Ben-Ami (1984: 37) sites the Wazana family as one of the renowned holy families of Morocco. For the centrality of the authority passed on among the Moroccan holy families see Deshen 1989.
2. According to Ben-Ami, Rabbi Avraham lived at the beginning of the nineteenth century (1984: 244).
3. According to one version, Rabbi Avraham was born in Skoura. Dra is associated with ancient traditions concerning kabbalists and miracle workers (Elior 1985).
4. Rabbi David Wazana appears in Ben-Ami's book as Rabbi Avraham's brother (1984: 317). Apart from the possibility that the versions are different because of the different sources, we might be talking about another *tsaddiq*, the uncle of Rabbi David in our story.
5. See Babylonian Talmud, Sanhedrin 22a.
6. For the possibility of a human being abducted by demons see Alexander 1991; Bilu 1979; and Tsfatman 1988.
7. For the transformation of certain places into the "inheritance" of different rabbis, see Ben-Ami 1984: 51.
8. As already mentioned, two of the family's *tsaddiqim*, Rabbi Avraham and Rabbi David, are recorded among the *tsaddiqim* of Morocco (Ben-Ami 1984: 244, 317).

Chapter 4

1. For more details of Jewish life in the Atlas Mountains, see Flamand 1959; Shokeid 1982; and Willner and Kohls 1962.
2. Regarding the legal status of Jews as an inferior minority within Muslim society (Dhimmi) see Bat-Yeor 1985; and Lewis 1984.
3. Jewish-Muslim relations in Morocco have been extensively researched by the anthropologist Lawrence Rosen, who worked in Sefrou near Fez (cf. 1972, 1984). For an analysis of Jewish-Muslim relations in Morocco with greater emphasis on the tensions and conflicts than on the harmonious existence claimed by Rosen, see Stillman 1978. Bilu and Levy 1996 and Shokeid 1982 offer a more integrated view of the relationship.

Notes

4. On the importance of *zekhut avot* (the privilege of the forebears) within the traditional healing system of Moroccan Jewry, see Bilu 1978, 1985a. There is a great deal of similarity between Jewish *zekhut avot* and the Muslim *baraka*. For the centrality of the latter in Moroccan life, see Eickelman 1976; Jamous 1981; Rabinow 1975; and Westermarck 1926.

Chapter 5

1. For example, the holy men of the village of Tabia were buried in Demnate and Netifa (Ben-Ami 1984: 389–91). Rabbi Shlomo Timsut from Imi-n-tanut was buried in Essaouira (Bilu 1990: 254).
2. The miraculous occurrence whereby the sun stands still allowing the *tsaddiq* to be buried before the Sabbath begins and thereby to enjoy the imminent holiness without profaning it, is a recurrent theme in stories of the death and burial of such famous *tsaddiqim* as Rabbi Amram Ben Diwan, Rabbi Rephael ha-Kohen, Rabbi Shlomo Ben Leḥans, and Mulai Irhi (Ben-Ami 1984: 63).
3. Cf. "Absalom, Absalom my son . . ." (II Samuel 19:5). This inference is apparent not only in the similarity of the opening phrasing (here "Ya'aqov, Ya'aqov my son") but also in the context of the subject matter: an anguished lamentation over the death of a loved relative. The style of the blessing—"May the Lord bless you and keep you"— echoes the priestly blessing of the Bible.

Chapter 7

1. It is worth emphasizing here that among the former Moroccan community, reading in the mystical Zohar and delving into the hidden secrets in general is less proscribed than we find with other Jewish communities and therefore was a more common phenomenon, relatively speaking (Goldberg 1990; and Shtahl 1980). Against this background, the fact that Wazana totally avoided using the kabbala for healing only serves to emphasize his estrangement from the practices of other healers.
2. For a description of the Sous magicians see Westermarck 1926: 359–63.
3. The existence of an intrinsically different time stream in the other world recurs in popular folklore and literature, although the common pattern is the opposite of that presented here: years are experienced as lasting days (see Thompson 1966: III:76 [motif F377: Supernatural time in fairyland]).
4. For the demon in Muslim society in Morocco, see Crapanzano 1973, 1980; and Westermarck 1926. For the status of the demon within Jewish Moroccan society, see Bilu 1979, 1980.
5. For the phenomenon of possession (*dybbuk*) in Jewish tradition, see Bilu 1985b; Nigal 1983.

Notes

Chapter 8

1. Demons hate salt and keep away from it. Salt is therefore commonly used as a defense to ward off demons (see, for example, Bilu 1979).

Chapter 9

1. On Joseph's exceptional beauty see Babylonian Talmud, Yoma 35b.

Chapter 11

1. The Muslims in Morocco similarly divide healing formulations into *herz rabbani* and *herz sitani* (see Westermarck 1926: 208).
2. The names required for the healing are written on paper that is immersed in a vessel full of water. The writing is thus erased and the water absorbs the healing attributes. The same result may be obtained by writing on the bottom of a plate and then pouring water into the plate. Sometimes, the paper containing the names is burned, thus endowing the smoke with the healing properties.
3. These are the Moroccan names for the healing substances. *Harmel* (*peganum harmala*) is used for keeping demons and the evil eye at bay. *Rota* (rue) has similar uses, and is also effective in the treatment of anxiety and worry. *Casbur* (coriander), *pasokh* (gum ammoniac), *seb* (alum), and *jawi* (benzoin) are used in fighting demons and have other uses besides. Thus, for example, *pasokh* is a protection against sorcerers, while *seb*, a crystalline mineral, has diagnostic uses: when dissolved, it hardens into different shapes. These shapes are "read" to reveal the sufferer's problems (similar to reading coffee grounds; see Bilu 1978: 372–73; and Westermarck 1926: 306–10).
4. On the vicissitudes of the powerful Glaoua family in the Atlas regions during the first half of the twentieth century see Maxwell 1966.
5. Childlessness among married couples was usually believed to be the result of infertility on the woman's part, unless proved otherwise (see Bilu 1978: 99; and Shokeid 1971: 126).
6. For the two universal principles of magic, contact and similarity, see Frazer 1952.
7. "Our rabbis taught: It is permitted to consult by a charm the spirits [princes] of oil or eggs, but that they give false answers" (Babylonian Talmud, Sanhedrin 101a). It appears that the sages permit the use of such diagnostic techniques just because they are unfounded.
8. It is likely that this book was ascribed to King Solomon owing to the popular myths regarding his ability to command the demons (see, for example, Ginzberg 1913: 149–54).
9. As the day of the destruction of the two temples, the ninth of Av, a day of fasting and mourning, is deemed particularly inauspicious.
10. The Jews supported the despotic pasha of Marrakech, Ḥaj Tehami, because he protected them. Many believed that the pasha's benevolent attitude toward them owed to the fact that Rabbi Pinḥas ha-Kohen,

a sage from Marrakech considered to be a saint, saved the pasha from several attempts on his life (Ben-Ami 1984: 175). Apparently, the informants attribute these stories to Wazana.

Chapter 13

1. A common technique for exorcising a demon or spirit was to place a burning rag in the person's nostrils and "smoking" it so that the entity within would be burnt or choked (see, for example, Nigal 1983: 47).
2. For the disappearing voice as a sign of demonic presence, see Westermarck 1926: 269.
3. Literally the days "between the straits," this period of time spans the three weeks between the collapse of the walls of Jerusalem under the Roman siege on the seventeenth of Tammuz and the destruction of the temple on the ninth of Av.
4. It is difficult to ascertain the medical reasons for Wazana's death based on the details provided; however, in view of his fondness for drink, we cannot rule out the possibility that the cause of death was cirrhosis of the liver, the primary cause of death in alcoholics. The confusion, memory interference, inability to hold on to objects, and the terrors that Wazana suffered are recognized symptoms of this disease. Internal bleeding, possibly accompanied by portal hypertension with upper gastrointestinal bleeding might have been responsible for the large quantity of blood Wazana vomited as he was dying (see Geffries 1971: 1379–80).
5. Some informants referred to Wazana's fatal affliction as *derba* ("an attack"). This term describes a demonic disease category considered to be a dangerous attack usually resulting in death. The short duration of this type of affliction gave birth to the term "*derbat (e)l-yom-uleyla*," i.e., an attack which sealed a person's fate within a single day. The duration of Wazana's sickness fits into this category. See Bilu 1978: 78–81.
6. This assurance is based on a wish rather than on fact. In my visit to Agouim in 1993, I found the Jewish cemetery, lying on a steep slope across from the village, untended and ruined, with only a few gravestones intact. Wazana's tomb could not be located. I did manage to find a piece of a broken tombstone with the Hebrew inscription Tammuz, which is the month of Wazana's death (see picture on p. 115).
7. On the option of being cured of an affliction by "transferring" it to someone else, see Bilu 1978: 169; and Westermarck 1926: 605–7.

Chapter 14

1. These are all traditional garments worn in Morocco. *Chamir* refers to a closed cloak with a collar. *Farajiya* is an open cloak with covered buttons. *Salam* is a fur overcoat worn in winter.

Notes

Chapter 15

1. The benefits of holding a book attributed to Wazana are illustrated in detail in the epilogue.
2. There was a widespread belief among Moroccan Jewry that a saint could appear to his followers in the form of a snake (see Westermarck 1926: 65–66).

Chapter 16

1. It is tempting to think of these items in terms of psychoanalytic object relations theory as transitional objects of the type of the doll or blanket with which young children develop a strong attachment. We can see that this attachment is, among other things, an attempt to cope with experiences of separation from the parents and to reduce the anxiety to which they give rise. "Transitional objects are created in loneliness. They are based on feeling alone, yearning for past intimacy, and the recreation of past togetherness. . . . [T]ransitional objects restore lost objects" (Kestenberg and Weinstein 1978: 90). The "fetishistic" relationship Wazana exhibited for his parents' belongings is compatible with the conceptualization outlined above. For the origin of the term "transitional objects" see Winnicott 1980.

   The term "linking objects," coined by the psychoanalyst Vamik Volkan, is even better suited for our purposes. As Volkan says, "I have found that patients with established pathological grief typically select an inanimate object—a symbolic bridge [or link] to the representation of the dead person. . . . The mourner sees them [linking objects] as containing elements of himself and of the one he has lost. By using his linking object, the mourner can keep alive the illusion that *he has the power either to return the dead person to life* or to 'kill' him" (Volkan 1981: 20, emphasis added). The items once belonging to his parents that Wazana guarded so closely should be regarded more as "linking objects" than "transitional objects." The former are usually used by the individual during adulthood to compensate for loss of a close figure, while the latter are initially manifested during childhood in the course of normal development.
2. For the dangers of calling demons by their explicit name see Westermarck 1926: 603.
3. For an illuminating analysis of the psychological similarities between reactions to grief, mourning, and loss and mystical experiences, see Aberbach 1987. For the association between the absence of fathers and religious commitment see Masson 1976; and Ullman 1989. On the wish to compensate for the loss of a parent that might lead to achievement and excellence in many areas see Eisenstadt, Haynal, Rentchnick, and De Senarclens 1989.

Notes

Chapter 17

1. On the "tendency" for *tsaddiqim* to be buried on Friday, prior to the commencement of the Sabbath, see note 2 to chapter 5.
2. For details of demons' attraction to blood see Westermarck, 1926: 104, 277.
3. See note 3 to chapter 13.
4. Rabbinic discussions of the Three Weeks add another layer of significance to Wazana's death date. It is indicated in the Talmudic (Pesakhim 111) and Midrashic (Lamentations Rabba) literature that in this period of the year, *ketev meriri,* a very dangerous demon, is particularly active. This time is also viewed as inauspicious for transactions with non-Jews. Thus, from a Jewish perspective, Wazana's overinvolvement with Muslims and demons during the Three Weeks period made him especially vulnerable. Note, however, that none of the interviewees explicitly discussed these associations with us.
5. For a structural analysis of the story of Wazana's death with emphasis on this aspect of harmony, disruption, and restoration, see Jason 1976.
6. My analysis of the lawful regularity of the binary oppositions between Wazana and his father that appear in the legends discussed is of course based on the structuralist approach, whose arch-proponent is Lévi-Strauss (cf. 1964, 1966). For an interesting attempt to integrate "time-less" structuralist explanations with a historical approach best suited to analyzing the legendary aspects of the life of Wazana as a historical figure, see Ardener 1989.
7. Turner developed and expanded the concept of liminality first used by Van Gennep (1960) in the context of rites of passage.
8. For discussions of the shaman's role see Eliade 1964; Halifax 1980; Harner 1973; and Rogers 1982.
9. This puzzling correlation happens to be historically true. In the early 1950s, when Wazana died, the struggle for independence led to violent clashes between Moroccan nationalists and the French colonial government (see, for example, Bernard 1968).
10. The motif of a world without limits, where the only restriction imposed is ignored, is a common folklore theme (Thompson 1966: I:526 [motif C 600–49: The one forbidden thing]).

Epilogue

1. The pieces appeared in *Yediot Haḥronot* (Yigal Sarna) and *Ma'ariv* (Nurit Baretski) on March 26, 1993.
2. Yosef's family name is disguised.
3. On Maghrebi traditions of saint apparitions in dreams see Bilu and Abramovitch 1985, and Crapanzano 1975.
4. If indeed Yosef adopted in fantasy the biblical ascription of Joseph son of Jacob, this could endow surplus mystical depth to the triangular relations between Wazana, Yosef, and myself. Note that in his decon-

struction of my name, Yosef presented me as partaking of "the House of Jacob."

5. In all probability, this title, "the Cat Scanner of Be'er Sheva," was inspired by the soaring success of a rabbi-healer from a neighboring development town, who was dubbed "the X ray of Netivot" for his diagnostic achievements.

Bibliography

Aberbach, D. 1987. Grief and Mysticism. *International Review of Psychoanalysis* 14: 509–26.

Alexander, Tamar. 1991. *Demonological Stories*. Jerusalem: Academon. [Hebrew].

Ardener, Edwin. 1989. The Construction of History: "Vestiges of Creation." In *History and Ethnicity*, ed. E. Tonkin, M. McDonald, and M. Chapman. London: Routledge.

Bar-Moha, Josef, and Danny Dor. 1995. *The Abu Ḥatsera Family— Legend and Reality*. Or Yehuda: Ma'ariv. [Hebrew].

Bat-Yeor, (pseud.). 1985. The Dhimmi: Jews and Christians under Islam. Rutherford: Fairleigh Dickinson University Press.

Ben-Ami, Issachar. 1981. The Folk-Veneration of Saints among Moroccan Jews: Tradition, Continuity and Change. In *Studies in Judaism and Islam*, ed. S. Morag, I. Ben-Ami, and N. A. Stillman, 283–345. Jerusalem: Magnes Press.

———. 1984. *Saint Veneration among the Jews in Morocco*. Jerusalem: Magnes Press. [Hebrew].

Ben-Ari, Eyal, and Yoram Bilu. 1987. Saints' Sanctuaries in Israeli Development Towns: On a Mechanism of Urban Transformation. *Urban Anthropology* 16: 243–72.

Bernard, Stephane. 1968. *The Franco-Moroccan Conflict*. New Haven: Yale University Press.

Bertaux, Daniel, ed. 1981. *Biography and Society*. London: Sage.

Bilu, Yoram. 1978. Traditional Psychiatry in Israel. Ph.D. Diss. Hebrew University.

———. 1979. Demonic Explanations of Illness among Moroccan Jews in Israel. *Culture, Medicine and Psychiatry* 3: 363–80.

———. 1980. The Moroccan Demon in Israel: The Case of "Evil Spirit Disease." *Ethos* 8: 24–38.

177

Bibliography

————. 1982. Pondering the "Princes of Oil": A New Light on an Old Phenomenon. *Journal of Anthropological Research* 37: 269–78.

————. 1985a. The Benefits of Attenuation: Continuity and Change in Jewish Moroccan Ethnopsychiatry in Israel. In *Studies in Israeli Ethnicity*, ed. Alex Weingrod, 297–315. New York: Gordon and Breach.

————. 1985b. The Taming of the Deviants and Beyond: An Analysis of Dybbuk Possession and Exorcism in Judaism. *Psychoanalytic Study of Society* 11: 1–32.

————. 1987. Dreams and the Wishes of the Saint. In *Judaism Viewed from Within and from Without: Anthropological Studies,* ed. Harvey E. Goldberg, 285–313. Albany: State University of New York Press.

————. 1988. The Inner Boundaries of Communitas: A Covert Dimension of Pilgrimage Behavior. *Ethos* 16: 302–25.

————. 1990. Jewish Moroccan "Saint Impresarios" in Israel: A Stage-Developmental Perspective. *Psychoanalytic Study of Society* 15: 247–69.

Bilu, Yoram, and Henry Abramovitch. 1985. In Search of the Saddiq: Visitational Dreams among Moroccan Jews in Israel. *Psychiatry* 48: 83–92.

Bilu, Yoram, and Galit Hasan-Rokem. 1989. Cinderella and the Saint. *Psychoanalytic Study of Society* 14: 227–59.

Bilu, Yoram, and Eyal Ben-Ari. 1992. The Making of Modern Saints: Manufactured Charisma and the Abu-Hatseiras of Israel. *American Ethnologist* 19: 672–87.

Bilu, Yoram, and André Levy. 1996. Nostalgia and Ambivalence: The Reconstruction of Jewish-Muslim Relations in Oulad Mansour. In *The Modern Sephardi and Middle Eastern Jewries: History and Culture,* ed. Harvey E. Goldberg, 288–311. Bloomington: Indiana University Press.

Blackman, M. B. 1992. The Afterlife of the Life History. *Journal of Narrative and Life History* 2 (1).

Bourguignon, Erika. 1979. *Psychological Anthropology.* New York: Holt, Rinehart and Winston.

Brettell, C. B. 1993. *When They Read What We Write: The Politics of Ethnography.* Westport, CT: Bergin and Garvey.

Bruner, Jerome. 1990. *Acts of Meaning.* Cambridge: Harvard University Press.

————, 1991. The Narrative Construction of Reality. *Critical Inquiry* 18: 1–21.

Castaneda, Carlos. 1968. *The Teachings of Don Juan.* Berkeley and Los Angeles: University of California Press.

Clifford, James, and George E. Marcus, eds. 1986. *Writing Culture: The Poetics and the Politics of Ethnography.* Berkeley and Los Angeles: University of California Press.

Crapanzano, Vincent. 1973. *The Hamadsha: A Study in Moroccan Ethnopsychiatry.* Berkeley and Los Angeles: University of California Press.

————. 1975. Saints, Jnun, and Dreams: An Essay in Moroccan Ethnopsychology. *Psychiatry* 38: 145–59.

————. 1980. *Tuhami: Portrait of a Moroccan.* Chicago: University of Chicago Press.

Crites, Stephen. 1986. Storytime: Recollecting the Past and Projecting the Future.

Bibliography

In *Narrative Psychology,* ed. Theodore R. Sarbin, 152–73. New York: Praeger.

D'Andrade, Roy G., and Claudia Strauss, eds. 1992. *Human Motives and Cultural Models.* Cambridge: Cambridge University Press.

De Mille, Richard. 1980. *The Don Juan Papers.* Santa Barbara, CA: Ross-Erikson.

Deshen, Shlomo. 1977. The *Hillulot* of Tunisian Immigrants. In *The Generation of Transition,* ed. Moshe Shokeid and Shlomo Deshen, 110–21. Jerusalem: Yad Ben-Zvi Press. [Hebrew].

———. 1989. *The Mellah Society: Jewish Community Life in Sherifian Morocco.* Chicago: University of Chicago Press.

Douglas, Mary. 1957. Animals in Lele Religious Thought. *Africa* 27: 46–58.

———. 1966. *Purity and Danger.* London: Routledge and Kegan Paul.

Edgerton, Robert B. 1971. A Traditional African Psychiatrist. *Southwestern Journal of Anthropology* 27: 259–78.

Eickelman, Dale F. 1976. *Moroccan Islam: Tradition and Society in a Pilgrimage Center.* Austin: University of Texas Press.

Eisenstadt, Marvin, Andre Haynal, Pierre Rentchnick, and Pierre De Senarclens. 1989. *Parental Loss and Achievement.* Madison, CT: International Universities Press.

Eliade, Mircea. 1964. *Shamanism: Archaic Techniques of Ecstasy.* New York: Pantheon.

Elior, Rachel. 1985. The Kabbalists of Dr'aa. *Pe'amim* 24: 36–73. [Hebrew].

Flamand, Pierre. 1959. *Diaspora en terre d'Islam: les communautés israélites du sud-marocain.* Casablanca: Presses des Imprimeries Réunis.

Frazer, J. G. 1952. *The Golden Bough.* New York: Macmillan.

Geertz, Clifford. 1968. *Islam Observed: Religious Development in Morocco and Indonesia.* Chicago: University of Chicago Press.

Geffries, G. G. 1971. Diseases of the Liver. In *Textbook of Medicine,* 13th ed., ed. P. B. Beeson and W. Mcdermott. Philadelphia: W. B. Sonders.

Gellner, Ernest. 1969. *Saints of the Atlas.* Chicago: University of Chicago Press.

Gergen, Kenneth G., and Mary Gergen. 1983. Narratives of the Self. In *Studies in Social Identity,* ed. Theodore R. Sarbin and Karl E. Scheibe, 254–73. New York: Praeger.

Ginzberg, Louis. 1913. *The Legends of the Jews.* Philadelphia: Jewish Publication Society of America.

Goldberg, Harvey E. 1978. The Mimuna and the Minority Status of Moroccan Jews. *Ethnology* 17: 75–87.

———. 1983. The Mellahs of Southern Morocco: A Report of a Survey. *The Maghreb Review* 8: 61–69.

———. 1990. The Zohar in Southern Morocco: A Study in Ethnography of Texts. *History of Religions* 29: 233–58.

———. 1992. Potential Polities: Jewish Saints in the Moroccan Countryside and in Israel. In *Faith and Polity: Essays on Religion and Politics,* ed. Mart Bax, Peter Kloos, and Andrianus Koster, 233–52. Amsterdam: VU University Press.

Good, Byron J. 1994. *Medicine, Rationality, and Experience: An Anthropolog-*

ical Perspective. Lewis Henry Morgan Lectures. Cambridge: Cambridge University Press.

Halifax, John. 1980. *Shamanic Voices: The Shaman as Seer, Poet and Healer.* London: Penguin.

Handelman, Don. 1967. The Development of a Washo Shaman. *Ethnology* 6: 444–64.

———. 1985. Charisma, Liminality, and Symbolic Types. In *Comparative Social Dynamics,* ed. E. Cohen, M. Lissak, and U. Almagor, 346–59. Boulder, CO: Westview Press.

———. 1991. Symbolic Types, the Body, and Circus. *Semiotica* 85: 205–25.

Harner, Michael. 1973. *Hallucinogens and Shamanism.* Oxford: Oxford University Press.

Ingham, John M. 1996. *Psychological Anthropology Reconsidered.* Cambridge: Cambridge University Press.

Jamous, Raymond. 1981. *Honneur et baraka: les structures sociales traditionnelles dans le Rif.* Paris: Editions de la Maison des Sciences de l'Homme.

Jason, Heda. 1976. Rabbi Wazana and the Demons: Analysis of a Legend. In *Folklore Today: Festschrift for Richard M. Dorson,* ed. L. Degli, H. Glassie, and F. Oinas, 273–90. Bloomington: Indiana University Press.

Kestenberg, Judith S., and Joan Weinstein. 1978. Transitional Objects and Body-Image Formation. In *Between Reality and Fantasy: Transitional Objects and Phenomena,* ed. S. A. Grolnik and L. Barakin, 75–96. New York: Jason Aronson.

Kilborne, Benjamin, and L. L. Langness, eds. 1987. *Culture and Human Nature: Theoretical Papers of Melford E. Spiro.* Chicago: University of Chicago Press.

Langness, L. L., and Gelia Frank. 1981. *Lives: An Anthropological Approach to Biography.* Novato, CA: Chandler and Sharp.

Lévi-Strauss, Claude. 1964. *The Raw and the Cooked.* Harmondsworth, England: Penguin.

———. 1966. *The Savage Mind.* Chicago: University of Chicago Press.

Lewis, Bernard. 1984. *The Jews of Islam.* Princeton, NJ: Princeton University Press.

Low, Setha M. 1988. The Medicalization of Healing Cults in Latin America. *American Ethnologist* 18: 135–54.

Marcus, George E., and Dick Cushman. 1982. Ethnographies as Texts. *Annual Review of Anthropology* 11: 25–69.

Marcus, George E., and Michael M. J. Fischer. 1986. *Anthropology as Cultural Critique: An Experimental Moment in the Human Sciences.* Chicago: University of Chicago Press.

Marcus, M. A. 1985. The Saint Has Been Stolen: Sanctity and Social Change in a Tribe of Eastern Morocco. *American Ethnologist* 12: 454–67.

Masson, Jeffrey. 1976. The Psychology of the Ascetic. *Journal of Asian Studies* 35: 611–25.

Maxwell, Gavin. 1966. *Lords of the Atlas: The Rise and Fall of the House of Glaoua, 1893–1956.* London: Longmans.

Bibliography

Munson, Henry Jr. 1984. *The House of Si Abd Allah: The Oral History of a Moroccan Family*. New Haven: Yale University Press.

Myerhoff, Barbara. 1976. Balancing between Worlds: The Shaman's Calling. *Parabola* 1: 6–13.

Nigal, Gedalia. 1983. *Dybbuk Stories in Jewish Literature*. Jerusalem: Reuven Mass. [Hebrew].

Obeyesekere, Gananath. 1981. *Medusa's Hair: An Essay on Personal Symbols and Religious Experience*. Chicago: University of Chicago Press.

———. 1990. *The Work of Culture*. Chicago: University of Chicago Press.

Rabinow, Paul. 1975. *Symbolic Domination: Cultural Forms and Historical Change in Morocco*. Chicago: University of Chicago Press.

Rogers, S. N. 1982. *The Shaman, His Symbols and His Healing Power*. Springfield, IL: Charles C. Thomas.

Rosaldo, Renato. 1989. *Culture and Truth: The Remaking of Social Analysis*. London: Routledge

Rosen, Lawrence. 1972. Muslim-Jewish Relations in a Muslim City. *International Journal of Middle East Studies* 3: 435–49.

———. 1984. *Bargaining for Reality*. Chicago: University of Chicago Press.

Schafer, Roy. 1981. Narrative in the Psychoanalytic Dialogue. In *On Narrative*, ed. W. J. T. Mitchell, 25–49. Chicago: University of Chicago Press.

Shokeid, Moshe. 1971. *The Dual Heritage: Immigrants from the Atlas Mountains in an Israeli Village*. New York: Manchester University Press.

———. 1982. Jewish Existence in a Berber Environment. In *Jewish Societies in the Middle East,* ed. Shlomo Deshen and Walter P. Zenner, 105–22. Washington, DC.: University Press of America.

Shtahl, Avraham. 1980. Ritual Reading of the Zohar. *Pe'amim* 5: 77–86. [Hebrew].

Spence, Donald. 1982. *Narrative Truth and Historical Truth*. New York: Norton.

Spiro, Meford E. 1993. Is the Western Conception of the Self "Peculiar" within the Context of the World Cultures? *Ethos* 21: 107–53.

Stillman, Norman A. 1978. The Moroccan Jewish Experience: A Revisionist View. *The Jerusalem Quarterly* 8.9: 111–23.

———. 1982. Saddiq and Marabut in Morocco. In *The Sephardi and Oriental Jewish Heritage,* ed. Issaschar Ben-Ami, 489–500. Jerusalem: Magnes Press.

Strauss, Claudia, and Naomi Quinn. 1997. *A Cognitive Theory of Cultural Meaning*. Cambridge: Cambridge University Press.

Thompson, Stith. 1966. *Motif-Index of Folk-Literature*. Bloomington: Indiana University Press.

Tsfatman, Sara. 1988. *Human-Demon Intermarriage*. Jerusalem: Academon. [Hebrew].

Turner, Victor. 1967. *The Forest of Symbols*. Ithaca, NY: Cornell University Press.

———. 1969. *The Ritual Process: Structure and Anti-Structure*. Chicago: University of Chicago Press.

———. 1974. *Dramas, Fields, and Metaphors*. Ithaca, NY: Cornell University Press.

Ullman, Chana. 1989. *The Transformed Self: The Psychology of Religious Conversion*. New York: Plenum.

Bibliography

Van Gennep, Arnold. 1960. *The Rites of Passage.* London: Routledge and Kegan Paul.

Volkan, Vamik D. 1981. *Linking Objects and Linking Phenomena.* New York: International Universities Press.

Waterbury, John. 1972. *North for the Trade: The Life and Times of a Berber Merchant.* Berkeley and Los Angeles: University of California Press.

Weingrod, Alex. 1990. The Saint of Beersheba. Albany: State University of New York Press.

Westermarck, Edward A. 1926. *Ritual and Belief in Morocco.* London: Macmillan.

Willner, Dorothy. 1969. *Nation Building and Community in Israel.* Princeton: Princeton University Press.

Willner, Dorothy, and Margaret Kohls. 1962. Jews in the High Atlas Mountains of Morocco: A Partial Reconstruction. *The Jewish Journal of Sociology* 4: 207–41.

Winnicott, Donald W. 1980. *Play and Reality.* London: Tavistock Clinic.

Index

Aberbach, D., 174n. 3

Abu-Ḥatsera: family of, 23, 34, 43, 44, 121, 128, 170n. 5; Rabbi Ya'aqov, 43; Rabbi Yisrael (Baba Sali), 27, 121, 128; Rabbi Yitzhak (Baba Haki), 128; Rabbi Yosef, 22–23, 76–77, 79, 137, 152

"affliction transference," 116, 173n. 7

afrit. See demons, *afrit* (giant demon)

Agouim, 19, 20, 21, 24, 35, 39, 41, 57, 60, 71, 77, 95, 96, 102, 103, 104, 105–7, 108, 109, 111, 114, 117, 120, 124, 128, 135, 149, 152

Ait Abas, 17

Ait Bouli, 17

Ait Budiel, 38, 39

Ait Wauzgit, 35, 41

Ait Wazana. *See* Wazana, family

Alexander, Tamar, 170n. 6 (ch. 3)

Amassine, 20, 24, 41, 50, 51, 53, 59, 103, 104, 106, 131, 137

amulet (*qame'a*), 49, 60, 89, 99, 111, 126

arak (*maḥia*), 79–82, 111, 112, 126

Ardener, Edwin, 175n. 6

aslai. See demons, illnesses caused by

Assarag, 18, 20, 35, 39, 45–46, 50, 53, 54, 55, 57, 58, 59, 70, 74, 98, 99, 105–6, 127, 149

Atlas Mountains, 29, 45, 62, 64, 105, 107, 121, 148, 160, 163

Atlit, 22, 23, 24, 128, 129

balance. *See* order

baraka, 171n. 4 (ch. 4)

bar mitzvah, 47

Bat-Yeor, 170n. 2 (ch. 4)

beads, 60, 119

Be'er Sheva, 31, 32, 120, 127, 154–59, 161, 162, 165, 166

bees, 54

Bein Hametsarim. *See* the Three Weeks

Ben-Ami, Issachar, 36, 37, 47, 49, 50, 139, 169n. 3, 170nn. 5 (ch. 2), 1, 2, 4, 7 (ch. 3)

Ben-Ari, Eyal, 154

Ben Gurion, 33

Beni Mellal, 18

Berbers, 18, 45, 84, 115

Bertaux, Daniel, 14

Bialik, 33

Bilu, Yoram, 47, 64, 67, 92, 154, 158, 160, 162, 163, 164, 169n. 3, 170nn. 5 (ch. 2), 6 (ch. 3), 171nn. 4 (ch. 4), 1 (ch. 5), 4, 5 (ch. 7), 173nn. 5, 7, 175n. 3 (epilogue)

Binyamina, 23

biography, 14, 148, 169n. 1 (ch. 1)

bkhur. See burning incense

Blackman, M. B., 153, 165

Bled es-siba, 46

blessing, 43, 47, 54

blood, 67, 114, 138

bordo (walking stick), 59–60, 108

Index

boundaries: keeping and crossing, 87, 109, 111, 114, 142–44, 147
Brettell, C. B., 153, 165
Bruner, Jerome, 14, 15
burning incense (*bkhur*), 68, 94, 98, 99

candles, 27, 112, 160
Casablanca, 33, 42, 47, 54, 74, 84–87, 98, 99, 100, 102, 144, 147
casbur. See healing, materials
Castaneda, Carlos, 169n. 1 (ch. 1)
cemetery, 17, 18, 36, 47, 51, 57, 69, 98, 101, 111, 112, 114, 116, 131, 135, 137
chamii, 119, 173n. 1 (ch. 14)
chicken, 38, 140, 141
cirrhosis of the liver, 173n. 4
Clifford, James, 153
"contraction of the road" (*qfitsat haderekh*), 36, 39, 51, 52, 97, 138, 139
couscous, 68, 92, 94
Crapanzano, Vincent, 15, 134, 171n. 4 (ch. 7), 175n. 3 (epilogue)
Crites, Stephen, 14
culture and personality. *See* psychological anthropology

D'Andrade, Roy, 14
Dar el-Beida. *See* Casablanca
Demnate, 18, 171n. 1 (ch. 5)
demons (*jnun*), 15, 40, 42, 56, 57, 60, 62, 65–69, 70, 72–76, 80, 89, 90, 91, 92, 93, 95, 98, 104, 108–16, 132–35, 137, 138, 140, 141, 142, 143, 144, 147, 156; *afrit* (giant demon), 68, 74; blind, 40, 42; characteristics of, 66–67; designations of, 66; as doubles, 66, 75, 95; illnesses caused by, 67, 76, 90, 108, 109, 173n. 5; *ketev meriri,* 175n. 4 (ch. 17); marrying humans, 66, 70, 72–76; methods for controlling, 68–69, 72, 74; as snakes, 108, 114, 140
derba. See demons, illnesses caused by
Deshen, Shlomo, 170n. 1 (ch. 3)
Dhimmi, 170n. 2 (ch. 4)
divination. *See istinzal*
doctor, 13, 103, 109
Don Juan, 169n. 1 (ch. 5)
Douglas, Mary, 144
Dra, 36, 48, 62
dream, 11, 30, 39, 50, 61, 121–27, 139, 154–56, 160, 164, 175n. 3 (epilogue)
dybbuk, 171n. 5

egg, 95, 103, 113
Eickelman, Dale, 47, 171n. 4 (ch. 4)
Eisenstadt, Marvin, 174n. 3 (ch. 16)
Eliade, M., 175n. 8
Elijah the Prophet, 37
emigration, 106, 121, 124, 146

falling sickness, 54
farajiya, 119, 173n. 1 (ch. 14)
festive meal (*se'udah*), 19, 23, 38, 77, 94, 106, 121, 123, 124, 128–29, 139
Fez, 30
Flamand, Pierre, 170n. 1 (ch. 4)
folk-literature, motifs of: The one forbidden thing, 175n. 10; Supernatural time in fairyland, 171n. 3 (ch. 7)
France, 85, 100
Frazer, J. G., 172n. 6
French, 57, 84, 85, 96, 106; commissar, 86; general, 84–86; governor, 96, 103; officer, 84–86

Geertz, Clifford, 9, 48
Gellner, Ernest, 48
Gergen, K. J., 14
Givat Ada, 22, 23
Glaoui, 90, 102
gold, 97, 109, 146
Goldberg, Harvey, 45, 47, 50, 169n. 4
Good, Byron, 14

Hadera, 24
Haj Tehami, 90, 102, 172n. 10
Halifax, John, 175n. 8
Hamadsha, 134
Hanukka, 51, 138
harmel. See healing, materials
Harner, Michael, 175n. 8
Hasan-Rokem, Galit, 154
Hassan II, 78
havdalah, 37
hazan, 50
healer, 11, 18, 19, 59, 62, 64, 65, 68, 69, 71, 73, 77, 80, 82, 88–93, 102, 103, 105, 109, 113, 133, 140, 145, 146, 151, 157, 161, 166; hazards of being, 63–64; and loss of a parent, 64, 133
healing, 62, 64, 88–90, 92, 102, 104, 113, 132–33, 137; materials, 89, 94, 99, 172n. 3; —, books, 63, 65, 89, 90; —, plate, 100, 122; writing (*ktiva*) for, 49, 54, 55, 63, 89, 113. *See also* Wazana, Rabbi Ya'aqov

184

Index

Heine, 33

hillula, 29, 30, 43, 48, 163, 169n. 2;
   of Rabbi David u-Moshe, 19, 30,
   77; of Rabbi Shimon Bar-Yohai, 26,
   126, 170n. 7 (ch. 2); of Rabbi Yosef
   Abu-Hatsera, 22. *See also* Wazana,
   Rabbi Ya'aqov, *hillula* of

horseman, Arab, 39, 139

Huichol, 146

hypnotic trance, 93, 95

Idirghan, 33, 39

Imini, 19, 24, 41, 106

Ingham, J. M., 16

invocations, 69, 92

Israel Folklore Archive, 18, 53, 54, 169n. 1

istinzal, 92–97, 103, 113

Jamous, Raymond, 171n. 4 (ch. 4)

Jason, Heda, 169n. 1 (ch. 2), 175n. 5

jawi. See healing, materials

jellaba, 29, 34, 65, 85, 101, 119, 156

Jerusalem, 35, 173n. 3

Jews: in Assarag, 45–48; and Muslims
   in Morocco, 45–46, 170n. 3 (ch. 4);
   vocations of, 45

jnun. See demons

kabbala, 63, 68, 89

kaddish, 128

kaid (local ruler), 38, 139–40

kaid Ibrahim, 90, 102

Kilborne, Benjamin, 16

Kiryat Gat, 19, 20, 151

Koran, 71

kosher, 56, 72, 144

ktiva (writing). *See* healing, writing for

Lag Ba'Omer, 26, 126, 170n. 7 (ch. 2)

Lele, 144

Lévi-Strauss, Claude, 175n. 6

Lewis, Bernard, 170n. 2 (ch. 4)

liminality, 145

limit. *See* boundaries: keeping and crossing

linking objects, 174n. 1 (ch. 16)

lion, 37

magic, 15, 18, 64; universal principles of,
   91, 172n. 6. *See also* sorcery; Wazana,
   Rabbi Ya'aqov

magician, 64, 65, 119

mahia. See arak

Marcus, George, 153, 165

Marcus, M. A., 163

Marrakech, 19, 47, 90, 102, 103, 105, 124

Masson, Jeffrey, 174n. 3

Maxwell, Gavin, 172n. 4

medium, 92–95

mellah (Jewish quarter), 37, 39, 106

Meron, 26, 28

mikveh. See ritual bath

Mimuna, 22, 169n. 4

mohel (ritual circumciser), 24, 47

moshav (semi-cooperative village), 10, 17,
   18, 20, 25, 122, 151; Atseret, 18–20,
   26, 116, 123, 151, 152; Kinus, 18, 19;
   Makor, 25, 151

Myerhoff, Barbara, 145, 146

names: holy, 62–64, 71, 88, 89, 90; impure,
   88, 89

Natanya, 24, 128

Netifa, 18, 171n. 1 (ch. 5)

Netivot, 128

Nigal, Gedalia, 171n. 5 (ch. 7)

ninth of Av, 98, 125

Obeyesekere, Gananath, 16, 135

order: between the worlds, 133, 140, 147;
   disruption of, 141, 147; social, 142–47

Ouarzazate, 18, 19, 23, 36–40, 43, 48, 62,
   90, 96, 97, 98, 105, 106, 117

pangolin (anteater), 144

Pardes Hana, 33, 150

Paris, 84

pasokh. See healing, materials

pilgrims, 26, 145

postmodern anthropology, 153, 165

prayer, 70–71, 107, 113, 128, 137, 139

psychological anthropology, 14–16

Rabat, 98

Rabbi Amram Ben Diwan, 18

Rabbi David Dra Halevi, 18

Rabbi David u-Moshe, 18, 19, 24, 30, 106,
   117

Rabbi Pinhas ha-Kohen, 172n. 10

Rabbi Shlomo Ben Lehans, 18

Rabbi Ya'aqov Wazana. *See* Wazana, Rabbi
   Ya'aqov

Rabinow, Paul, 171n. 4 (ch. 4)

Ramle, 128

restitution, 109, 116, 140

Index

Books in the Raphael Patai Series
in Jewish Folklore and Anthropology

The Myth of the Jewish Race, revised edition, by Raphael Patai and Jennifer Patai, 1989

The Hebrew Goddess, third enlarged edition, by Raphael Patai, 1990

Robert Graves and the Hebrew Myths: A Collaboration, by Raphael Patai, 1991

Jewish Musical Traditions, by Amnon Shiloah, 1992

The Jews of Kurdistan, by Erich Brauer, completed and edited by Raphael Patai, 1993

Jewish Moroccan Folk Narratives from Israel, by Haya Bar-Itzhak and Aliza Shenhar, 1993

For Our Soul: The Ethiopian Jews in Israel, by Teshome G. Wagaw, 1993

Book of Fables: The Yiddish Fable Collection of Reb Moshe Wallich, Frankfurt am Main, 1697, translated and edited by Eli Katz, 1994

From Sofia to Jaffa: The Jews of Bulgaria and Israel, by Guy H. Haskell, 1994

Jadid al-Islam: The Jewish "New Muslims" of Meshhed, by Raphael Patai, 1998

Saint Veneration among the Jews in Morocco, by Issacher Ben-Ami, 1998

Arab Folktales from Palestine and Israel, introduction, translation, and annotation by Raphel Patai, 1998

Profiles of a Lost World: Memoirs of East European Jewish Life before World War II, by Hirsz Abramowicz, translated by Eva Zeitlin Dobkin, edited by Dina Abramowicz and Jeffrey Shandler, 1999

Jewish Poland—Legends of Origin: Ethnopoetics and Legendary Chronicles, by Haya Bar-Itzhak, 1999

Without Bounds: The Life and Death of Rabbi Ya'aqov Wazana, by Yoram Bilu, 2000.